ELIZABETH TAYLOR

A NEW BIOGRAPHY BY
David Bret

ELIZABETH TAYLOR

THE LADY, THE LOVER, THE LEGEND
1932—2011

GREYSTONE BOOKS

D&M PUBLISHERS INC.

Vancouver/Toronto/Berkeley

Greystone Books
An imprint of D&M Publishers Inc.
2323 Quebec Street, Suite 201
Vancouver BC Canada v5t 4s7
www.greystonebooks.com

Published simultaneously in the United Kingdom
by Mainstream Publishing Company (Edinburgh) Ltd
7 Albany Street
Edinburgh UK EH1 3UG

Cataloguing data available from Library and Archives Canada
ISBN 978-1-55365-440-7 (pbk.)
ISBN 978-1-55365-985-3 (ebook)

Cover design by Peter Cocking
Cover photograph by Francois Lochon/Gamma Rapho/Getty Images
Printed and bound in Canada by Friesens
Text printed on acid-free, 100% post-consumer paper
Distributed in the U.S. by Publishers Group West

THIS BOOK IS DEDICATED TO

Barbara, La grande chanteuse Amália Rodrigues,
Joey Stefano, Dorothy Squires, Henry, Eden, Fritzi, Adeline .
and Les Enfants de Novembre

N'oublie pas . . .
La vie sans amis
c'est comme un jardin sans fleurs

ACKNOWLEDGEMENTS

WRITING THIS BOOK WOULD NOT HAVE BEEN POSSIBLE had it not been for the inspiration, criticisms and love of that select group of individuals who, whether they be in this world or the next, I will always regard as my true family and autre coeur.

Barbara, Irene Bevan, Marlene Dietrich, René Chevalier, Axel Dotti, Dorothy Squires and Roger Normand, *que vous dormez en paix*. Lucette Chevalier, Jacqueline Danno, Hélène Delavault, Tony Griffin, Betty and Gérard Garmain, Annick Roux, John and Anne Taylor, Terry Sanderson, Charley Marouani, David and Sally Bolt. Also a very special mention for Amália Rodrigues, Joey Stefano, those *hiboux*, *fadistas* and *amis de foutre* who happened along the way, and *mes enfants perdus*.

Very many thanks to Bill Campbell and the munificent team at Mainstream. Likewise my agent Guy Rose and his lovely wife, Alex. Also to my wife, Jeanne, for putting up with my bad moods and for still being the keeper of my soul.

And finally a *grand chapeau bas* to Elizabeth, for having lived it.

David Bret

CONTENTS

INTRODUCTION

LIZABETH TAYLOR WILL GO DOWN IN HISTORY FOR
making more turkeys than acclaimed films, for having an
on-screen voice that more than frequently grates and for rarely
maintaining the acting standards of her co-stars. Additionally, she
will be recalled as one of three Hollywood creations who made
the successful transition from precocious child prodigy to adult
movie star – the others were Judy Garland and Natalie Wood –
not by talent alone, but by maternal push. Not that this constant
surveillance and carping from the wings fashioned lasting success
for these women. Judy's mother was an ogre who actively endorsed
the enforced feeding of uppers and downers to keep the show
on the road – a selfish action that directly contributed to the
early demise of her daughter, something that Ethel Gumm was
not around to witness. Maria Gurdin, Natalie Wood's mother,
was considerably worse, possessed of an overwhelming ego and
diminished mental capacity, which caused her to genuinely believe
that her machinations were for her daughter's good. Sara Taylor
was a combination of the two. And who may deny, sifting through
the evidence, that she was more than partly responsible – assisted
by the negative elements of the Hollywood dream factory – for *her*
daughter's instability, which threw open the floodgates to a whole

catalogue of calamities, suicide attempts, collapsed marriages and sabotaged relationships?

Although one cannot doubt that without these ubiquitous Svengalis none of these young women would have made it to the top so quickly, if at all, one cannot ignore the irreparable damage they inflicted on their fragile charges, whose whole lives would be dragged out under enormous clouds of impending gloom. Montgomery Clift, Joan Crawford, Errol Flynn and Elvis Presley may also have endured monster mothers, but they knew how to fight back. Elizabeth Taylor never found the strength to.

The film critic Alexander Walker called her a born survivor, but, as will be seen, this was only partly true. Despite the many genuine concerns about her health, she alone orchestrated the weapons of self-destruction throughout her entire life, deliberately aggravating situations brought about by her own recklessness and folly, often solely for the purpose of contenting the media and keeping her name in the headlines. This she did better than anything witnessed on the screen.

Elizabeth Taylor derived some sort of ghoulish pleasure from home-based drama and self-inflicted adversity, and, as such, remains *the* prima donna of the world's show-business elite. Her story all too often makes for grim reading, but it is nevertheless a fascinating one, from which absolutely no punches have been pulled.

ONE

MOTHER'S LITTLE DIVIDEND

ELIZABETH TAYLOR WAS BORN INTO MONEY, AND THROUGH-out her entire life never had to compromise or go without. Her father, Francis Lenn Taylor, was born in Springfield, Illinois, in 1897 but raised in Arkansas, Kansas, by parents who ran an express-mail and messenger service. As a youth, he fell for aspiring actress Sara Viola Warmbrodt, one year his senior and the daughter of a local German émigré laundry manager.

Any initial romance between the two was, however, short-lived. In November 1918, when Francis turned 21, he was offered an apprenticeship with entrepreneur Howard Young, his uncle on his father's side. Young, who hailed from St Louis, had amassed much of his fortune from shrewd oil investments and ploughed this back into a successful art-dealing business. The following year, he and Francis opened the Howard Young Gallery in Manhattan.

Sara, meanwhile, had left home to study acting in Kansas City and changed her name to Sara Sothern. By 1922, she was playing a minor role in a Los Angeles production of magician–illusionist Channing Pollock's *The Sign on the Door* (1921). Pollock next put her into *The Fool* (1925), playing the part of 15-year-old Crippled Mary Margaret – aka Mary Magdalene – in this modern version of the St Francis of Assisi story. The critical panning this received coincided with Sara's meeting with the great Russian actress and silent-movie icon Alla Nazimova, a close friend of Rudolph Valentino and the doyenne of Hollywood's closeted lesbian clique.

That Sara had even been acknowledged by this powerful, feisty woman almost certainly means that she would have been invited to join Nazimova's infamous lesbian 'sewing circle'. This met regularly at The Garden of Alla, Nazimova's mansion on Sunset Boulevard, where the 'baritone babes' included both of Valentino's wives, Lili Damita (who later married Errol Flynn) and Dolly Wilde (Oscar's niece, described by the hostess as 'the only Wilde who likes women'). Even so, Sara's membership of Nazimova's circle must have been fleeting for, despite its dreadful reviews, *The Fool* opened on Broadway at the end of the year. Here, the lead was played by James Kirkwood, already a name in the New York gay community – many years later, Sara's daughter would appear in his *There Must Be a Pony* (1986).

In September 1926, *The Fool* opened at London's Apollo Theatre. The sensation in the British capital at this time was the outrageous Tallulah Bankhead, another Nazimova aficionado affectionately known as the 'Queen of the Gallery Girls' – in other words, London's 'uncloseted' lesbian community. Tallulah was in the middle of a nine-month run of another piece of hokum, *The Creaking Chair*. For a while, she and Sara competed for the attention of the Sapphic Sisterhood, an organisation run by a woman named Fat Sophie. Any rivalry ended, however, when Tallulah bobbed her famous, lovely waist-length hair one evening before going on stage. Her 'galleryites' very quickly followed suit, and Fat Sophie set her gang onto Sara to 'crop' her outside the Apollo – their revenge, they said, on this fake for attempting to emulate their heroine. When *The Fool* closed in March 1925, Sara returned to New York. Several flops followed, including *Arabesque*, an unlikely pairing with Bela Lugosi. It was here, early in 1926, when she was thinking of giving up the stage, that Sara bumped into her former beau, Francis Lenn Taylor.

Theirs was a 'lavender' courtship, clearly setting the stall for things to come. Photographs of Sara Sothern taken at the time in

The Little Spitfire, her latest play, show her with close-cropped hair and looking decidedly butch – a true protégée of Nazimova. Francis, at 28, was already a promiscuous homosexual. Why the couple decided to date may have baffled their friends: even in those days, homosexuality was less frowned upon in artistic/theatrical circles than in Hollywood, so neither would have encountered serious problems pursuing their respective careers. Howard Young, however, had offered Francis the management of a new gallery about to open in London and had apparently made it clear that if his nephew was going to relocate overseas and extend the company's good name, it would be as a family man. Naturally, he chose Sara to be his bride, and when she married him at the end of 1926, it was on the proviso that she give up the boards for ever. For the rest of their marriage, Sara would resent this and never miss out on an opportunity to remind her husband who wore the trousers in the Taylor household.

The Taylors, like their daughter, never did things by halves. The Great Depression, felt by much of the world, did not affect them at all. According to an interview she granted *The Ladies Home Journal* in February 1954, Sara claimed that she had arrived in London in February 1929, two months ahead of Francis, to go house hunting. This might well have been one of her 'tall tales', one to hammer home the fact that she was boss. Another was the description of the property she settled for: Sara might have seen 'tulips almost three-feet high, forget-me-nots and yellow lavender violas', but it is unlikely that there had been 'flaming snapdragons and roses' in early March.

In fact, it was the politician Victor Cazalet, who had met Sara during the London run of *The Fool*, who found the Taylors their first home: 11 Hampstead Way was a two-bedroom Victorian cottage, backing onto the heath. Using this as a base, the pair travelled back and forth to the Continent, snapping up valuable works of art for well-heeled clients. And when Sara introduced her husband to the wealthy 38-year-old bachelor famed for his stance on anti-Semitism, it was love at first sight. Not only did Cazalet become Francis's lover, he became the Taylors' unofficial sponsor – with Sara more than willing to ignore what they might have been getting up to in private so long as Cazalet was helping Francis to feather their nest by introducing them to all the right connections.

When Sara learned that she was pregnant towards the end of 1928, she made up her mind *not* to be a regular housewife – a characteristic that would be handed down to her daughter. The Hampstead home might have been on the small side, but she hired a cook, a maid and a chauffeur, and upon the birth of her first child in June 1929 – baptised Howard in honour of the Taylors' benevolent uncle – she hired a nurse to look after him.

Naturally, the Hampstead house was by now overcrowded, and the Taylors bought Heathwood, a large mock-Tudor property on nearby Wildwood Road, courtesy of Uncle Howard. The house had around a dozen rooms, servants' quarters, a tennis court and access to a private wood. Some 50 years down the line, their daughter, unable to bear anyone else having something that had once been hers, failed in an attempt to buy it back.

The Taylors socialised with the St John's Wood–Chelsea artists' clique, becoming friends with Laura Knight, Augustus John and John Flanagan, Gracie Fields's paramour with whom she had recently set up home in Augustus John's former studio. Leaving little Howard at home, Francis and Sara travelled extensively to auctions at home and abroad, snapping up Old Masters for the gallery, which were sold at a huge profit. This stopped in the autumn of 1931 when Sara discovered that she was pregnant again. On 27 February 1932, she gave birth to a daughter, Elizabeth Rosamond – the first name in honour of both her grandmothers (Sara's mother had recently died), the second after Grandmother Taylor's maiden name.

The little girl appeared to have been born with a cowl and was suffering from hypertrichosis – a coating of fine, dark facial hair, though this disappeared by the time she reached three months. The condition, of course, might have been pure invention, enabling Sara when persistently reminded in later years that Elizabeth was far more beautiful than she had ever been to say something along the lines of, 'Well, she wasn't always so!' In early pictures, Elizabeth's eyes, an unusual shade of violet, appear sunken in a head that looks too large for her body on account of her shoulders being too narrow. Neither does she appear to have been baptised: as a half-hearted Christian Scientist, Sara disapproved of such 'rituals'. Victor Cazalet, Francis's *amour* – and probably Sara's too – insisted upon being Elizabeth's godfather – in an unofficial capacity, owing to the lack of ceremony – with the added advantage that he was also a Christian Scientist.

When Cazalet moved to Grand Swifts, a magnificent retreat near Cranbrooke in the heart of the Kent countryside, he loaned the Taylors Little Swallows, a 15-room Tudor house on the estate, which they visited most weekends. He also plied Elizabeth with expensive gifts, including a pony for her fifth birthday, which she baptised Betty. This set a precedent in her life that material possessions were all that were required for a person to prove their love and worth. Cazalet also supported Sara's aspirations for her daughter's career on the stage – her theory being that with the right amount of push Elizabeth might one day achieve the goals *she* had once set for herself. Movies were not even considered: in Sara's opinion, whilst stage actors represented status, movie stars were vulgar.

Sara always maintained that Elizabeth and Howard were enrolled at the grandly titled Madame Vacami Dance Academy – actually run by an unglamorous Mrs Rankin from an attic in Knightsbridge. According to research conducted by Alexander Walker (*Elizabeth*, 1990), the academy denied that the pair had ever been there. Similarly, Sara boasted that Elizabeth had appeared at the London Hippodrome in a 'command performance' before the Duchess of York (later the Queen Mother) and the Princesses Elizabeth and Margaret. Elizabeth herself recalled in her memoirs (*Elizabeth Taylor*, 1965), with typical exaggeration, 'the isolation, the hugeness, the feeling of space and no end to space', of her alleged debut stage performance – it was a detailed memory considering she had been just four years old at the time. And, again, it was untrue, as was almost certainly Sara's admission that she had been a guest at George VI's coronation a few years later. As for the 'recital', this was no more than an end-of-term concert at the local parish hall.

Sara had already placed Howard at the Arnold House Preparatory School, and in September 1937 she enrolled Elizabeth at Byron House in London's Highgate. No record survives as to how she fared with her lessons or which, if any, were her favourite subjects – only that she lived for the weekends when she could escape to the house in Kent and her pony. This idyll ended, however, as the war clouds gathered over Europe. In the spring of 1938, with Victor Cazalet footing the bill, Sara and her children were put aboard the SS *Manhattan* bound for New York. During the voyage, very much against her better judgement, Sara permitted them to watch their first movie: *The Little Princess* (1939), starring wunderkind Shirley Temple. The trio spent several days in the city, then travelled by train to Pasadena, where Sara's father had a chicken ranch. A few months later, having tied up his business interests in London and bid a presumably tearful farewell to Victor Cazalet, Francis joined them there.

For such self-appointed society folk as the Taylors considered themselves to be, a modest chicken farm was regarded as an inappropriate base from which to conduct their affairs, and in the spring of 1940 they relocated to southern California, where Sara had formerly nurtured her own dreams of stardom. Here, she set about fashioning her children's futures – though there was no question that Elizabeth would always remain her favourite. Sara and Francis bought a decent-sized bungalow in Pacific Palisades, within a stone's throw of the ocean, and rented a suite at the Chateau Elysée Hotel, where Francis opened a gallery. Here, he set about amassing a sizeable fortune – selling 'works of art' he had mostly purloined in London to gullible clients who might not have recognised a Laura Knight or an Augustus John if it had jumped up and hit them. John, in particular, had been in the habit of making dozens of preliminary sketches before starting on a major work – most of these he screwed up and tossed into the waste bin. Initially, Francis had visited John's studio with a genuine interest in securing the artist's paintings to sell on to his clients – but towards the end of the Taylors' residence in London, he had gone there to rummage through the rubbish. What sketches had been salvageable had been ironed, framed and crated up for the gallery in America – with the artist completely unaware that he had been effectively ripped off by a friend. The deception had not stopped there: with many European Jewish socialites going into exile to evade Nazi persecution at that time, particularly in Germany and France, Francis had 'relieved' them of their art treasures, buying them for a song and selling them to wealthy Americans at a vast mark-up. Many years later, one of these would cause Elizabeth considerable embarrassment.

Elizabeth and Howard were ensconced at a typical Hollywood school, where education came second to their parents' hobnobbing with the rich and famous who turned up at the gates each evening to collect their offspring. In London, this 'tiresome' task had been assigned to the Taylors' nanny or butler. Here, however, Sara needed to be seen and even learned to drive so that the other parents would not think her socially beneath them. Regular scholars would have hour-long lessons in mathematics, geography and English, but these were often substantially reduced to fit in the 'essentials' of Tinsel Town's education system for Elizabeth: photography sessions, wardrobe and make-up trips, etc.

Sara had always counted upon one or both of her children to provide meal tickets for the future. She had infiltrated London society, working her way into parties and receptions if invitations had not been forthcoming, hoping that Elizabeth or Howard might marry appropriately and elevate the Taylors to the upper classes, where Sara was convinced they belonged. When Howard began displaying rebellious qualities at an early age, Sara concentrated her efforts solely on Elizabeth and applied the same tactics in Hollywood as she had in London, being far more interested in her pretty ebony-haired, violet-eyed daughter becoming the next Deanna Durbin or Shirley Temple than she was in Elizabeth getting good marks at school. Therefore, instead of politicians and the landed gentry, Sara homed in on Hollywood's 'royalty' – working her way through the ranks, she would, one way or another, seduce producers, directors, cameramen and, eventually, one or two of the moguls themselves.

First, Sara decided that the family would have to make the sacrifices necessary for social elevation. Francis, very much under the thumb and to all intents and purposes enjoying being dictated to by this horrendously manipulative martinet, transferred his gallery to the Beverly Hills Hotel on Sunset Boulevard, and no sooner had the crates been unpacked at the Pacific Palisades bungalow than the family upped sticks and moved to a villa on the more fashionable Elm Drive – Elizabeth's home until her first marriage. She and Howard were installed in the more upmarket Hawthorne Elementary, a snooty establishment where they were ribbed on account of their 'clipped colonial' accents. Howard ignored the taunts or sometimes employed his fists to restore decorum. Elizabeth, who had to be the centre of attention even then, mocked them by affecting a shrill Southern accent, which, frequently and annoyingly, would crop up in her films.

Sara enrolled Elizabeth for after-school song-and-dance lessons. By hook or crook, she acquired her an audition with MGM producer John Considine, who had scored a big hit with *Boys Town* (1938) and had recently completed *Third Finger, Left Hand* (1940) with Myrna Loy. Exercising a brief routine, Elizabeth must have impressed him, because Considine arranged for her to audition for the Messiah himself – the all-powerful Louis B. Mayer, who had set Judy Garland on the Yellow Brick Road towards immortality. Mayer was decidedly put off by Elizabeth's tuneless voice – although this was not a major problem, as she could be dubbed by someone else – but still offered her a contract to be renewed every six months, providing that she lived up to the studio's expectations. Her starting salary was to be $100 a week, a tidy sum for a nine-year-old girl. Sara rejected the offer. A recent client at Francis's gallery had been Andrea Berens, the fiancée of Universal's chairman J. Cheever Cowden, who had purchased several of the purloined

Augustus Johns. Sara soon inveigled an introduction to Cowden himself, an audition was arranged and Universal offered Elizabeth the same contract as MGM but with a salary of $200 a week. Sara was also placed on the studio payroll as her daughter's chaperone/adviser, obligatory in those days when the contractually bound was a minor.

Sara's victory over Louis B. Mayer was pyrrhic, because although Elizabeth was on a higher salary, Universal had a glut of child stars at that time and did not know what to do with her, which of course prompts the question: why sign her up in he first place? She was given a small part in *There's One Born Every Minute* (1942) – heading the credits was child star Carl 'Alfalfa' Switzer, unfairly regarded as the first actor to suffer the 'Liz Taylor curse'. In 1959, Switzer, whose speciality as a member of 'Our Gang' was singing off-key, would be shot dead in a drugs-and-drink-fuelled brawl, aged 40. Elizabeth's film with Switzer was released at end of 1942, by which time Universal had dropped her on account of Sara Taylor's persistent on-set meddling.

Intent on making Elizabeth's a household name, Sara unwisely solicited the attentions of Louella Parsons and Hedda Hopper, Hollywood's arch-rival gossip columnists – the idea being that if one of these influential ladies reviewed Elizabeth favourably, fame and fortune would be sure to come her way. Louella refused to attend Elizabeth's next audition, claiming that she had better things to do. As for Hopper, there appears to have been some sort of link with Francis Taylor's benefactor/lover Victor Cazalet. Some sources suggest that Cazalet's sister Thelma had befriended Hopper during her trips to London – others that Cazalet had once had an affair with the columnist's ex-husband, stage actor William DeWolf Hopper. Sara maintained that one of the Cazalets had furnished her with a letter of introduction to Hedda Hopper. However, the likeliest theory is that Sara approached her, taking advantage of the fact that she was a friend of a friend who ironically might just prove an invaluable ally. Hopper was kind enough to invite mother and daughter to her home, but she was not impressed. She observed in her autobiography *The Whole Truth and Nothing But* (Doubleday, 1963) of the pre-teen Taylor vocals, 'Sara had never gotten over Broadway, and she wanted to have a glamorous life again through her child . . . It was one of the most painful ordeals I have ever witnessed.'

Luck appears to have been on Elizabeth's side – largely because Hopper did not refer to this 'ordeal' in her syndicated column – during the summer of 1942 when Louis B. Mayer was having problems finding a little girl with an 'English rose' accent for his debut exercise in Technicolor, *Lassie Come Home* (1943), which was about to go into production. Mayer's first choice had been Marie Flynn, the soon-to-be-forgotten child prodigy who had appeared with Ingrid Bergman in *Intermezzo* (1939). During her screen test, however, she was deemed 'mousy-looking and unphotogenic for color'. Mayer, or more likely one of his assistants, remembered Elizabeth and dispatched one of his lackeys to sweet-talk her mother into letting him have her. Elizabeth was offered the part without making a screen test (the four other unnamed child actresses who did tests failed because they could not do English accents) but was compelled to take a drop in salary. This, she later said, had been worth it for the opportunity making the film gave her to form what would be a lifelong friendship with its star Roddy McDowall.

London-born fellow evacuee Roddy McDowall had made his name as a child star in *John Halifax, Gentleman* (1938) three years before taking Hollywood by storm in *How Green was My Valley* (1941). He would be the first in a long line of closeted gay actors who would regard Elizabeth Taylor as some sort of protectress/surrogate-mother figure. Cynics have ignobly dubbed her a 'fag hag', but this title is unfair. Despite her selfishness towards many, her flighty reputation, her neurasthenia and her inability to hold herself together at times, for these men she proved nothing less than a rock and a loyal and discreet tower of strength, and as such commanded untold respect from the world's gay community. Even the small section of this community who disliked her could not help but admire her for the unselfish qualities she displayed in her tireless rallying to raise funds for AIDS research. Also, one must not lose sight of the fact that in the days of the intensely homophobic studio system, she too ran the risk of being ostracised by the film community by befriending gay actors and sharing in their 'secret' lives. That this sort of thing was still prevalent was brought to the public's attention, along with her loathing of hypocrisy, in September 1992 when Elizabeth pronounced on Whoopi Goldberg's television show, 'The creativity of homosexuals has made so much possible in this town. Take out the homosexuals, and there's no Hollywood.' The next month, she would go one step further and attack the US government on account of the biggest health crisis to hit the country since the flu epidemic during the early part of that century. 'I don't think President Bush is doing *anything* at all about AIDS,' she told an International AIDS summit in Amsterdam. 'In fact, I'm not sure he even knows how to *spell* AIDS!'

Lassie Come Home, directed by Fred Wilcox, was a smash at the US box office, and even more so with British audiences who welcomed the heartrending boy-and-dog scenario as an antidote to the horrors of war. Elizabeth played Priscilla, the granddaughter of the Duke of Rudling (Nigel Bruce, aka Dr Watson in the Sherlock Holmes films), to whom Lassie is sold, the story centring around her flight back to her rightful owner Joe Carraclough (McDowall). It spawned the first in a long line of Lassie movies. (The lead was played by a male dog called Pal, who earned more than the rest of the cast added together, Hollywood's biggest canine star since Rin Tin Tin.) In no way can this film be attributed to making Elizabeth a name – she appeared in four scenes only, was on screen for ten minutes, and was not seen in trailers and on playbills – but, as part of a hugely successful package comprising the cream of the British thespian crop (Donald Crisp, Elsa Lanchester, Nigel Bruce, Dame May Whitty, Edmund Gwenn), Elizabeth was assured of being retained on the Metro roster, albeit in minuscule letters.

Elizabeth was not yet a star, as she and her mother liked to think when recalling the period, just one of any number of disposable kiddie actresses at a time when there was a surfeit of these. Because she was closer to the bottom of the MGM list than the top, and because they had nothing for her to do after *Lassie Come Home*, she was loaned out to Twentieth Century Fox – the studio that, two decades hence, her foibles would come close to bankrupting.

Fox had begun shooting *Jane Eyre* (1944) with Joan Fontaine as the adult Jane and Orson Welles as Rochester. Though her name does not figure in the credits, she acquitted herself extremely well as Helen Burns, the girl who befriends Jane. For once, Sara was justified in complaining that such a stellar performance was not recompensed by her daughter's name being added to the credits (though today Elizabeth's name frequently appears above that of Peggy Ann Garner), but her protestations backfired on her. The director Robert Stevenson complained to Louis B. Mayer, who issued Sara with the first of several verbal warnings when Elizabeth returned to MGM.

The next film was *The White Cliffs of Dover* (1944), a tribute to British wartime heroism headed by Irene Dunne and Alan Marshall – a non-event so far as Elizabeth's contribution was concerned. She appeared briefly in just two scenes, and, as if to punish her further for her mother's interference, Mayer ensured that, once more, her name did not appear in the credits.

TWO

MOVE OVER,
SHIRLEY TEMPLE

PRECISELY HOW ELIZABETH CAME TO BE GIVEN THIRD lead in *National Velvet* (1944) has been swallowed by Hollywood folklore. Sara Taylor claimed that it was on account of her daughter's rave reviews for *Lassie Come Home*, but there had been none. MGM talent scout Lucille Ryman Carroll claimed in an interview with *People* magazine in November 1987 that Elizabeth had stormed into her office and announced, 'You're wasting your time auditioning anyone else. I'm going to be playing Velvet Brown!' One finds it hard to imagine her getting away with such audacity. A third, more plausible, explanation appeared in several movie magazines: Carroll and the producer, Pandro S. Berman, had taken Elizabeth's riding skills into consideration and concluded that it would be easier to offer her the part, rather than train someone else. Luckily, they made a good choice, though the back injury she sustained falling off her horse during rehearsals would plague her for the rest of her life because it was not properly tended to at the time.

Based on the novel by Enid Bagnold, the script for *National Velvet* had been commissioned by Paramount for 30-year-old Katharine

Hepburn back in 1935, but it was, not surprisingly, rejected by her (Velvet Brown is only 12 years old) and subsequently sold to MGM, who had kept it on ice since. The story is far-fetched, though the film itself provided an entertaining touch of whimsy for post-war audiences eager to embrace a world hopefully cleansed of oppression. It is marred only by the occasional 'British' accents of some of the leads: Anne Revere is not too bad and Mickey Rooney kept his American accent, because he was in the middle of his Andy Hardy period and MGM did not want his fans to be confused, but the Bronx twang of child star Jackie 'Butch' Jenkins is dreadful.

The unprecedented success of *National Velvet* led to Louis B. Mayer upping Elizabeth's salary to $200 a week – and, bizarrely for a man whose stinginess was legendary, this was not her only reward. Mayer brought in an interior designer who fashioned her a *National Velvet* bedroom, complete with the most expensive riding equipment money could buy and a wooden horse. Naturally, this came in handy for photo shoots. And, finally, Mayer paid her an unprecedented $15,000 bonus, adding to the speculation that, as had happened with Judy Garland after *The Wizard of Oz* (1939), this acknowledged connoisseur of underaged girls might have had an ulterior motive.

Mayer was certainly acting with shrewdness, because one of the terms for her receiving the bonus was that her current contract would be extended by another year, binding her to him for what was anticipated would be the remainder of her childhood before puberty set in. As for Elizabeth, she had a condition of her own before permitting Sara to sign on the dotted line: she wanted to keep the horse King, with whom she had bonded on the picture. Mayer acquiesced, and photographs of her being presented with the horse – no longer of use to the studio because he was lame – flooded the press.

In October 1943, to counteract one journalist's comment that the horse was far too big for Elizabeth, a statement was issued to the *Hollywood Reporter*, purporting to have come from her:

He would never hurt me. You don't have to worry about King when you get on his back – you just leave everything to him, and I think that he likes to know that I leave it to him, that he's the boss, and I trust him.

These would almost certainly have been Sara's words, but they presented an interesting analogy with the way in which Elizabeth regarded the men in her life in years to come. Similarly, cynics would draw comparisons between the way she related to the loss of her animals – the speed with which each 'irreplaceable' furry creature was replaced – and the way in which she got over her break-ups with her small army of husbands and lovers.

This love of four-legged creatures would be further documented in a *Life* magazine feature of February 1945 – who could resist a cute little girl cuddling up to one of her many pets, at that time a kitten, three dogs and a chipmunk? The chipmunk, the first in a series all baptised Nibbles, became a minor celebrity: first, with a cameo appearance in *Courage of Lassie* (1946); then when a New York publisher brought out *Nibbles and Me*, a 77-page tome recounting the story of Elizabeth's friendship with the little fellow(s). Her name appeared on the title page, although it is unlikely that she contributed to it other than to pose sweetly with her cherished pet. The book was essentially a gimmick cooked up by Sara and MGM's publicity department to promote the child star and her latest movies – location shots from *Courage of Lassie* and *National Velvet* were included.

Nibbles and Me was serialised in *Photoplay*, and much was made of the fact that Elizabeth had it drilled into her by her mother that tears were useless when one of the chipmunks died. Sara explained that death did not exist so long as the departed loved one was retained in the memory, according to the edicts of Christian Science. Elizabeth would recall her mother's words many times over the years – only to go to pieces each time she lost someone dear, frequently, it has to be said, for the benefit of the media.

One syndicated column, whose contributor perhaps wisely opted to remain anonymous, labelled Elizabeth 'a modern-day St Francis of Assisi', having been alerted by Sara that her daughter was what would today be called a horse-whisperer. 'She whinnies like a horse,' observed the *Los Angeles Times*'s Louis Berg. 'And she also chirps like a squirrel and makes bird noises.' MGM attempted to capitalise on this by purchasing the screen rights to William Henry Hudson's 1904 novel *Green Mansions*, offering her the central role of Rima. Accepting this would have been a terrible mistake. Though she genuinely possessed the innocent appeal required to play the timid forest girl who converses with the fauna and falls in love with a handsome stranger, she was already too voluptuous and, through no fault of her own, would have turned the part into a joke. Sara realised this. The project was shelved until 1954, when Vincente Minnelli tried to foist it upon the equally unsuitable Italian siren Pier Angeli. It was eventually filmed in 1959 when Mel Ferrer directed his then wife Audrey Hepburn in the definitive portrayal opposite Anthony Perkins.

To make up for Elizabeth losing out on Rima, and for the benefit of those unfamiliar with America's latest pre-pubescent sensation, an 'official' biography was syndicated in columns across America in the hope of someone coming forward with a role as close to 'real life' as possible. In much the same way as Tasmanian scallywag Errol Flynn had been reinvented as an all-round sporting jock from Ireland, so Elizabeth became a wunderkind talent plucked from the London Blitz – one who had danced before the king of England and who had also been amazed to learn of her ability to communicate with animals. It was pure hogwash, of course, but peacetime readers lapped up ever syrupy sentence – although the hoped-for role never came.

As had happened with Joan Crawford and Judy Garland, Elizabeth was welcomed into Louis B. Mayer's 'family circle' and invited to call him 'Papa'. However, away from the studio with her real family, Elizabeth's life was anything but convivial. Francis, who was involved with Gilbert Adrian – MGM's chief costume designer since 1927 and in a lavender marriage with actress Janet Gaynor at that time – moved into a hotel, taking Howard with him, whilst Sara was sleeping with director Michael Curtiz, whom she had met on the set of *Life with Father* (1947), all in the interest of elevating her daughter's position on the Tinsel Town ladder.

Sara is also known to have set her sights on Louis B. Mayer himself, no doubt unaware that she was a generation too old for his tastes. Her ardour dimmed, however, when she learned that Mayer had denounced her as 'gutter-class', though it was Elizabeth who committed the unpardonable sin of squaring up to the messiah. Barging into his office unannounced, she told him exactly what she thought of him, and before she slammed the door behind her, she yelled, 'You and your studio can go to hell!' Mayer did not fire her, but for the rest of his life, he and Elizabeth loathed one another: she never entered his office again and only spoke to him under duress.

Mayer, of course, knew the monetary value of his temperamental young star and, cashing in on the latest canine phenomenon, gave her a part in *Courage of Lassie* – a misnomer if ever there was one, for the 'Lassie' in question, still played by Pal, was called Bill! Like its predecessors, the film was shot in glorious Technicolor and showcased the famous collie's talents as an Allied agent-combatant more capable of outsmarting the Nazis than its human counterparts, despite suffering from shellshock. Starring Frank Morgan and Tom Drake, it was a big success – but again not on account of Elizabeth's contribution, which was minimal and overshadowed by her quadruped co-star, as it had been in the last Lassie vehicle.

Elizabeth was next whisked through a quartet of kitchen-sink dramas in an attempt to draw as much adolescent mileage out of her as possible – just in case her star burned itself out with the advent of adulthood, as had happened with other Hollywood child prodigies. Louis B. Mayer had delayed this in Judy Garland's case by ordering her to plait her hair and strap down her budding breasts. Sara was having none of this and began pestering the studio to turn Elizabeth into a young woman at a time when she was still legally regarded as a child, well aware that this would bring protests from the moralists. By the age of 15, Elizabeth had had more than her share of on-screen kisses and a betrothal – whilst *off* the screen, Sara fiercely guarded her morals and refused to let her out of her sight for a single moment. If anyone walked up to Elizabeth and asked a question, the reply always came from Sara.

Elizabeth was promoted as the home-loving girl who respected her parents and who eschewed the bright lights in favour of helping Mama with her chores. Photographed in an apron and rubber gloves, she could be seen 'labouring' over the stove or hunched over the sink, contemplating the dirty pots. The fake scenarios, arguably the closest Elizabeth ever got to doing actual housework, took place on a film set but were swallowed by the fans, who also clipped snaps taken of her at 'high-school parties', convinced that she was just as normal as they were – save that that these too were staged on a back lot and the 'students' were young bit-part players and extras.

Sara's affair with Michael Curtiz paid off. *Life with Father*, in which Elizabeth worked as a loan-out to Warner Brothers, was an Irene Dunne–William Powell comedy set in 1880s New York. Elizabeth made a nuisance of herself, courtesy of Sara, by being frequently absent during shooting. It was the unwritten law of some studios in those days that A-list actresses were permitted to leave the set during their menstrual cycle, providing this had been squared with the on-set nurse, who was not averse to examining them to ensure they were telling the truth. So far as the astonishingly naive outside world was concerned, adolescents such as Shirley Temple, Judy Garland and Elizabeth were 'late developers' who did not yet *have* periods – the moguls' way of convincing the public that they were not yet watching young women. Sara took Elizabeth home for the least little thing – a slight cough, aching feet, a pimple, a single sneeze – resulting in questions being asked by Warner Brothers' insurers, who, stupidly believing that teenage girls only 'fell sick' once a month, wanted to know why she was having 'periods' at the rate of one a week.

In keeping with her fake studio biography, Elizabeth was not allowed to date and was not permitted to venture anywhere – not even the bathroom – unless chaperoned. Though they did not employ the actual word, the movie magazines reminded their readers that, despite the on-screen amours, Elizabeth was very much a virgin. Little girls who smiled a lot and posed for photographs with fluffy animals were not supposed to even *know* about sex, let alone indulge in it. Such was the naivety of cinemagoers. Therefore, when Elizabeth was observed to be developing breasts, MGM 'extended' her childhood by casting her in *Cynthia* (1947) with George Murphy and Mary Astor. Promoted as 'a teenage Camille', she played Cynthia Bishop, the consumptive, shy girl who cannot have the puppy she so desires because of her allergies – but whose overprotective parents do allow to go on her first date with a young marine, who escorts her to the end-of-term prom.

Elizabeth got on well with the famously feisty Mary Astor, but the feeling was not mutual. Astor found her scheming, even back then, and could not help comparing her with the much more amenable Judy Garland, with whom she had appeared in *Meet Me in St Louis* (1944). 'Judy was warm and affectionate and exuberant,' she wrote in her memoir, *A Life on Film* (Delacorte, 1971). 'Elizabeth was cool and slightly superior . . . There was a look in those violet eyes that was somewhat calculating. It was as though she knew exactly what she wanted and was quite sure of getting it.'

To reassure the public that, like herself, Elizabeth's character was not flighty, the young man who swept her off her feet in the film was James Lydon, her beau from *Life with Father*. As the gangly, inarticulate youth in the Henry Aldrich series, Lydon had been America's favourite wartime teenager after Andy Hardy. Since then, he had matured into an inordinately handsome, hunky young man. Even so, where American audiences were concerned, Lydon was still the kind of boy no one would associate with leading a girl astray.

That Elizabeth *was* thinking about such matters was, however, evident on 13 July 1947 when she appeared on Louella Parsons' radio show for a 'modest' fee of $3,000. Parsons was aware that the Taylors had separated and that Elizabeth had been the centre of attention at Roddy McDowall's 18th birthday party the previous September – dancing with several older men. 'Boys of my own age are so young,' she told Louella. She also refused to acknowledge her parents' split – Elizabeth claimed that her father was away from home on business and that Sara wanted to join him but that she was too busy chaperoning her back and forth to the studio. And, Louella wanted to know, what were her aspirations for the future? Elizabeth's response was that two things were on her mind: becoming a great actress and ensnaring a husband. She did not add that she was not *old* enough to marry but did give the impression that any husband would do so long as he spirited her away from her overbearing mother.

The fact that Louella Parsons 'overlooked' the Taylors' marital problems in her syndicated column perturbed MGM: whatever scandal or crisis Louella failed to pick up on, they knew, Hedda Hopper almost certainly would. Both hacks were therefore fed the story that Francis *was* away on business, discussing the opening of a new gallery with Howard Young. When Louis B. Mayer heard of the split, he decided to take no chances and opted to put an even greater distance between them – hoping to achieve the maxim 'Absence makes the heart grow fonder'. Elizabeth had worked hard over the past year, Mayer told the press. She was beginning to make a name for herself, and, with no project on the immediate horizon, Mayer felt that she was entitled to a holiday. The studio would pick up the tab, naturally.

At the end of July, Elizabeth and Sara sailed for Southampton on the *Queen Mary*. They spent two months in London, shopping and revisiting old haunts, until a cable from Mayer summoned Elizabeth home for her first musical – co-starring with Jane Powell and Wallace Beery in *A Date with Judy* (1948). The film was produced by Joe Pasternak, the man responsible for reviving Marlene Dietrich's career after she had been branded box-office poison. It was a great success, primarily on account of Brazilian bombshell Carmen Miranda's ferociously camp rendition of 'Cuanto Le Gusta' and Wallace Beery's club-footed dance routine. As for Elizabeth, she provided little more than colourful scenery, and the moralists frowned upon the scene where, still underaged, she vied with Powell for the attentions of 28-year-old Robert Stack. Even so, at least one influential critic was impressed, Irving Hoffman of the *Hollywood Reporter* singling her out as 'a 14-carat, 100-proof siren of the future'.

Next came *Julia Misbehaves* (1948) – essentially a showcase for the phenomenal talents of Greer Garson and Walter Pidgeon – a production with distinct but inadvertent references to the crisis within the Taylor household. Elizabeth played wealthy debutante Susan Packett, whose aim was to reconcile her divorced parents whilst attempting to break away from their dominance so that she might have a life of her own with a man of her choosing. The critics – and Garson-Pidgeon aficionados who had never accepted them extant of their pairing in *Mrs Miniver*-style dramas – were not impressed.

Elizabeth's first major relationship, at least the first to make the press, was with 23-year-old West Point-graduate-turned-footballer Glenn Davis, whom she met during the summer of 1948. Until this time – adopting the maxim 'Look by all means, but please don't touch!' – wearing a succession of outfits by Francis's designer lover Adrian, she had been encouraged to flutter her eyelashes at just about every man in sight, particularly the older, unattractive ones, because, according to Sara, these were the ones with the money and power. Sara and Francis had even bought Elizabeth her first car (courtesy of MGM), a powder-blue Cadillac convertible, to help her get noticed – not that this was necessary, and in any case she was not yet permitted to drive it.

The relationship with Davis was almost certainly platonic, an exercise stage-managed by MGM to gain essential publicity after Elizabeth's last few films had failed to match up to the success of their predecessors. Davis had announced his plans to enlist for military service.

Elizabeth and Glenn Davis met up most weekends during the summer/fall of 1948. He would occasionally collect her from the studio where she was shooting *Little Women* (1949). Directed by Mervin LeRoy, this had an all-star cast – headed by June Allyson as Jo March, the heroine of Louisa M. Alcott's classic novel – all of whom were better than Elizabeth, whose squeaky histrionics were lost when pitted against the quiet dignity of Mary Astor, the poetic innocence of Margaret O'Brien and the distinctive presence of that grand old man of the British theatre, C. Aubrey Smith, who sadly died before the film was released. In her blonde wig, it is only towards the end of the film, when she almost comes into her own, that one realises one has been watching Elizabeth Taylor. However, as Amy March, she inadvertently displays some of the later Taylor characteristics of selfishness and impetuosity – she grabs the best costumes and even manages to steal someone else's intended.

On 8 September 1948, Elizabeth was photographed kissing Glenn Davis a tearful farewell when he left to fight in Korea. Afterwards. she appeared in public, looking glum, wearing his 'ALL AMERICA' sweatshirt and the 'lucky' gold football chain he had given her. It was all staged, of course.

Elizabeth coped with her 'war bride' status by travelling to London in November 1948 to star opposite 37-year-old Robert Taylor in a lacklustre espionage thriller, *Conspirator*. Sara told the press that whilst in England, still recovering from wartime food shortages, she and her daughter would 'cut corners' the same as everyone else. To prove this point, the two of them travelled 'by common cab' to the Ministry of Food to collect their ration books – then had the driver convey them to Claridge's.

Conspirator was promoted as 'Elizabeth Taylor's First Adult Love Story'. Both leads were woefully miscast. At 16, Elizabeth was hopeless as Robert Taylor's 21-year-old wife, whilst he seemed way out of his depth playing the villain, the British officer who spies for Russia and is instructed by his superiors to kill her. There were also rumours of an off-screen romance between the two – fuelled by the studio to prevent Taylor's homosexuality from becoming public knowledge.

Such had been MGM's concern for one of their brightest stars that they had forced Taylor into a lavender marriage with 'baritone babe' Barbara Stanwyck. When Taylor was suspected of hunting for 'rough trade' around Soho, the MGM publicity machine went into overdrive, and once again Elizabeth was appointed the inadvertent stooge for a gay man. Taylor was snapped 'lusting' over Elizabeth in her strapless, low-cut gown, which, of course, only caused more controversy – though nothing quite as bad as his lusting over rent boys would have done. Alternatively, he was photographed looking all forlorn in his dressing-room, penning one of his daily love letters to his wife, who was back in Los Angeles with her wardrobe-mistress lover. What Stanwyck and the press did not yet know was that Taylor, who was tired of the charade, was about to file for divorce.

Away from the set, there was little time for sightseeing in the British capital – Sara told reporters that when the cameras were not rolling, her daughter was receiving essential schooling or was safely tucked up in bed. Of course, if that was the case, this posed the question of how could she have been 'involved' with Robert Taylor?

Elizabeth and Sara did get around to visiting their former home on Wildwood Road, now loaned out to the Women's Voluntary Services. They also spent time with Victor Cazalet's sister Thelma – Cazalet had died in an air crash during the war – and it was she who introduced them to the actor Michael Wilding. Twenty years Elizabeth's senior, Wilding would, of course, figure strongly in her life in later years. The pair are known to have dated, apparently with Sara's blessing, and Wilding was photographed kissing Elizabeth goodbye in the VIP lounge at Heathrow.

More controversially, upon her return to America early in 1949, Elizabeth, very much against her will, became 'involved' with super-recluse Howard Hughes, who had been monitoring her progress by way of cinema newsreels and movie magazines for months. At the age of 44, Hughes was one of the country's wealthiest tycoons, although he was already mentally unbalanced, and he believed that he could have any woman – or man – in the world as long as he offered hard cash and lots of it. His conquests are thought to have included Ginger Rogers, Hedy Lamarr, Ava Gardner, Lana Turner, Carole Lombard, Errol Flynn and Cary Grant – whilst Jean Harlow, Italian beauty Gina Lollobrigida and French revue artiste Zizi Jeanmaire famously spurned his advances.

Hughes possessed a massive collection of Elizabeth Taylor photographs, from the flat-chested ones of her *National Velvet* days to the more recent ones in which she displayed a more than ample cleavage. He emerged from his mansion bolthole to visit Francis's gallery, striking up a friendship and purchasing several paintings he had absolutely no use for, and eventually invited Francis and his family to his home. Hughes is said to have offered $1 million in cash for Elizabeth's hand in marriage – moreover, as her father's permission was required for such a union to take place, Francis is said to have accepted the offer. Elizabeth, however, had stood up to the mighty Louis B. Mayer, so she was unafraid of the scruffy Texan billionaire. Hughes was unceremoniously sent packing.

No sooner had Hughes exited the scene than Glenn Davis arrived home from Korea, hoping to take up with Elizabeth where they had left off. Their reunion would be brief. The press compared their sporting–showbiz love affair with that of French singer Édith Piaf and world boxing champion Marcel Cerdan – the two couples frequently appeared on the same front pages. But whereas Piaf and Cerdan stuck it out – until his death in a plane crash in October 1949 – Elizabeth and Davis would have no such luck.

According to American press reports, Davis turned up at Elizabeth's 17th-birthday party with an expensive cultured-pearl necklace – and a diamond-and-ruby engagement ring. The latter, however, stayed in his pocket when he was introduced to one of the guests. 'She had started dating that rich guy Pawley, and, let's face it, he showed her a better time than I did,' Davis told biographer Kitty Kelley in 1980. 'I stayed there for about a week or ten days of high-stepping and then I took off.' In 1951, Davis married Hollywood starlet Terry Moore, arguably one of the most popular of the 'studio stooge' dates. In her time, Moore would keep the 'outing' hacks from the doors of numerous gay stars, including Rock Hudson, George Nader, Anthony Perkins and James Dean. The marriage lasted less than a year.

Elizabeth had had the new beau waiting in the wings for a while, setting yet another precedent. Twenty-eight-year-old William Pawley was heir to the multimillion-dollar Miami Transit Company. He and Elizabeth met in March 1949. As usual for her, it was love at first sight, and Pawley did not hang around for someone else to muscle in on his territory. First, he wrote Elizabeth a series of love letters, telling her how much he worshiped her. Receiving a positive response, he flew to Los Angeles to gain the approval of her family – in other words, Sara. This was, of course, forthcoming, and soon afterwards, having consulted with Louis B. Mayer, Sara escorted her daughter to Miami to meet the future in-laws. They were mobbed by thousands of fans at the airport and were trailed by hundreds of camp followers as Pawley showed his guests around his home territory. Occasionally, 'shriekers' would be employed by MGM's Florida representatives to incite excitement amongst the crowd, if it was not already evident. They gathered outside theatres and restaurants, allowing the couple scarcely a moment's peace. It was painful for Pawley, although Elizabeth lapped up this adoration whilst pretending to be unnerved by it all.

Though many would submit to the humiliation of doing so in the future, William Pawley made it clear that he would never walk in a movie star's shadow. Sara was actually in favour of this, seeing as the pickings were suitably rich, whilst Elizabeth, as usual, didn't know what she wanted – except as much attention as possible. She had just been contracted to *The Big Hangover* (1950) with Van Johnson and *Father of the Bride* (1950) with Spencer Tracy and Joan Bennett – the latter her biggest break to date – and she tentatively promised that once these were in the can she would retire.

Pawley did not know Elizabeth well enough not to believe her. He tried to expedite matters by asking her to marry him, and on 2 June 1949 she was photographed wearing an emerald-cut diamond ring. Whilst Pawley refused to divulge how much this had set him back, only that Elizabeth was worth every penny, she told *Photoplay*, 'In Hollywood, I would not be anything but Elizabeth Taylor. In Miami, I'll be Elizabeth Pawley. I like that!'

Then, as would happen with just about every relationship Elizabeth embarked upon, the rot set in. Pawley reminded her of her promise and began 'moulding' her into what he saw as the ideal wife – telling her how to dress and conduct herself in public, instructing her on what she should and should not eat, and giving her suggestions on how she should speak and to whom. The further the engagement progressed, the more Elizabeth worried that her own marriage might turn out like that of her parents. She was, and forever would remain, hopelessly insecure where men were concerned. She had virtually no female friends or confidantes to turn to for advice and therefore found herself stewing over problems which as yet did not exist – even when things were going well, she was persistently searching for reasons why they should not be.

In her own bizarre way, Elizabeth must, therefore, have been grateful for the release that came prior to shooting *The Big Hangover*, when she was informed that, before going on to *Father of the Bride*, she would be working as a loan-out in an even bigger project, sharing top-billing with Montgomery Clift in Paramount's $2-million remake of *An American Tragedy* (1931). The finicky director George Stevens chose Elizabeth not, it is alleged, because he considered her to be in Monty's class, which she certainly never was, but because he was convinced that their combined beauty would 'set the screen alight'. Pawley offered her an ultimatum: unless she renounced the film, there would be no wedding. Elizabeth chose the film, and, initially, Pawley adopted a Machiavellian front, accompanying her to the wedding of her friend Jane Powell in the September. The next day, taking a leaf out of the book of the

Hollywood system he so despised, he called Hedda Hopper – not Elizabeth – to announce that the engagement was off.

Elizabeth, in all probability, could not have cared less. On 22 August, her photograph had adorned the cover of *Time* magazine. The gist of the accompanying feature was that the golden greats of yesteryear – Dietrich, Stanwyck, Davis and Crawford – had passed their sell-by date and that Hollywood was now embracing a new type of goddess. 'MGM has . . . turned up a jewel of great price, a true star sapphire,' the editorial read. 'She is Elizabeth Taylor!' The studio disapproved of the analogy. Elizabeth was still only 17 and still a minor, promoted by them as being the archetypal, pure-as-the-driven-snow girl next door. So far as is known, she was still a virgin, never having been let out of her mother's or chaperone's sight for a moment. And this is how a very naive public would have viewed her, despite the fact that she was a busty, beautiful teenager. Her next film, however, would help her to grow up in the eyes of the public.

THREE

WITH THIS FIST,
I THEE WED

EW MEN WOULD PROVE AS IMPORTANT AS THE NEXT ONE who entered Elizabeth's life – one who, equally rarely, would stay the course, because theirs was a relationship that almost certainly never progressed beyond the platonic.

Edward Montgomery Clift was born in Nebraska in October 1920 with a whole set of silver spoons in his mouth, the son of the vice president of the National Bank of Omaha and an ordinary housewife, although she was even more domineering and grasping than Sara Taylor. Having dragged Monty and his siblings around the world to teach them the rudiments of culture, and always living beyond her means, Sunny Clift had enrolled Monty with an exclusive modelling agency when he was still in his early teens. She had encouraged his acting bug, which had seen him treading the boards professionally at the age of 15. After ten successful years on Broadway, Monty had been persuaded to make his first film, playing John Wayne's highly strung adopted son in the acclaimed Howard Hawks western *Red River* (1948).

Monty had loathed the whole Hollywood experience, scrawling the words 'VOMIT, CALIFORNIA' across the tops of the envelopes when writing home. The problem was not the film capital itself, but the hypocrisy of its hierarchy. In the theatre, Monty had been able to choose male lovers without fear of reprisal, but once he hit Hollywood he became so hung up about his sexuality – he was much less ashamed of sleeping with men than in having to remain closeted about his preferences for the sake of his career – that he forced himself to sleep with any number of women in an attempt to determine on which side of the fence he truly belonged. One has to remember that this was an age when there was no such term as bisexuality: one was either a 'regular guy' or a 'fairy', and if a man privately professed to liking men *and* women, this merely meant that he had not yet emerged from the closet. In Monty's case, the torment of uncertainty had driven him to drink and drugs. On top of this, he suffered poor health on account of recurring amoebic dysentery for most of his tragically short life, despite his hunky frame.

The two women in Montgomery Clift's life as the 1950s dawned could not have been more different: Libby Holman, the 40-something bisexual torch singer who had once stood in the dock accused of shooting dead her 22-year-old gay husband, tobacco heir Zachary Smith Reynolds, and 18-year-old Elizabeth Taylor, whose voluptuous assets, Monty's confidants assured him, would be sufficient to turn any gay man straight.

Monty had received rave reviews for *Red River* and had gone on to make *The Search*, directed by Fred Zinneman, *The Big Lift* (1950) and *The Heiress* (1949) opposite Olivia de Havilland, establishing himself as one of America's leading young actors. All of these classic films, however, would be eclipsed by *A Place in the Sun* (1951), the new title for George Stevens's reworking of Theodore Dreiser's 1925 novel *An American Tragedy*, first filmed in 1931 with Phillips Holmes and based on an actual New York murder trial of 1906.

In October 1949, Paramount, worried about Monty's steadfast refusal to cease cruising for rough trade amongst the gay haunts of downtown Los Angeles, opted to 'normalise' him for the benefit of the press by supplying him with Elizabeth as his date for the premiere of *The Heiress*. For her part, she was delighted at the prospect of meeting the most beautiful man in Hollywood, though Monty was indifferent and would have much preferred to have taken his latest boyfriend. He is even down on record as having declared, 'Who the hell is Elizabeth Taylor?', although he must have known. He also fought against the studio's publicity gimmick that because they were going to play lovers on the screen, it might not be a bad idea if they appeared to be so in real life.

Monty realised that Elizabeth was considerably more than just a pretty face and fabulous body – she is said to have impressed him by uttering innumerable profanities, aimed at Sara, in the back of the limousine en route to Grauman's Chinese Theater – and discovered just how much they had in common, not least of all their horrendously overbearing mothers. Monty christened Elizabeth 'my Bessie Mae', a term of endearment that, like their close friendship, lasted for life. Hedda Hopper jumped the gun, as only she of course could, when she saw Elizabeth straightening Monty's bow tie at the theatre entrance. 'Those magnificent lovebirds are very soon going to be married,' she wrote in her syndicated column. In fact, Monty chain-smoked all evening, looked fed up and snarled at a reporter who rushed up to him to praise *The Heiress*: 'You *love* it? I hate the fucking thing!'

George Stevens was lucky to be making *A Place In The Sun* in the first place. The 1931 version, directed by Dietrich's Svengali, Josef von Sternberg (also for Paramount), had so watered down the political content of Dreiser's book that he publicly denounced it, and it had subsequently flopped at the box office. Stevens had no little clout in Hollywood. In the 1920s, he had worked as assistant cameraman on a number of Laurel and Hardy shorts, he had directed his first feature in 1933, and two years later had been requested by Katharine Hepburn to direct her in *Alice Adams* (1935). He had similarly triumphed alongside Ginger Rogers and Fred Astaire, and Cary Grant and Barbara Stanwyck. Despite such plaudits, however, Stevens was not entirely indispensable, like just about everyone else in Hollywood, and he now took an uncalculated risk and threw a spanner into the works by informing the Paramount executives that he wanted to follow the Dreiser story to the letter. A lesser director might have been fired. Stevens was politely reminded (as if he did not know already) of the still present ill-feeling and suspicion in the wake of the McCarthy witch-hunt, and he quickly capitulated; even the names of the central characters had to be changed.

For the sheer beauty and grace of its two leading players, *A Place in the Sun* remains one of the finest American films of all time. For much of the movie, however, Elizabeth in her first authentic adult role serves solely as pretty scenery, and it is Montgomery Clift who carries the production from start to finish. Both Fred Zinneman and Edward Dmytryk, who later directed Elizabeth and Clift in *Raintree County* (1957), avowed in a 1989 television documentary (*Monty: His Place in the Sun*) that Monty's acting prowess had been such that he had been able to coax more out of his co-stars than even the best director.

In the film, Monty played doomed drifter George Eastman, who gets one girl (Shelley Winters) pregnant whilst falling for rich-bitch Angela Vickers (Elizabeth), who is initially attracted to his sadness – as happened with Monty away from the screen. In fact, there is much mirroring of the Taylor–Clift relationship here, particularly during the famous balcony scene where, *en profile* and in the most stunning close-ups since Garbo and Gilbert's *Flesh and the Devil* (1926), they let themselves go. 'How can I tell you how much I love you? How can I tell you all?' he murmurs in the flickering light, whilst she responds, 'Tell Mama . . . Tell Mama all!' To get this scene spot on, Elizabeth and Monty rehearsed in the privacy of his apartment, with Monty later telling his friend Libby Holman that Elizabeth would allow her hands to wander, hoping to turn him on – always to no avail. Later in the film, when Eastman is about to go to the electric chair for 'murder by thought', Angela visits him in his cell and swears that she will love him until the day she dies. Many years later, she repeated those words in the message she sent to Monty's family after his death.

Monty's sensitive portrayal of George Eastman was essentially an extension of himself: the loner who does not fit in. The role

WITH THIS FIST, I THEE WED

earned him an Oscar nomination in the same year that his nearest rival, Marlon Brando, was nominated for *A Streetcar Named Desire* (1951) – both were upstaged by Humphrey Bogart, who won the award for *The African Queen* (1951). Even so, the film received tremendous praise, with scarcely an adverse review. Charlie Chaplin, not one to offer compliments lightly, called it 'the greatest movie ever made about America'. The *New York Times*'s usually acerbic Bosley Crowther singled out Monty as 'terse, hesitating, full, rich, restrained and poignant', whilst distinguished film critic Andrew Sarris later observed in *American Cinema* (Dutton, 1968):

> Clift and Taylor were the most beautiful couple in the history of the cinema. It was a sensuous experience to watch them respond to each other. Those gigantic close-ups of them kissing were unnerving – sybaritic – like gorging on chocolate sundaes.

Al Hine observed in *Holiday*:

> George Stevens has placed Elizabeth Taylor in a part where all the uncomfortable, preening mannerisms that have brought a touch of nausea to her recent portrayals are valid. The conceit, artificiality and awkwardness which mar her playing in most ingénue roles are not only acceptable but essential to her rendition of Miss Rich Bitch 1951.

Many of those close to the two stars believed that Elizabeth genuinely wanted to marry Monty, particularly when Paramount attempted to exploit their friendship by announcing that they were considering changing the title of the film to *The Lovers*. When they met, Elizabeth was sufficiently naive not to be aware that Monty was gay – despite them being frequently accompanied on their outings by his latest rough-trade lover – and, unable to tell him to his face how she felt about him, she put pen to paper. These love letters disturbed him so much that he later gave them away to another lover.

Elizabeth has never kissed and told, despite her hectic love life, so it is very unlikely that we will ever know if their relationship was in any way sexual. What they *did* share progressed way beyond the mere physical. Though 12 years his junior, Elizabeth would be mother, sister, soulmate and lover, all neatly fit into one decidedly pretty but above all sympathetic package. That they were on exactly the same wavelength is further demonstrated by their love scenes in *A Place in the Sun*. The final rehearsals for these were conducted entirely without speech, with Elizabeth and her dishy co-star 'thinking' their lines and communicating by eye contact, a process which intensified and added to the value of their on-screen romance.

Whilst shooting the film, Elizabeth had met 23-year-old 'Nicky' Hilton, the wealthy playboy heir to the $150-million hotel chain, and around Christmas 1949 they began dating, encouraged by Elizabeth's parents, who were far more interested in her marrying into money than in being the escort of an acknowledged bad lot of ambiguous sexuality. Hilton was the arch seducer. Though he held an executive position in his father Conrad's hotel conglomerate (as honorary manager of the Bel Air Hotel), he used this and his wealth to coax as many women – and more than a few men, who were paid to secure their silence – into the sack. Handsome but virtually devoid of charisma, Hilton had attended the prestigious Loyola College but dropped out at 19 to join the navy. Here, he had had any number of male lovers. Later, for the sheer hell of it, he seduced the formidable siren Zsa Zsa Gabor – his father's second wife – with her boasting to all and sundry that he had a ten-inch penis and the sexual stamina of a racehorse.

Had Elizabeth and her parents searched beyond the dollar signs and done their homework, they would have discovered a decidedly unpleasant young man who saw Elizabeth primarily as a status symbol, the first prize in a lottery draw that every red-blooded male in America would have entered, given the chance. Like Elizabeth, Hilton had had no childhood to speak of. Since nursery school, he had been groomed to one day take over the family emporium. As she had been a child star, so he had been a 'child hotelier', never allowed to have friends. However, whereas Elizabeth had had a more or less stable upbringing – although her parents had slack morals, they had nevertheless striven to protect their own – Hilton had not. Essentially, he was bad news: a drunkard who was hopelessly addicted to sex, gambling and drugs. One of his cronies was Texan oil magnate Glen McCarthy, upon whom the James Dean character in *Giant* (1956) would later be based.

Hilton also had a fondness for brawling: he had more than once been cautioned by the police for knocking his girlfriends around. He thought nothing of spending thousands of dollars on some trinket to impress a lover who would only learn what he was like the hard way. He often had black or Jewish lovers, who would then have to listen to his virulently racist or anti-Semitic ranting when he had had too much to drink, which was often. Hilton would later have relationships with Natalie Wood and Marilyn Monroe, and treat them both badly. He was convinced that one of these mistreated lovers or a vengeful partner might want to kill him, *so* despised was he, that he kept a loaded gun on his bedside cabinet – with a rosary wrapped around it for good luck.

Hilton was a swift mover. Aware of Hollywood's strict, unwritten chaperoning laws, he courted Elizabeth conventionally – hitting the town once she was safely tucked up in bed. Their first dates were supervised. Elizabeth and her parents visited the Hiltons' 64-room mansion in Bel Air's Bellagio Road and were knocked sideways to observe how the 'other half' lived. This was opulence way beyond Elizabeth's and Sara's wildest dreams – it was a display of wealth that, certainly from Sara's point of view (if not Elizabeth's, too), far exceeded the need for physical attraction towards the man. Elizabeth might have thought herself in love with Nicky Hilton, but would she have felt the same way had he been poor? And if she could end up living in a place like this, who cared what the husband was like? Not for the first time, unbridled greed for the almighty dollar would cloud Elizabeth's judgement.

Hilton, for his part, 'slummed' it by dropping in on the Taylors – once the press had been alerted to catch him arriving. Occasionally, there would be family outings to Arrowhead Springs. If the couple *did* go out 'alone' – always with an MGM chaperone hovering in the background – Elizabeth insisted upon being taken to downtown drugstores and hamburger joints, hoping that the press would report that she was *not* interested in Hilton's money, whilst revealing the opposite by showing off the latest costly bauble he had given her. Hilton, the manic spendthrift, fixated her with another pastime that set a precedent for the rest of her life: spending for spending's sake.

When Nicky Hilton asked Francis Taylor for his daughter's hand in marriage, permission was granted and the news 'leaked' to the media. On account of her treatment of Glenn Davis and William Pawley, Hedda Hopper had baptised her 'Liz the Jilt', and the columnists now reminded their moralist readers – who nevertheless loved nothing more than a juicy scandal – that Elizabeth looked like she might be aiming for the hat-trick, particularly when Hilton announced that he was expecting her to give up her career so that they could start a family at once.

The press also mentioned that not only was Elizabeth still a minor, but that she had yet to graduate – legally essential, but no problem for MGM, who organised a diploma and slipped her into a graduation ceremony at Los Angeles High in front of hundreds of fellow graduates who were seeing her for the first time and who must have been irked that whilst they had had to study hard for their diplomas, she had not. In February 1950, a few days before Elizabeth's 18th birthday, Conrad Hilton announced that his son was officially engaged to 'the movie star', and the next day she showed off her ring to the press. Hilton had gone one better than William Pawley by buying her a 4.5-carat diamond.

The studio publicity machine, though well aware of Hilton's near-psychotic, abrasive nature, went into overdrive, promoting Nicky and Elizabeth as the perfect all-American couple. Elizabeth had merely been pencilled in for the role of Kay Banks in *Father of the*

Bride, but now shooting began in earnest as the studio rode on the back of the phenomenal amount of press coverage afforded to her forthcoming nuptials. This deflected from the back-lot gossip concerning its director Vincente Minnelli, then married to Judy Garland but not averse to having a not-so-discreet fling with Francis Taylor, the real father of the bride.

The film, recounting a middle-class family's tribulations during the run-up to their only daughter's wedding, is reminiscent of the hugely popular Ernst Lubitsch comedies of the previous generation. In retrospect, of course, its true star is Spencer Tracy, who, as per usual, steals the show. Tracy plays tightwad Stanley Banks, who reflects upon the event which has crippled him financially. In an actress-character juxtaposition, Kay has been a busy girl – seven serious boyfriends in the last few months – but now she has met Buckley Dunstan (Don Taylor), the man she wants to spend the rest of her life with. Stanley does all he can to discourage her, worrying that Buckley might not be good enough, or worse still a crook. He tries to save money by suggesting the couple elope, finally dipping his hand into his pocket and allowing the ceremony to take place – an Elizabeth Taylor extravaganza that sees the society caterers moving in and the house stripped of its furniture to accommodate the hundreds of mostly unwanted guests.

Father of the Bride was scheduled to go on general release to coincide with Elizabeth's wedding, which meant that *A Place in the Sun* was deferred for release until the following year. Much had been made in the press that Elizabeth and Montgomery Clift had extended their love affair beyond the screen, although the studios hoped that such rumours would have been quelled by then. The official reason for the delay was George Stevens's usual excuse that he had used so much film, shooting every scene dozens of times, that it would take this long to cut and edit.

Elizabeth is said to have developed cold feet on the eve of the ceremony, spending some time in New York with Montgomery Clift. In her definitive biography *Montgomery Clift* (Harcourt, 1978), Patricia Bosworth quotes an unnamed friend of Monty telling her that Elizabeth had pleaded with him to marry her so that she could get out of marrying Nicky Hilton. 'Elizabeth's prime objective in life was to find a husband,' the friend is claimed to have said, suggesting that even a neurotic, drunken, partner-beating thug like Hilton might have been better than no husband at all. Elizabeth is also known to have been against the prenuptial agreement drawn up by Hilton's lawyers, avowing that any children the couple had would be brought up in the Catholic faith, though he was a lapsed Catholic who rarely went to church.

The wedding took place on 6 May 1950 at the Church of the Good Shepherd in Beverly Hills and was hailed *the* society event of the year. There were a couple of hitches. First, the press had been requested not to mention Hilton's age – ridiculously, so that he would not be accused of 'child-napping' – and as such he was refused the licence until offering proof that he was over 21! Second, there was a bust-up between Sara and the officiating priest, Monsignor Patrick Concannon, when he informed her that the ceremony would have to be conducted *outside* the altar rail because although she had signed the documents to marry into the Catholic Church, Elizabeth had never been baptised.

This was no ordinary wedding, of course. The bride's real family were not the Taylors but MGM, who had more or less organised everything and were not averse to picking up the tab. After all, this was good publicity for *Father of the Bride*, about to go on general release. The 500 hand-picked guests included the very cream of the MGM crop, many of whom had never met Elizabeth Taylor, and more than a few who could not stand her, Hilton or both of them. Ginger Rogers, Gene Kelly, Phil Harris and Alice Faye, the Van Johnsons, and William Powell only attended because Louis B. Mayer had instructed them to. Hedda Hopper and Louella Parsons were there, hoping to pick up some juicy titbit concerning the groom's still-hectic love life. There were, of course, the genuine close friends – Mickey Rooney, Arthur Loew Jr, Spencer Tracy, Roddy McDowall, Joan Bennett and, for the moment, Debbie Reynolds – along with

4,000 fans who endured the 100-degree heat and who definitely wanted to be there.

Elizabeth looked ravishing in a near-replica of the dress she had worn in *Father of the Bride*. The dress of white satin, embroidered with hundreds of seed-pearls, was made by MGM's Helen Rose at a cost of $3,500, but as it was officially studio property, it would have to be returned after the ceremony. Elizabeth was allowed to keep the mink stole given to her by Sara – paid for by Louis B. Mayer. Her other gifts included a Frans Hals original from Francis, 100 shares of stock from Conrad Hilton and a $60,000 diamond-and-platinum ring from Howard Young. The bridesmaids, whose yellow dresses were also on loan from MGM, included Jane Powell, Hilton's sister Marilyn and Mara Reagan, who would soon marry Howard Taylor. Elizabeth, in what would be the first in a series of stock statements, told the sea of reporters, fronted by Hedda and Louella, 'He's my darling. I'll love no other man until my dying day!'

Maybe Elizabeth already knew that she was kidding herself. Hilton, if he had not been aware of the fact before, now realised that he would henceforth be second in running to the 'Queen of Hollywood' – although as Elizabeth's consort, he was apparently even more in demand as the stud who only had to snap his fingers for the girls – and boys – to come running. Within days of the ceremony, he was up to his old tricks, photographed drunk in the bar of the Carmel Country Club at the start of his honeymoon with two call girls he had picked up. News of this was relayed to Louis B. Mayer, who had coughed up for the honeymoon proper, scheduled to begin on 23 May when the couple were to board the *Queen Mary* bound for Europe. Had Elizabeth been stepping out of line, Mayer would have been able to bring the situation under control. Hilton, however, was a law unto himself, and to have alerted Elizabeth to her new husband's indiscretions – taking into account his mercurial temperament – might only have made matters worse. Mayer was left with no alternative but to cross his fingers and hope that they would be able to sort out any differences 'on neutral territory' – in other words, whilst at sea.

According to reports at the time, the couple argued non-stop throughout the voyage, mostly over Hilton's drinking and the $100,000 he blew in the ship's casino, turning the air blue with their language. There were other rows over their accommodation. Hilton had demanded the bridal stateroom, but despite offering to pay over the odds, this was unavailable: the Duke and Duchess of Windsor were on board, and the shipping company's unwritten rule declared that this room should always be offered to them free of charge whenever they crossed the Atlantic. Neither were these arguments exclusively verbal. Elizabeth often repeated the story to friends that Hilton, in a drunken rage, had stormed into the bathroom whilst she was showering one evening and punched her so hard in the stomach that she had miscarried. There is no evidence that she was ever hospitalised for this, although several of Hilton's other female conquests – never the male ones, who would have probably hit him back – have made similar claims that he managed to win every fight by employing his fists, always hitting them in places where the bruises would not show.

The charade, with Hilton's gambling and extra-marital romps taking precedence over his honeymoon, continued in London, where the couple attended the premiere of *Father of the Bride*. Elizabeth thought nothing of standing outside the theatre for two hours, chatting to fans and signing autographs, compelling her husband to hover in the background. Until then, hardly anyone in London had even heard of Nicky Hilton, and he was aggrieved to be persistently addressed as 'Mr Taylor'.

In Paris, there was a surprise reception hosted by 'holy terror' columnist Elsa Maxwell, Hedda Hopper's and Louella Parsons' arch-rival, who had for many years headed an international sewing circle, along the lines of Nazimova's, despite her considerable girth and unattractiveness. Maxwell was an acclaimed seducer of pretty young women. Many celebrities, such as opera star Maria Callas, succumbed to her charms solely because of the prestige brought about by having a favourable review in her *New York Post* column.

Her attempts to include Elizabeth in her roster of 'Gillette Blades' – in other words, women who 'cut both ways' – failed, although Elizabeth was impressed with her hostess's pulling power so far as the guest list was concerned. This included President Auriol, several heads of state, Jean Cocteau, Édith Piaf, Gérard Philipe and the ageing revue star Mistinguett, who told the press, 'She [Elizabeth] can't act, her voice sets your teeth on edge, and all she does is flash her diamonds and show off her cleavage. I guess she'll go a long way!'

The couple travelled to Rome and then back to Paris for a bash which was attended by more photographers than guests, because word got out that Elizabeth would be wearing $15,000 worth of loaned diamonds. The evening signalled the end of the marriage when a very public slanging match wound up, word for word minus the expletives, on the front pages of the next day's newspapers – in some instances accompanied by pictures of the sobbing bride. Not long afterwards, the couple flew back to New York, where the press were informed that they had separated.

In New York, whilst Nicky Hilton embarked on another sex-and-gambling spree, this time with a well-known actor, Elizabeth – on the verge of what would be the first of many nervous breakdowns – called MGM and begged the studio to send someone to escort her home and protect her from the press, who would not leave her alone, although the 'publicity-holic' only had herself to blame. In an attempt to fool reporters, whose editors kept them on 24-hour standby, Elizabeth announced that she would be flying back to California but instead flew to Chicago. Here, she made a rod for her own back by meeting up with Nicky Hilton. The pair were snapped kissing and she declared how she had never stopped loving him, that their problems had been brought about by outside interference and that to keep her marriage strong she planned to enrol on a course of cookery lessons and learn how to be a proper housewife. 'Elizabeth Taylor in a kitchen?' Marlene Dietrich scoffed to me some years later. 'She wouldn't have known how to boil water without burning it!'

The Hiltons moved to Los Angeles, where Hilton rented a house in Pacific Palisades instead of buying one – it later emerged because a rented property would be easier to dispose of once the marriage had collapsed completely. It was offered a temporary reprieve by Elizabeth's next film. *Father of the Bride* had brought in so much money that MGM commissioned a sequel with the same cast and production team. *Father's Little Dividend* (1951) began shooting in the September. It was not a patch on the original, did not do nearly so well at the box office and does not stand up on its own.

Work might have taken Elizabeth's mind off her marital problems, although she also appears to have been deliberately starting out on a Judy Garland-style 'trail of self-destruction'. In the film, she looks very thin, having lost a stone in weight whilst in Europe, and she was smoking two packs of cigarettes a day in an attempt to calm her nerves and ease her depression. Also, she was becoming addicted to sleeping pills. She had flaked out on the set of *Father's Little Dividend* more than once, and each time Nicky Hilton had dropped in on her at work there had been another row. By October 1950, just five months into her marriage, Elizabeth had had enough. She flew to New York to stay with the only person in the world she felt she could trust – Montgomery Clift.

Monty had also been in Europe, attending the London premiere of *The Heiress* then travelling on to Rome, contravening the studio's instructions, to engage in what he called a 'marathon fuckathon' – a series of wild sexual escapades, which were, from his point of view, a welcome antidote to the restraints of Hollywood. He later said that he might have been content to stay overseas indefinitely, such was his loathing of the film capital and its bigotry, but an emergency had brought him home: Libby Holman's 17-year-old son Christopher had been killed in a climbing accident on Mount Whitney. The tragedy had resulted in a dramatic increase in Holman's already heavy drugs dependency and her ability to drink every one of her hard-drinking friends under the table, bar Monty.

Monty had disapproved of Elizabeth marrying Nicky Hilton, and although they had spoken on the phone and had exchanged letters regularly, this was their first meeting since before the wedding. Both were shocked by the changes in one another: Elizabeth looked gaunt and was a bag of nerves; Monty was matching Libby Holman glass for glass, pill for pill, and was heavily into therapy.

It was effectively a case of the blind leading the blind. Ten years down the road, the worn-out Monty would be guiding a similarly jaded Marilyn Monroe through her paces during *The Misfits* (1961), one of her last films. Monty and Elizabeth were seen shopping in Bloomingdale's and dining at his favourite Italian restaurants – she was one of the few people unaffected by watching him devour his regular fare of raw meat using his fingers, whilst he tended to ignore her habit of belching loudly – and, on the odd occasion, he took her home to meet his parents, still failing to shock her by addressing his mother as 'Cunt'.

It was Monty who convinced Elizabeth that divorcing Nicky Hilton was her only option and that confiding in her parents would be a big mistake. Sara, he said, thought only of material possessions and would urge her to patch things up and suffer Hilton's cruelty for the sake of what the Taylors could get out of him. The news hit the headlines on 8 December, courtesy of Louella Parsons' column in the *Los Angeles Herald-Examiner*, and took the MGM moguls by surprise. The last thing the studio needed prior to releasing *A Place in the Sun* was adverse publicity, particularly as those critics privileged to have watched the rushes were forecasting that this would be *the* movie of 1951.

Parsons, Hopper, et al., had been keeping tabs on the Hilton fiasco from the word go, relaying details of every row, though they had been prohibited from enlarging on the stories of physical abuse – not least of all Elizabeth's claims that her husband had once punched her so hard in the stomach that she had miscarried in the bathroom. 'Other young people quarrel, but before *we* have time to kiss and make up, it's in the papers,' she complained to Louella. This would be the only one of her marriages where she shared no blame for it turning into a disaster – for not even Hilton's closest friends had known what he had been like behind the bedroom door, and those on the receiving end of his fists had been too dignified, it would appear, or maybe too afraid, to speak out. An MGM spokeswoman whom Hilton had bedded almost let the cat out of the bag, telling Louella, 'They always fight about the same thing: his gambling and playing around, his ignoring her as a wife, and they *both* have a temper.' The interview had been orchestrated by Louis B. Mayer, wishing to ensure that public sympathy remained on the side of his star, though in this instance he was not wrong in painting Hilton as the archetypal Bluebeard-villain who deserved all that was coming to him.

The Hiltons' split proved a bitter blow for Elizabeth's grasping mother. Sara had tolerated her son-in-law's philandering – her own husband was little better. The gambling, too, had not perturbed her unduly, for his supply of cash had always appeared limitless. Being made aware for the first time of his psychotic streak *did* concern her, but only because this had driven Elizabeth away from him before she had had time to find a suitable, similarly wealthy replacement.

The divorce was preceded by another incident that set a Taylor precedent: mental or physical collapse in the wake of a dramatic experience, frequently overplayed for the benefit of the media. Having struggled through the initial filming of *Love Is Better Than Ever* (1952) with frayed nerves and what was reported to be 'recurring ulcerative colitis', on 9 January 1951 Elizabeth booked herself into the Cedars of Lebanon Hospital under the name Rebecca Jones. She stayed there for a week, with the columnists refusing to believe the story put out by the studio that she was running up a several-thousand-dollars bill just to be treated for the flu. Some of the tabloids even hinted at a suicide attempt, but there was no evidence to support this. Equally curious, she was allowed out of the hospital each day to attend studio meetings and reshoot key scenes for the inappropriately titled *Love Is Better Than Ever*.

The Hiltons' marriage ended in the Santa Monica divorce court on 29 January 1951 (with the final decree to become effective one year hence), eight months after it had begun, on the grounds of mental and physical cruelty. Elizabeth asked for no alimony but got to keep the shares of Hilton stock given to her by her former father-in-law and around $250,000 of wedding presents. Nicky Hilton did not attend the hearing. He instead sent his lawyer to petition the judge into forcing Elizabeth to sign a document annulling the marriage so that he would be able to remarry in church. The judge declared that the choice was entirely hers, and she refused. Elizabeth also cited Hilton's 'abusive language' as a reason for wanting him out of her life – which might have been a bit rich from a woman who, even then, was renowned for her ability to out-curse the best of them.

'I never want to hear that man's name mentioned again,' Elizabeth told the sea of reporters waiting outside the courthouse. She would be good to her word. When Nicky Hilton died of a drugs-related heart attack in February 1969, aged just 42, she neither commented nor sent flowers to his funeral.

FOUR

ENGLISH WITHOUT TEARS

LIZABETH EVADED MUCH OF THE PRESS BACKLASH THAT followed her divorce by staying with Montgomery Clift in New York. They are said to have slept in the same bed, though this does not necessarily mean that they were in any way lovers – it is a well-known fact that, prone to nightmares, Monty frequently slept between his best friends, actor Kevin McCarthy and his wife Augusta Dabney, without the slightest hint of sexual activity. Quite simply, with Elizabeth and Monty it was a case of two soulmates helping one another through a difficult patch. They are also known to have only socialised amongst Monty's circle, sometimes accompanied by Monty's 'fuck buddy', and Elizabeth's old friend, Roddy McDowall. The trio visited leather bars and gay clubs, where Monty could pick up his favourite rough trade and where, according to both men, Elizabeth could curse to her heart's content.

It had almost been a case of jumping out of the frying pan and into the fire when on the eve of her divorce Elizabeth had made *Love Is Better Than Ever* with Larry Parks, an actor who had been virtually unknown until playing the Oscar-nominated lead in *The Jolson Story* (1946) and its sequel *Jolson Sings Again* (1949). The McCarthy witch-hunt was at its zenith at that time, and just about everyone in Hollywood knew, thought they knew or thought they knew someone who knew a communist. In February 1950, Senator Joe McCarthy's unproved claim that much of the country had been infiltrated by 'Reds' sparked off a wave of mass hysteria that would achieve little other than tarnishing the film community for decades to come and led to a state of paranoia in America in the early 1950s. McCarthy claimed to be in possession of a 205-name list of communists working in the State Department, and it did not take long for 'sublists' of alleged allies and sympathisers to appear – few of these more influential, the senator pointed out, than the ones the public were flocking to see each day on their cinema screens.

Heading the HUAC (House Committee on Un-American Activities), which had vetted the script for *A Place in the Sun*, was Congressman J. Purnell Thomas, who would later be jailed for payroll padding. And in charge of the long-winded Anti-Communist Motion Picture Alliance for the Preservation of American Ideals was John Wayne, a man who had publicly lampooned gay/bisexual stars such as Robert Taylor, Robert Montgomery and Tyrone Power as 'unnatural men'. However, whilst these actors had been decorated for their bravery during the Second World War, the supposedly gung-ho Wayne had made any number of excuses not to fight for his country. Wayne's fanatical right-wing allies included Clark Gable, Gary Cooper, Barbara Stanwyck, Howard Hughes, Hedda Hopper, Lola Rogers (the mother of Ginger), Walt Disney and two of the actors he had mocked, Robert Taylor and Robert Montgomery. One wonders how Wayne slept at night. Opposing the purge, which very quickly got out of hand, were Tallulah Bankhead, Gene Kelly, Humphrey Bogart and Lauren Bacall, Danny Kaye, director John Huston, and future president Richard Nixon.

Directors Elia Kazan and Edward Dmytryk (one of the so-called 'Hollywood Ten' who had been jailed for their beliefs) were but two who shopped their suspected communist colleagues. Careers were needlessly destroyed: those of playwrights Lillian Hellman and Dashiel Hammet, actor Melvyn Douglas, and actresses Gale Sondergaard and Anne Revere, who had twice worked with

Elizabeth. John Garfield, a brilliant actor who had raved over Elizabeth's performance in *A Place in the Sun* and had wanted to work with her, died a broken man in 1952 at the age of 39. The worst casualty from Elizabeth's point of view, however, was Larry Parks, because she was indirectly involved with him when the proverbial blast hit the fan. So far as some of Senator McCarthy's aides were concerned, if someone was the partner, lover or best friend of a suspected communist – or even of you were someone who played a character on screen who seemed to lean in that direction – it figured that they too might have such tendencies – absolute piffle, of course!

Neither did Elizabeth do herself any favours in the wake of her messy, very public divorce by having an affair with the director of *Love Is Better Than Ever*, Stanley Donen – so far as is known, her first relationship with a married man. Eight years her senior, Donen had teamed up with Gene Kelly as a Broadway dancer/assistant choreographer in 1941, aged just 17. The two had worked together ever since, their films having included *On the Town* (1949), which Donen had co-directed. Their subsequent successes would include *Seven Brides for Seven Brothers* (1954), *Funny Face* (1957) and *Charade* (1963). Kelly had just signed Donen for *Singin' in the Rain* (1952) and was keen to have his protégé report back with the names of any 'Reds' who might be hiding in the closet. It was almost certainly Kelly who shopped Larry Parks to the HUAC.

Parks could have extricated himself from a tricky situation, as many did during this silly political soap opera, by repeating a stock statement at his impromptu hearing: 'I respectfully decline to answer the question [that I am a Communist] on the grounds that this is privileged information under the Fifth Amendment of the United States Constitution.' Instead, he admitted that he had once been a member of the Communist Party. Threatened with incarceration (the Hollywood Ten had served up to twelve months in jail, depending upon the gravity of their 'crimes'), Parks was compelled to name, or invent, twelve Reds and was promised that he would be allowed to continue with his career. He refused, and for him it was the end of the road. *Love Is Better Than Ever* would be assigned to oblivion, and he made just two more films – his swansong being *Freud* (1962) with Montgomery Clift – before his death in 1975, at which time he was running his own real-estate firm.

Elizabeth was never summoned before the HUAC, though not through lack of trying on Howard Hughes's part. Having already been twice rejected by her, the tycoon had obviously not learned his lesson. Despite the power his enormous wealth generated, even Hughes would not have dared report Elizabeth to the HUAC without some proof, even fabricated, so he 'leaked' her name to committee member Hedda Hopper – the method in his madness being that he would 'rescue' her, marry her and they would live happily ever after. Elizabeth might have coped with the absurdity of this had it not coincided with her affair with Stanley Donen hitting the headlines. Mrs Donen – the dancer Jeanne Coyne – filed for divorce and threatened to cite the 19-year-old Elizabeth as co-respondent, which, of course, she had every right to do. There then followed a nasty, very public argument with Sara Taylor when Elizabeth took her lover home to meet the family – this also ended up on the front pages.

Shortly after this episode, Elizabeth was rushed into hospital. Depending upon which report one heeded, she was either suffering from exhaustion or it was because of a suicide attempt. No sooner had she recovered from this ordeal than she was once again diagnosed with colitis and a peptic ulcer.

Despite the trouble caused by her relationship with Stanley Donen, Elizabeth refused to give him up, and when she turned up for the premiere of *Father's Little Dividend* clutching his arm, MGM stepped in. She had been contracted for a cameo role as herself in *Callaway Went Thataway* (1951) with Fred MacMurray and Howard Keel, but after that nothing major was planned other than the release of *A Place in the Sun* later in the year. The studio held an emergency meeting, and it was decided to get her out of the country as soon as possible so that they could put an end to her affair with Donen with her out of the frame. She was signed up as Robert Taylor's love interest in *Ivanhoe* (1952), scheduled to begin shooting in England during the summer.

Medieval dramas, musical revivals, biblical spectaculars and period thrillers were on the rise again at this time because of the McCarthy hearings. The studios, so as not to be caught out, opted for non-contemporary, non-political themes: *Quo Vadis* (1951) was amongst the first and was followed by *Scaramouche* (1952), *The Prisoner of Zenda* (1952) and *Knights of the Round Table* (1953). Another massive threat to the movie industry was the new medium of television – despite the cynics' claims that this 'newfangled contraption' would never take on, in the spring of 1951 one-in-five American homes possessed one.

Some organisations, such as NBC, attempted to draw away some of the rapidly escalating advertising funds from the television network by launching radio programmes such as *The Big Show*, a $50,000-a-time, 90-minute extravaganza hosted on Sunday evenings by the no-holds-barred Tallulah Bankhead. This featured the most dazzling array of stars ever assembled in a single studio, from all walks of life. The likes of Bing Crosby, Frank Sinatra and Édith Piaf were treated with the utmost respect, but Tallulah went out on a limb to offend artistes she regarded as 'jokes'. Ethel Merman, whose contract insisted that no reference be made to her age, was greeted with, 'Hello, Ethel, darling. And may I say, you don't look a day over 60!' Tallulah might only have been ribbing when she threatened to inform her listeners on live radio that Elizabeth had once been married to 'the biggest man in the hotel trade' – an indiscreet reference to Nicky Hilton's legendary endowment, which she had personally sampled. Even so, Elizabeth was taking no chances, and Tallulah got to 'interrogate' his stepmother/mistress Zsa Zsa Gabor instead.

With profits plummeting as more and more people stayed home to watch television, big changes were being effected by the studio, particularly at MGM. Louis B. Mayer, the invincible tyrant who had made every star but Garbo quake in their boots and whose health was starting to fail, resigned in 1951 and was replaced by the much younger Dore Schary, who had joined MGM as a scriptwriter in 1937. Schary, to cut down on costs, was forced to release some of his major stars so that they could work freelance, including Spencer Tracy, Clark Gable and Greer Garson. MGM and the other studios compensated for their losses by searching beyond the confines of Hollywood for 'package deals' – outfits comprising directors, producers, lead players, scriptwriters and cameramen, mostly from Europe. Though Elizabeth and her contemporaries might not yet have been aware of the fact, fierce competition was just around the corner – a whole galaxy of stars who were not just pretty faces, but considerably more talented than their American counterparts were on their way: Leslie Caron, Gina Lollobrigida, Vittorio Gassman, Hildegarde Knef, Juliette Gréco, Gérard Philipe and sex-kitten Brigitte Bardot. In short, for every contract player the studio placed on suspension for not toeing the line, two more were waiting in the wings.

It might well be that Elizabeth was threatened with suspension when she tried to get out of going to England to do *Ivanhoe*, claiming that she had suffered a nervous breakdown – true – but when her pleas fell on deaf ears, following a brief sojourn in New York with Montgomery Clift, she elected to soldier on. On 18 June 1951, she sailed on the *Liberté*, accompanied by her secretary Peggy Rutledge and MGM publicist Malvina Pumphrey, who had been instructed to keep an eye on her. No sooner had she settled into her London hotel suite than she received a call from Michael Wilding. Sara Taylor later claimed (in an August 1952 interview with *Motion Picture*) that she had encouraged Elizabeth to set her sights on Wilding – another 'tall tale' considering that Sara had bemoaned the family losing out on Nicky Hilton's wealth, and Wilding was not a wealthy man by any means.

Like Howard Hughes before him, Wilding had been monitoring Elizabeth's progress from afar, though not for the same selfish reasons. He invited her to dinner, and, as per usual for her, it was love at first sight. Over the next two months, the pair were rarely apart when she was not working on *Ivanhoe*.

Born in Westcliff-on-Sea in 1912, Michael Wilding had spent much of his childhood in Russia, where his father had worked for British Intelligence. Upon leaving the prestigious Christ's Hospital, otherwise known as the Bluecoat School, he had aspired to become an artist, but the acting bug had bitten, and he had made his debut in *Pastorale*, an Austrian film, in 1933. Dashing and debonair, with a clipped accent and slightly slurred (on account of epilepsy) delivery, he had teamed up with Anna Neagle for a tremendously successful series of post-war sugary romantic comedies – most notably *Spring in Park Lane* (1948) and *Maytime in Mayfair* (1949) – directed by Neagle's husband, Herbert Wilcox. All three were insufferable snobs but curiously had mass appeal with the working classes, whom they had always looked down upon.

Wilding had had a very public affair with Marlene Dietrich, his recent co-star in Hitchcock's *Stage Fright* (1950), who was understandably peeved to have been shunted aside for a younger model. 'They said I was jealous because Elizabeth Taylor was much younger than me,' Marlene told me in 1990, 'but that's untrue. I was angry at the time because she wasn't a star, just a tart with breasts and very little talent. Her voice used to set my teeth on edge!' Wilding also had a lengthy off-on affair with Stewart Granger, who later sued Hedda Hopper for outing them in her autobiography. This relationship would continue well into his association with Elizabeth.

Worried by the scandal that would erupt by her dating a man old enough to be her father, MGM's British representatives tried to fix Elizabeth up with golden-boy teen-idol Tab Hunter, who was in London shooting *Saturday Island* (1952). The move was an attempt to keep an allegedly salacious story out of the press and made this the third time Elizabeth had been used as a stooge-date for a gay man – one who would years later wear his sexuality with great pride. She enjoyed Hunter's company but made it clear that she was only interested in Wilding. At the end of August 1951, Elizabeth and Wilding became secretly engaged, mindless of the fact that he was still married to the actress Kay Young and that

Elizabeth's own decree would not become absolute until January 1952. Also, as she was still under the age of 21, she would not be permitted to marry without her parents' permission. With this in mind, she had the gall to send a telegram home, signed 'Elizabeth and Michael Wilding'.

Ivanhoe was an entertaining slice of historical hokum, awash with dodgy wigs and false beards, the kind of fare that appealed to Saturday-morning matinees. Adapted from Sir Walter Scott's novel, it was 'Hollywoodised' and later denounced by Elizabeth as 'a piece of cachou'. It did well at the box office, however, and was nominated for best film at the Oscars in 1952, losing to *The Greatest Show on Earth*.

Robert Taylor and George Sanders, at 40 and 45 respectively, were a little too old to play the swashbuckling hero and cheesy villain, de Bois-Guilbert, and Taylor's Nebraska drawl is out of place in medieval England. Elizabeth makes her appearance almost half an hour into the film as Rebecca of York, the 'Jewish infidel' who as an outsider must hide her face in public. Some of the anti-Semitic comments levelled at her transcend fiction, paralleling what was happening in Hollywood at the time, and make for uncomfortable viewing.

Having completed the film, and after spending a few days in the south of France, Elizabeth returned to New York and more shindigs with Montgomery Clift and Roddy McDowall. The trio stayed at the Plaza Hotel, where the management offered them a long-weekend suite free of charge in appreciation of the fabulous reviews earned by *A Place in the Sun* – although it was actually paid for by Paramount. Michael Wilding had asked Elizabeth to marry him, and, as had happened with Nicky Hilton, the sojourn appears to have been another attempt to 'cop out' on her accepting. In *Montgomery Clift*, Patricia Bosworth quotes an anonymous friend of the actor as telling her, 'I remember being at Monty's apartment when Elizabeth phoned from the Plaza, where she was staying, and begged him to reconsider marrying her before Wilding arrived in New York. Monty was sweet [in refusing], but adamant.'

Sara and Francis Taylor might not have entirely forgiven their daughter her trespasses, but MGM flew them to New York all the same. They were celebrating their silver-wedding anniversary, and for a couple of days everyone played happy families. There was controversy, however, after the Taylors left and Elizabeth, Monty and McDowall stayed on at the Plaza for another week – expecting Paramount to pick up the tab. Rather than pay the excess $2,500 – though goodness knows how they managed to run up such a bill in so little time – the trio moved to a cheaper hotel, where in a drunken spree they wrecked their room and ran up another bill. Feeling guilty, Elizabeth paid for the damage and bought gifts for those responsible for cleaning up after her.

Then it was on to 'Chez Clift' and more newspaper headlines when Nicky Hilton breezed into town and invited Elizabeth to dinner for old time's sake. She accepted, the press were of course alerted and less than a week later she was photographed in the same restaurant with Michael Wilding – having learned of her latest 'calamity', Wilding felt that she might need a friendly shoulder to cry on.

Wilding had tagged along with Anna Neagle and Herbert Wilcox, who were in America to promote *The Lady with the Lamp* (1951), their sanitised version of the Florence Nightingale story in which Wilding had a cameo. MGM, who had condemned Elizabeth for her behaviour in New York, saw photographs of her wearing the sapphire ring Wilding had given her (paid for by Elizabeth herself, because his quickie divorce had left him broke) and now declared that she had gone too far by getting involved with a man who was too old for her. They were also annoyed that he was, like Nicky Hilton, a known bisexual – albeit without Hilton's thuggish traits – and, like Stanley Donen, very much married when his relationship with Elizabeth had begun. There were further complications when Elizabeth and Wilding were seen socialising with Jean Simmons and her husband Stewart Granger, the very man Wilding was suspected of having an affair with.

Dore Schary, who was proving only marginally more popular with his stars than Louis B. Mayer had been, worked behind the scenes, trying to ensure that the Wilcoxes' visit was briefer than planned, even if this meant 'pulling' their film. His plan backfired. When they and Wilding returned to London in the middle of February, Elizabeth gave the gossips something to talk about by travelling with them. She also gave every indication that she might be pregnant, particularly when Wilding announced that he was going to make 'an honest woman' out of her as soon as possible.

Hollywood was robbed of cashing in on the publicity this time around when Elizabeth married Michael Wilding on 21 February 1952, six days before her twentieth birthday. She had wanted the ceremony to take place at a church on Victor Cazalet's estate but was told that this would take around a month to organise. Although waiting would have been the respectful thing to do – King George VI had died two weeks earlier, and the capital was still in mourning – Elizabeth would not hear of it. She was too impatient to wait and, in any case, would not be told what to do, neither then nor in the future.

The ten-minute ceremony took place at Caxton Hall. Because he claimed he was 'counting the pennies', Wilding accepted the Wilcoxes' offer to pay for everything, including the reception at Claridge's. Elizabeth financed the honeymoon and set a precedent for this particular marriage: each time she saw an expensive bauble that she liked but which Wilding could not afford, she paid for it herself and told everyone that it had come from him.

The bride wore another Helen Rose creation. The Wilcoxes were witnesses, whilst Ben Goetz (the head of British MGM) and his wife stood in for Elizabeth's parents, who did not attend. Howard Taylor had wanted to be there but was doing military service in Korea. Outside the registry office, the Wildings were cheered by 3,000 fans, many wearing black armbands. And as had happened on the 'happiest day' of her life with Nicky Hilton, Elizabeth delivered the speech, variations of which would crop up over the years: 'All I want is to be Michael's wife and have his children. I'm never going to put my career first!'

The honeymoon – two weeks in the French Alps and innumerable gratis society parties – is said to have been blissful; certainly, there were no reported arguments. Another month was spent in his plush flat in Mayfair's Bruton Street – according to Wilding, 'I was learning Elizabeth the rudiments of the housewife!' Sara Taylor scoffed at this and in interviews repeated what she had told *Photoplay* in September 1951: 'What she can't do around the house includes almost everything you could mention.' When the *Daily Express*'s David Lewin asked Elizabeth if she really was intent on relinquishing her career, she as per usual piped up with the first thing that came into her head: 'A career is not all *that* important, anyway!'

Then, it was back home and back to work. MGM had heard the rumour that the fiercely independent, anti-Hollywood Montgomery Clift had tried to persuade Elizabeth to drop off the studio-system bandwagon and spread her wings – or rebel against it, as he had, and accept only the roles she really wanted. They therefore upped her salary to $6,000 a week, loaned her $50,000 for the house in Beverly Hills that had taken her fancy and offered her husband a $3,000-a-week three-year contract, which he certainly did not merit at the time. Prior to leaving England, Wilding also received a £40,000 tax demand that Elizabeth is thought to have paid.

Like the proverbial fish out of water, Michael Wilding did not make it big in Hollywood. His first film there, opposite Greer Garson in *The Law and the Lady* (1951), was a hopeless rehash of Joan Crawford's *The Last of Mrs Cheyney* (1937) and saw both leads panned by the critics. His second (of which more later) was *Torch Song* (1953) with Crawford herself. It was a part that any good-looking actor with a British accent could have played – it was Crawford's film, period.

Elizabeth's first film as Mrs Wilding was the portentously titled *The Girl Who had Everything* (1953), perhaps MGM's way of warning her, with the emphasis being on the past tense, what would happen if she failed to knuckle down to marriage number two. Like the Wilding outing, it was a rewrite of an earlier smash, *A Free Soul*, which had earned plaudits for Cark Gable, Norma Shearer and

Lionel Barrymore in 1931. Elizabeth plays rich-girl Jean Latimer, who falls for a handsome Latino (Fernando Lamas), becomes his mistress, then finds out he is a crook being hunted by mobsters who eventually kill him. There is also a very bold suggestion for the time of an incestuous relationship between Jean and her father, played by William Powell. However, with Lamas attempting to step into Gable's shoes, even though he possessed not one fraction of his raw animal magnetism, and Elizabeth shrieking much of the time and merely looking decorative, the film was nothing to write home about.

In fact, so far as MGM were concerned, Elizabeth had stepped out of line by getting pregnant within two months of her wedding and not announcing her condition until well into the shooting of the film. And rather than grant her maternity leave, as any reputable employer would, Dore Schary put her on suspension as soon as the film was in the can. Unusually, though, rather than stop her salary, they trimmed it to $2,000 a week.

Michael Wilding also suffered Schary's wrath for failing to toe the line. When he was offered a part in *Latin Lovers* (1953) with Lana Turner and Ricardo Montalban, he criticised the script and refused to report to the set until his lines had been changed. With no success in Hollywood and while enjoying a much larger salary than most established character actors, Wilding's should have been a case of beggars not being choosers. He, however, was Elizabeth Taylor's husband and considered himself to be on a higher pedestal than most mortals, which was why Schary opted to bring him back to earth with a bang. Wilding was replaced by John Lund in *The Latin Lover* then suspended without pay until the picture was completed.

Montgomery Clift was also having a rough time finding good parts after *A Place in the Sun*, though this was mostly his own fault. He had turned down *Sunset Boulevard* (1950), declaring that the scenario of the fading star falling for the younger man smacked of his own relationship with Libby Holman. Monty had played the tortured priest in Hitchcock's *I Confess* (1953) with great conviction, and he had moved audiences to tears with his portrayal of the ill-fated Prewitt in *From Here to Eternity* (1953), securing Frank Sinatra's comeback by getting him a part in the film, since which time he had rejected one script after another – over 50 by the end of 1952!

Although Monty had refused to see Elizabeth during her marriage to Nicky Hilton – he had not been far out by giving them just six months – he took to Michael Wilding and was a frequent visitor to their Hollywood home. Cynics suggested at the time that Monty had some kind of ulterior motive, that despite his homosexuality he believed that he would marry Elizabeth some day and that in the meantime he was looking out for her. The aforementioned anonymous friend interviewed by Patricia Bosworth went one step further by suggesting that Monty and Wilding were actually *competing* for Elizabeth's affections, concluding, 'Monty felt very loving and protective and rather superior when it came to Elizabeth Taylor.'

There is little doubting that Monty's professional fussiness rubbed off on Elizabeth during his extended stays with the Wildings. She turned down *All the Brothers were Valiant* (1953) with Robert Taylor and Stewart Granger – as it happened, another paltry rehash of a Joan Crawford film (*Across to Singapore*, 1928) – and *Roman Holiday* (1953), later a huge success for Audrey Hepburn. MGM rewarded Elizabeth by extending her suspension.

On 6 January 1953, Michael Howard Wilding, Elizabeth's first child, was born by Caesarean section, and the press reported Taylor and Wilding 'deliriously happy and in love'. Montgomery Clift showered the baby with gifts and constructed a 'mini-nursery' in his apartment for when Elizabeth came to stay. MGM released Elizabeth from her suspension only to extend her punishment by loaning her out to Paramount for *Elephant Walk* (1954). The theme of the film was something of a cross between *Rebecca* (1940) and the later *Giant*. Elizabeth plays Ruth Wiley, the new wife of a tea planter (Peter Finch) who has tremendous difficulty fitting in when she and her husband relocate to a plantation in Ceylon. That she was miscast goes without saying, particularly in the scenes where her husband eschews his marital bed to spend time with his drinking cronies because he does not find her attractive. What red-blooded male, the critics unanimously demanded, would *not* wish to spend the night with Elizabeth Taylor?

Hedda Hopper suggested the title of the film most appropriate, because Elizabeth's weight had ballooned to 150 pounds following the birth of her son. Elizabeth asked for a salary increase, which was refused. Indeed, she was told to consider herself fortunate to be employed, period. Neither had she been first choice for the film. British actress Vivien Leigh, then married to Laurence Olivier, had completed most of the location scenes before collapsing from nervous exhaustion, in what turned out to be the onset of mental illness. Elizabeth's hell-raiser co-stars Peter Finch and Dana Andrews recognised her as a 'regular guy' and invited her to join their 'Fuck You Club' – a select group of extras and studio personnel who made it a preoccupation to shock everyone in sight with their foul language and atrocious table manners. For the rest of her life, Elizabeth would belch loudly and break wind in front of dinner guests she believed needed to be put in their place. MGM received $150,000 for loaning her out, around eight times the salary she received from Paramount, and the budget eventually soared to a record (for that studio) $3 million. In an attempt to save on expenditure, Paramount retained all of Vivien Leigh's long shots, though they are thought to have coughed up for the medical expenses when Elizabeth was hospitalised upon her return to Hollywood. A wind-machine had blown a piece of grit into her right eye, and this had become so deeply embedded that surgery was required to remove it, after which there were complications when an ulcer developed. Elizabeth later recalled that she had been lucky not to lose the eye. The bandages were barely removed when she began work on her next film, *Rhapsody* (1954). It is interesting to note that her co-star for this should have been one Richard Burton, but he had been reassigned to *The Robe* (1953) on account of the delay caused by Elizabeth's injury.

Michael Wilding, meanwhile, had been given the invidious task of supporting Joan Crawford in her first Technicolor film, *Torch Song*. Joan played musical-comedy star Jenny Stewart – an amalgamation of all the gay icons of the day, collectively baptised as 'The Victory Red Brigade' owing to their predilection for the famous Elizabeth Arden lipstick. Édith Piaf, Maria Callas, Bette Davis, Judy Garland, Tallulah Bankhead and Joan herself were rarely seen in public without lashings of the stuff. Wilding played her pianist love interest who had been blinded during the war. The film was shot in just 24 days and was directed by Charles Walters, who had triumphed with Judy's *Easter Parade* (1948) and *Meet Me in St Louis*. Walters had planned as near as possible to have an all gay/bisexual production and to present its male characters as essentially weak, whilst the Crawford character would monopolise the proceedings, again reflecting real life. His big mistake was in failing to realise that Joan Crawford/Jenny Stewart would never have given a meek, mumbling and mild man such as Michael Wilding the time of day, let alone lean on him for support.

Joan made it more than clear that she did not want Wilding anywhere near the picture, but the $125,000 fee from MGM helped change her mind. Even so, there were problems as soon as shooting began – caused by Elizabeth, who was naturally apprehensive about her husband working with a nymphomaniac renowned for sleeping with her leading men. In Joan's defence, however, it must be said that it was only through Elizabeth's pushing that Wilding had been given the part in the first place. She was shooting *Rhapsody* on a nearby lot, so she made a point of checking up on Wilding every day to ensure that Joan was not leading him astray. What she did not know was that the *director* had set his sights on him, though nothing appears to have come of this.

Some years later, Joan told Roy Newquist in *Conversations with Joan Crawford* (Citadel, 1980), 'I think Elizabeth Taylor, in one of her rare good films [*Rhapsody*], is great to watch.' In the spring of 1953, however, she regarded the young star as an upstart, publicly referring to her as 'Princess Brat', and took exception to Elizabeth 'swanning' onto *her* set, without permission, *and* ignoring her. Joan sent a message to Elizabeth via her publicist which read, 'You tell that little bitch never to walk in here again without acknowledging me. I want you to teach her some manners!' She then posted a guard at the soundstage door – at her own expense – to prevent Elizabeth from getting in.

Elizabeth tried to fight back but, aside from her colourful language, was no match for the ferocious, hugely feared but respected Joan, a far greater actress than she would ever be. When Hedda Hopper's syndicated column reported Elizabeth as having said, 'Mike Wilding is playing a blind man – that way he won't have to *look* at Crawford during their movie,' Joan hit back with an unprintable comment about Elizabeth almost losing her sight in *Elephant Walk*. Some years later, when spiralling production costs, largely on account of Elizabeth's illnesses and indispositions, threatened Twentieth Century Fox with bankruptcy and saw them laying off 200 workers, Joan recalled Elizabeth's behaviour on the set of *Torch Song* and told reporters (Sean Considine, *Bette & Joan: The Divine Feud*), 'Miss Taylor is a spoilt, indulgent child – a blemish on public decency.'

FIVE

A DATE WITH JIMMY AND ROCK

I N *RHAPSODY*, ELIZABETH PLAYED LOUISE DURANT, YET another spoilt rich girl, who flees the comfortable family nest to fall for a couple of self-centred musicians, played by John Ericson and Vittorio Gassman. At that time, Gassman, a brooding, exceedingly handsome slab of beefcake who had recently married Shelley Winters, was Italy's leading actor. He should have been perfect as the moody violinist, but, like everyone else, he appears to be stumbling around the set much of the time.

Naturally, Louise marries the wrong man (Ericson), realises her mistake when he turns to drink and leaves him for his rival. However, because MGM was still ruled by the Motion Picture Code of Decency at that time, she eventually learns the error of her ways and returns to her husband. The film was best summed up by the *New York Herald Tribune*, which observed, 'Her animation is only the animation of the doll with the strings being pulled behind the scenes . . . even her evident and genuine beauty seems at times to be fake.' Elizabeth and Ericson merely shrugged off the bad reviews, but for Vittorio Gassman it was the last straw. Like Michael Wilding, he had seen his roles deteriorating since coming to Hollywood; by the end of the year, he would have returned to Europe and his former glory. As for Wilding, after *Torch Song* he would soon revert to his usual Hollywood tosh – he looks positively embarrassing in tights as Prince Charming in *The Glass Slipper* (1955).

Elizabeth always claimed to have hated *Beau Brummell* (1954), in which she starred opposite Stewart Granger, still reputedly 'friendly' with Michael Wilding. First filmed in 1924 with real-life Lothario John Barrymore in the title role, as far as costume dramas go it is not that bad, but most of the critics gave it the thumbs down on account of 'regular guy' Granger playing a dandy, the adviser to an even more affected Prince of Wales (later George IV), aka Peter Ustinov. As his paramour, Lady Patricia, Elizabeth was poor – 'Decorative, but something less than usual as a heroine,' opined the *New York Herald Tribune*. It was filmed in England during the summer of 1953, and the next year it would be selected for the Royal Command Film Performance.

In the September, leaving Michael junior with Elizabeth's in-laws, the Wildings flew from London to Copenhagen for a series of personal appearances – for some inexplicable reason, the very bland *The Girl Who had Everything* was packing Scandinavian cinemas. No sooner had they checked into their hotel than Elizabeth fell victim to viral flu – worse than this, a Danish consultant diagnosed mild tachycardia. Fearing she might die on the plane home, she sent for her baby and recovered at once. Next, the happy family headed for Madrid – where Elizabeth threw a fit at a bullfight upon discovering that they killed the bull – then Capri, where she upset the customers at Gracie Fields' La Canzone del Mare complex by ignoring the hostess and ordering her staff around.

MGM were clearly intent on getting their money's worth out of Elizabeth – before she developed a genuine illness and actually died on them, according to one anonymous spokesman, which was perhaps being a little too cruel – for no sooner had *Beau Brummell* wrapped than she was rushed into the screen adaptation of F. Scott Fitzgerald's *The Last Time I Saw Paris* with Van Johnson, her fourth film in less than a year.

Told mostly in flashback, it is a good film that might have been better with a more charismatic leading man – Johnson's utter lack of warmth prevents the audience from ever sympathising with him. Elizabeth, on the other hand, is at her most alluring as doomed American in Paris, Helen Ellswirth. The soundtrack of contemporary French *chansons* is mesmerising – composed not by the credited Conrad Salinger, but by Charles Trenet and Henri Contet. Elizabeth also requested that her favourite song at the time, Édith Piaf's 'La vie en rose', should be included.

Elizabeth surprised everyone by getting along with the film's director Richard Brooks, a man almost as renowned for his harsh approach and vulgarity as he was for his gritty scripts and ace direction. Brooks had co-scripted *Key Largo* (1948) and would go on to win an Oscar for *Elmer Gantry* (1960), but like Michael Curtiz had a knack of bullying his actresses in an attempt to draw better performances out of them. Alexis Smith, Pier Angeli and the equally foul-mouthed Bette Davis had given as good as they got, maintaining that complaining about Brooks's anti-social behaviour only made matters worse. Elizabeth, it is reported, merely ignored him.

Probably still acting on Montgomery Clift's advice, Elizabeth turned down *The Barefoot Contessa* (1954) – which subsequently went to Ava Gardner – whilst her husband went one better. Wilding denounced the part of the pharoah in *The Egyptian* (1954) as a 'stuffy nightshirt role' and set about finding a role on the legitimate stage, which he said would better befit his talents – only to reject, earning Rex Harrison's eternal gratitude, the part of Professor Henry Higgins in a nationwide tour of *My Fair Lady*. When later asked why he had refused the role of a lifetime, he merely shrugged his shoulders and quipped, 'I guess I just must be lazy!'

The Wildings' second son, Christopher Edward (the Edward after Montgomery Clift, whose first name this was), was born on 27 February 1955 – once again by Caesarean section – it is said so that Elizabeth might have the ultimate 23rd birthday present. By now, their spending was spiralling out of control. However, claiming that their current home was now beneath their 'ultra-celebrity couple' status, the Wildings persuaded MGM to extend their loan to enable them to relocate to a luxury steel, glass and baked-earth residence at 1375 Beverly Estate Drive, in the then largely untouched Benedict Canyon. Designed by Los Angeles architect George McLean and on the market for $150,000, one of its sheer glass walls overlooked the valley below. In next to no time, visitors would be describing the house as filthy on account of the menagerie they had amassed – cats, dogs and ducks, which were given the run of the place and not house-trained. Wilding was oblivious to the mess and his wife's sloppy habits. 'She hangs her clothes on the floor and is obsessed with collecting magazines with her lovely face on their covers,' he told Louella Parsons. Most of the time all *he* was interested in was hanging around the pool, smoking his pipe and painting.

It was only when she learned that Grace Kelly had been pencilled in for one of the leads in George Stevens's *Giant*, which had already spent three years on the stocks, that Elizabeth became interested. The fact that the film was to be made by Warner Brothers interested MGM even more. Elizabeth's last few films for the studio had been deemed mediocre – Hollywood was still using *A Place in the Sun* as a yardstick to measure her by. Dore Schary was hoping that as a loan-out she would bring in a nice return and not be in a position to demand a salary rise or cause them any problems with her convoluted personal life. Schary pulled all the necessary strings, and she got the part.

Despite his near-legendary status, George Stevens preferred the title of 'independent director'. As such, he lacked the financial backing of a major studio. Unable to afford the film rights to Edna Ferber's epic bestselling novel (20 *million* copies sold by 2004), which critiqued the all-American dream, he formed a profit-sharing corporation with 67-year-old Ferber and producer Henry Ginsberg to get the project off the ground. Alan Ladd and Clark Gable had been considered for the central role of racist bigot Bick Benedict but were dismissed as being 'over the hill'. William Holden had also been tested, but the part was given to Rock Hudson, Universal's resident B-movie beefcake who had impressed everyone with his recent moving performance opposite Jane Wyman in *Magnificent Obsession* (1954).

With Elizabeth signed to play Bick's long-suffering wife Lesley, Montgomery Clift was signed to be the film's third lead, the rebellious outsider Jett Rink, more or less upon her recommendation, only for him to be declared too much of a risk by Warner Brothers' insurance company on account of his much-publicised drink-and-drugs dependency. Instead, Stevens brought in his biggest scoop: 24-year-old James Dean, straight out of the yet-to-be-released *Rebel Without a Cause* (1955). Completing what would be the ultimate exercise in camp iconography were Mercedes McCambridge, Joan Crawford's pseudo-lesbian sparring partner from *Johnny Guitar* (1954), James Dean's 16-year-old lover Sal Mineo, who had starred with him in *Rebel*, Dennis Hopper and *Baby Doll* (1956) sex-kitten Carroll Baker.

The interiors of *Giant*, regarded by critics as George Stevens's finest hour, began shooting in Los Angeles in May 1955. As had happened when Monty Clift had monopolised *A Place in the Sun* (and, of course, on account of the tragedy just around the corner), it was James Dean's film. Although only *East of Eden* (1955) had been released at that time and the public at large were yet to be captivated by his spellbinding talent, Jimmy was already being variously hailed as a lost cause, a cock-hungry schizophrenic and a pre-'Brat Pack' prima donna whose only truly happy but not entirely sane moments occurred when he was creating merry hell. Like Valentino before him, he was the supreme control freak whose every nuance and photogenic gesture had to be meticulously rehearsed and perfected.

Like Elizabeth, Jimmy was stubbornly independent and never let the studios push him around as they did everybody else. When MGM tried to prevent him from cruising for rough trade – the rougher the better – Jimmy sought out his own bizarre heterosexual conquests: Maila Nurmi, television's Vampira, and, according to lover James Gilmore (*James Dean*, Robson, 1995), a one-legged woman with whom Jimmy had liked to watch Gilmore have sex – but only after he had drawn a face on her stump. And yet James Dean's single-handed championing of American youth at a time when the country was recuperating from the ravages of McCarthyism and many parents failing to furnish their offspring with decent role models, made him the icon of an entire generation. Elizabeth Taylor and Rock Hudson might have considered themselves the essential ingredients of *Giant* during the first few weeks of shooting, but when Jimmy joined the production for the locations in Marfa, Texas, they and their peers very soon realised that regardless of the fact that his screen time would run to just twenty minutes of a three-hour-plus film, Jimmy was the icing on the cake. His chance remark on the set one day to buddy Dennis Hopper, comparing himself with his two idols, would soon enter Hollywood folklore: 'You know, I think I've got a chance to really make it because in this hand I'm holding Marlon Brando saying "Fuck you!" and in the other hand saying "Please forgive me!" is Montgomery Clift. Fuck you, please forgive me, fuck you. And somewhere in between is James Dean!'

Elizabeth, with her innate sense of seeking out men who were different, got on like a house on fire with James Dean and Rock Hudson, though initially there was no love lost between the two male actors, with Rock calling Jimmy 'that little scruff' and Jimmy denouncing Rock as 'having the acting talent of a lump of wood'. Then – and for the rest of her life as the undisputed champion of the oppressed, troubled homosexual – she comforted and defended the two men with unswerving loyalty. Just as Elizabeth had done with Monty Clift, she would embrace Dean and Hudson as surrogate sons, though they too were older than her. She was also one of the few who knew at the time *why* Rock was being pressurised into courting his manager's secretary, Phyllis Gates – to prevent the trash magazines from publishing stories about his homosexuality.

Unaware that Montgomery Clift had a monopoly on the name, Rock baptised his new friend 'Bessie', and she addressed him as 'Rockabye'. Hudson and Phyllis Gates spent many contented hours with the Wildings at their Benedict Canyon home. Elizabeth's theory, drummed into her by Monty, was that they should inject a little 'Method' into their on-screen performances – in other words, in order to find out how they would get along as Mr and Mrs Benedict, they would have to spend as much off-screen time together as possible. This involved getting drunk a lot and regularly throwing up on the set – and Rock and Phyllis being third parties to the Wildings' rows as their marriage crumbled, partly on account of their incompatibility and age difference, and partly on account of the press. *Confidential* – the doyenne of the trash mags, which had been trying for some time to out Rock Hudson, hence the set-up with Phyllis Gates – had recently published a shattering exposé on Michael Wilding, claiming that he had organised a noisy pool party complete with strippers whilst his wife had been away filming on location.

It may well be that Elizabeth calmed the waters between Rock Hudson and James Dean, who were worlds apart professionally. Jimmy's Method training – in the same school that had produced Brando, Clift, Lee J. Cobb and a handful of distinguished thespians who had initially triumphed on the stage – had taught him that if the two characters hated each other on the screen, as Bick Benedict and Jett Rink did, then it would also be necessary for them to hate each other in the rehearsal room. Rock, on the other hand, had graduated from the Henry Willson Academy of Glamour. The academy was run by a gay, sexually voracious agent named Henry Willson, whose *truc* was to seduce every one of the 50 or so young actors who ended up on his roster – then threaten them with press exposure unless they toed the line. Rock had used sex as his primary means to achieve fame; acting ability had been picked up on the way – or, as in the case of other Willson recruits Tab Hunter, Guy Madison and several others, not at all. Jimmy, by far the better actor, resented this. However, he was also very obviously attracted to Rock, the superbly packaged slab of beefcake. That Rock and Jimmy had an albeit brief sexual relationship, almost certainly instigated by Elizabeth's machinations, is more than likely.

Speaking to *Star* magazine in 1987, she said, 'After I found out the truth about Rock, I began to feel a strong affection for Jimmy. But my feminine intuition told me that a mysterious understanding was being born between the two actors, and at times I felt like an uncomfortable third party.'

The Marfa locations for *Giant* were dominated by the huge $200,000-neo-Gothic Benedict mansion, erected to rise spookily out of the blistering desert sands and allowed to crumble back into them once the film was finished. Shooting was hampered by fierce heat and a severe water shortage that resulted in the consumption of too much alcohol – and frayed tempers.

To James Dean's way of thinking, it was possible for him to walk out of a room ten minutes after having had sex with a co-star, as happened with Rock Hudson, and immediately begin attacking him physically and verbally in a scene. Compared to the six-foot-four-inch, two-hundred-and-twenty-five-pound Rock, Jimmy was diminutive and wiry, but immensely strong and agile, wholly fearless and capable of challenging any man to a fight, even if he knew he was going to come off the loser. Elizabeth was witness to much of this and is said to have derived enormous pleasure out of watching Jimmy 'psyching' up for a scene – stomping his feet on the ground for ten minutes at a time, then tearing around the set screaming like a banshee! – and the effect this had on onlookers. Likewise, the entire cast was irked with George Stevens's habit of demanding that everyone be on the set in full costume from the crack of dawn, even if they were not going to be called for a scene until later in the day. On top of this, he would shoot scenes dozens, sometimes hundreds, of times, from every conceivable angle, often using over a thousand feet of film for a few seconds of screen time. For *Giant*, Stevens used 700,000 feet of film, of which 25,000 feet formed the finished 198-minute print.

Edna Ferber had based her book on the real-life rags-to-riches story of Texan oil magnate Glenn McCarthy, the aforementioned friend of Nicky Hilton. The film also inspired the glossy television soap-opera *Dallas* and its resident tyrant, J.R. Ewing – the latter taking his initials from those above the podium from which Jett Rink delivers his rambling, slurred speech in the film's final.

As had happened with Monty Clift in *A Place in the Sun*, there are many thinly veiled references to Elizabeth's off-screen relationships with James Dean and Rock Hudson, many of these sailing above the heads of the general public. When wealthy Texan Jordan 'Bick' Benedict (Hudson) arrives at the Maryland home of the lovely Leslie Linton (Elizabeth) to purchase the black stallion she is exercising, he drawls, 'That sure is a beautiful animal,' not meaning the horse. Later, she poses the question that almost got Rock outed by the press: 'Why aren't *you* married, Bick?' In the next scene, she is his wife and kills the off-screen rumours: if Rock Hudson could lust after Elizabeth Taylor, there was no way he could be gay!

Similarly, in a scene buzzing with sexual tension – the only one in the film – played against the haunting score by Dimitri Tomkin, Leslie sees a picture of herself (actually an Elizabeth Taylor publicity shot) on the wall of bad-boy Jett Rink's (Dean) shack and realises that he has a crush on her. Before making the film, Jimmy had told a friend that nothing had turned him on quite so much as the Victory Red-painted mouths of Elizabeth, Édith Piaf and Tallulah Bankhead, and that nothing would have given him more pleasure than having all three fellate him. Repeating her earlier question to Bick, she asks, 'When are you going to get married, Jett?' Jimmy, unlike Rock, never hid his life under a bushel, of course, and he responds only with his eyes. In a poignant moment, he serves her tea, taking (unscripted) a large slug of liquor to give him courage.

Jimmy was so nervous about shooting his first scene with Elizabeth – the zenith of which sees him standing in his famous mock-Crucifixion pose with his rifle threaded between his outstretched arms behind his lowered head, whilst Elizabeth emulates Mary Magdalene by crouching at his feet – that before the camera started rolling, he strolled out of its range to face the huge crowd of onlookers that George Stevens had allowed on to the lot. Smiling coyly, he unfastened his 'shit kicker' denims, urinated, then shook his penis at the sea of astonished onlookers. Later, he told Dennis

Hopper, 'I figured that if I could pee in front of 4,000 people, then I could do anything on film.' (British journalist Donald Zec was afforded a rare interview at around this time and in his memoirs, *Put the Knife in Gently* [Robson, 2003], said that Jimmy had wanted to stand on a Hollywood rooftop and urinate upon the throng below. And whilst most people found Jimmy fascinating but a little odd, Zec observed, 'I found [him to be] a scruffy, disgruntled misfit, manifestly in need of a bath.')

Soon after this point in the film, *Giant* starts to lose its credibility, particularly in the scenes where the characters have aged. James Dean relied on Method to age him, telling George Stevens, 'Wrinkles come only with good acting.' With his ever-present shades, greying temples and receding hairline, *he* looks authentic – whereas Elizabeth and Hudson resemble crude caricatures, with absolutely no facial lines and *blue* hair! Even so, the film remains a masterpiece, if only for the aforementioned scenes.

Surprisingly, considering the on- and off-set gossip surrounding Rock Hudson and James Dean (particularly with Jimmy's boast to all and sundry, 'I've had my cock sucked by five of the biggest names in Hollywood – all of them guys!'), it was the rumour that Rock was having an affair with Elizabeth that brought Phyllis Gates and Michael Wilding rushing to Marfa halfway through *Giant* – the latter accompanied by their two children to remind her that she was still a wife and mother. Elizabeth later confessed that she had been attracted to Rock but that like Montgomery Clift he would never be hers other than platonically. After his death, she recalled, 'I looked at Rock, so handsome and so apparently masculine. But I soon realised that no woman would succeed in igniting *his* enthusiasm.'

Some 30 years down the line, Phyllis Gates confessed that she had been worrying over nothing. Writing in her memoirs, *My Husband, Rock Hudson* (Doubleday, 1987), she observed, 'Was I jealous? Not really. I realised that no normal male could resist the fabulous charms of Elizabeth Taylor.' And referring to the brevity of Elizabeth's relationships and marriages, she added coyly, 'If there had been an affair, I doubted that it would last.'

Elizabeth rejoined Michael Wilding and the children in Hollywood, though the death knell had long since sounded on their marriage. On 30 September 1955, she and the whole of America were stunned by the death of James Dean. Though Jimmy's personal life had always been in turmoil, the real passion in his life over the last few months had been 'Little Bastard', his Porsche Spyder – top speed 170 mph – which his Warner Brothers contract had prohibited him from driving whilst shooting *Giant*. Jimmy had been scheduled to race professionally (he had won numerous trophies) at Salinas a few days after finishing the film, and, ironically, his last celluloid appearance was for a road-safety commercial. 'Take it easy driving,' he told actor Gig Young on behalf of the National Highway Committee. 'The life you might save might be mine!'

In the fading evening light that had rendered his silver Spyder almost invisible, Jimmy and his mechanic friend Rolf Wutherich crashed into another car at the intersection of Highways 41 and 466 near Chalome. Wutherich was thrown clear, but Jimmy died almost instantly, throwing open the floodgates to the most intense, unprecedented wave of grief and idolatry since the sudden death of Rudolph Valentino in 1926.

Jimmy's future had been well assured, with a $1-million contract in the pipeline for nine films to be made over the next seven years, beginning with *Somebody Up There Likes Me* (1956), the biopic of boxer Rocky Graziano. His death affected everyone who had known him personally. Montgomery Clift, who had been desperate to have an affair with Jimmy, is reported to have 'thrown up over his satin bed sheets'. In her book, Phyllis Gates claimed to have found Rock Hudson sobbing like a child – his character had detested Jimmy's in the film, and he was paranoid that the public would think him pleased that his 'enemy' was dead. Elizabeth was so overcome with shock that she had to be sedated and hospitalised overnight.

With a wealth of dubbing and retakes to be done before George Stevens wrapped up his production, the cast of *Giant* were allowed little time for mourning. Not one of the company attended Jimmy's funeral the following week in his home town of Fairmont, Indiana, though many sent flowers and messages of condolence to his family. Following an on-set altercation with Stevens during the dubbing – over the director's comments that Jimmy's death had not been unexpected on account of his reckless driving – Elizabeth collapsed with abdominal pains, resulting in yet another two weeks' hospitalisation, leaving critics to make of this what they wanted. Most agreed that she had been best away from Jimmy's funeral, because her presence would have turned it into a circus. Jett Rink's drunken speech in the stateroom at the end of the film – a scene in which the effects of an all-night bender had left Jimmy's voice inaudible – was dubbed over by Nick Adams, his ex-lover who had appeared alongside him in *Rebel Without a Cause*.

The trash mags continued their attacks on Michael Wilding throughout the winter of 1955. Unable to credibly out him for his homosexual affairs now that he was married to the most voluptuous woman in Hollywood, they were similarly peeved that she was unhappily tied to a much older man of dubious talent. It mattered little that Wilding had been offered no roles to get his teeth into and prove his worth, as had happened in England. Rather than being portrayed as a 'deviant', he was depicted as the archetypal lecher, and the tabloids ran numerous 'exclusives' concerning his supposed poolside romps with strippers. Heading the pursuit was *Confidential*, whose motto 'Tells the Facts and Names the Names' appeared on the cover beneath the title. 'We all read it,' Marlene Dietrich told me. 'Not because it was any good – it was rubbish and worse than some of the garbage you get on news-stands nowadays – but to find out if you were in it. Sometimes you never had an inkling until it was too late.'

Confidential had been launched in 1952 by Robert Harrison, whose 'brainwave' had come following the televised Senator Estes Kefauver crime investigations. According to Kefauver, America was grasped in a wave of vice, organised crime, corruption and gambling scams that was rapidly transforming it into a Mafia state. Harrison had elected to infiltrate and expose the nucleus of this 'den of iniquity' – Hollywood – and had thus far managed to keep ahead of orthodox scandalmongers Hopper, Parsons and Maxwell by employing unscrupulous methods. Neither was he too keen on checking the authenticity of his sources before running a particular story – usually alongside unflattering or suggestive photographs that frequently had nothing to do with the accompanying feature.

In 1954, *Confidential* was selling 4 million copies per issue, and Robert Harrison was doling out large amounts of cash to prostitutes of both sexes to coerce stars into compromising situations. Often a tiny microphone would be concealed in the bedroom, capturing not just the sex act itself, but the equally important post-coital small talk. Jealous or thwarted stars were encouraged to rubbish rivals whenever important parts were up for grabs so that they could step into their shoes. For 'special' cases, such as Errol Flynn (two-way mirrors), Rock Hudson and Elvis Presley (homosexuality), and Lana Turner (threesomes), Harrison furnished his 'detectives' with sophisticated miniature infrared cameras.

For Michael Wilding, Harrison had provided the strippers – failed bit-part players who needed the money. When it was reported back to him that this had caused a huge bust-up between Wilding and Elizabeth, the odious Harrison had the couple followed to Morocco, where Wilding was filming *Zarak* (1956) with Anita Ekberg and Victor Mature. Unable to link the Swedish actress with Wilding – she was about to marry the British actor Anthony Steele – Harrison printed a story hinting that Elizabeth had had a fling with Mature.

The source of the widening rift between the Wildings, of course, centred around his being compelled to walk in the shadow of his wife. In terms of their professional lives, he was a virtual nobody, the 'Mr Taylor' who could have resurrected his flagging career had he not been so lazy and fussy – the rejection of *My Fair Lady* being a prime example. Working with Elizabeth might have helped, but she does not appear to have wanted this – quite possibly because he was in his mid-40s and too old to play her love interest without looking ridiculous. Therefore, whilst he was seconded to dire television movies such as *Verdict of Three* (1958) and *Danger*

Within (1959), Elizabeth was signed up for MGM's $5-million Civil War blockbuster *Raintree County*, billed as '*Gone with the Wind* from the North's point of view', with her beloved Montgomery Clift. She was paid $100,000 – Monty, the biggest star, received three times this amount. Little did she know then that she would end up becoming his mentor and saviour.

SIX

LIZZIE SCHWARTZKOPF, MY JEWISH BROAD!

MGM HAD WANTED *RAINTREE COUNTY* TO BE DIRECTED by Richard Brooks, who since last working with Elizabeth had triumphed with *Blackboard Jungle* (1955), a sizzling exposé of the New York education system. Monty, however, wanted nothing to do with him. The studio next approached William Wyler, who had recently directed *Friendly Persuasion* (1956) – which Monty had turned down because he had not wanted to work for him! Therefore, in a typical Hollywood volte-face, considering their treatment of him during the McCarthy witch-hunt, MGM – this time with Monty's approval – brought in Edward Dmytryk, recently riding the crest of a popularity wave following the success of *The Caine Mutiny* (1954).

Monty was about to enter that final phase later identified as 'the longest suicide in movie history'. He was still involved with singer Libby Holman, still surviving on a diet of pills, alcohol and rough trade, still refusing to 'sort out' his sexuality for Hollywood's benefit and *still* a massive box-office draw, as *I Confess* and *From Here to Eternity* had proved. Even so, in May 1954 he had rejected more lucrative offers (including *East of Eden* and *High Noon*, 1952) in favour of returning to Broadway for 80 sell-out performances of Chekov's *The Seagull* with his friend Kevin McCarthy, after which he had given every indication that he had turned his back on the movie industry. He had vented his spleen on the 'establishment' very publicly. Attending the premiere of *Guys and Dolls* (1955), he had stood up in the auditorium and bellowed, 'Brando is vomitable, and this goddam picture stinks!' before storming into the foyer and punching his fist through the display case containing photographs of the cast. Yet the worst said of him was when the press agent for the film observed, 'Montgomery Clift still radiates class, even when urinating in the gutter.'

Why Monty had chosen *Raintree County* is not difficult to discern: Ross Lockridge Jr, its author, had also found it tough handling fame and fortune. In 1947, Lockridge, an English teacher from Indiana, where the story is set, had won MGM's annual Best Novel Award for his 1,066-page blockbuster, collecting $150,000 and guaranteed film rights. The following year, aged just 34, he had committed suicide, since which time the script had lain gathering dust in a studio vault.

Monty had called or written to Elizabeth almost every day since her marriage to Michael Wilding, and when visiting the couple, had frequently acted as intermediary during their now persistent quarrels. Sometimes he would spend time with one or the other on neutral territory, psychoanalysing the details of the latest crisis, but never taking sides. In his autobiography *Apple Sauce* (Allen and Unwin, 1982), Wilding called him 'an interpreter for two people who no longer spoke the same language'. Though he had known Elizabeth longer, Monty had tremendous respect for Wilding, probably on account of their common ground: sexuality, sophistication and theatrical training.

So far as Elizabeth was concerned, Monty was returning a favour. Time and time again, she had listened to and sympathised with his woes, ignoring the trash-mag innuendo that she and Monty might be having an affair, though Wilding himself was frequently questioned on the subject. Some years later, he told Monty's biographer, Robert

LaGuardia, 'I was happy that she had such a dear friend, and I knew how important he was to her. I never felt that they were too close or anything like that.' Wilding knew, of course, that by this time Monty was exclusively gay, that there could never be anything physical between him and Elizabeth, and also that what they had, something she would never share with Wilding, went beyond the carnal.

Neither was Elizabeth perturbed that Monty's name would be appearing above hers in the credits or that he was being paid more than her for his portrayal of John Shawnessy – in her opinion, he had worked hard to get to the top and deserved every cent. She severely criticised MGM for taking out special insurance on account of his 'delicate health' and in case he didn't finish the film – claiming that with her on his side, Monty would not falter. What she did not know was that a studio executive had visited Monty's New York brownstone to examine the contents of his 14-foot bathroom cabinet and had reported back that it contained 'every remedy known to mankind'. Even Monty's doctor friends were astonished by his knowledge of pills, potions and their various effects when combined. Monty also carried his infamous grey leather vanity case everywhere, a gift from an Italian lover, which contained thousands of pills of every kind.

For the duration of the shooting schedule, Monty rented a house in Dawn Ridge Road, not far from the Wildings' Benedict Canyon home. MGM, still reeling from James Dean's death – or rather the lost future revenue this had brought about – had provided Monty with round-the-clock chauffeurs so that he would not have to drive. Shooting commenced in April 1956, and the first few weeks are reported to have gone well, with Monty cutting down on his liquor consumption. He was, however, still taking prescription drugs, which Elizabeth later claimed she knew nothing about. One afternoon, director Edward Dmytryk was ordered to search his trailer and found 200 different types. Then came the reports of him flaking out in mid-conversation at dinner parties, with the other guests simply rolling him under the table or tucking him away in a corner of the room until he came round, rather than summoning a doctor.

On 12 May, Monty attended an intimate gathering at the Wildings, apparently against his will because he was tired. Elizabeth insisted on his presence, and he did not wish to let her down, which some critics interpreted as her having put a jinx on him, with her predilection for always wanting things her way. Also present were Rock and Phyllis Hudson (their 'arranged' marriage had taken place the previous November), and Kevin McCarthy. It is alleged to have been a muted if not miserable evening, with everyone but McCarthy feeling down in the dumps about something or other. Wilding spent much of it semi-prostrated with a slipped disc. Elizabeth also had a bad back, a recurrence of her injury sustained during *National Velvet*. Monty was depressed because he wanted to change huge chunks of the *Raintree County* script, and Edward Dmytryk would not hear of it. Meanwhile, the Hudsons' sham marriage was already in strife. Rock Hudson's manager, Henry Willson, had bought off yet another *Confidential* story. Virtually every move Rock made was shadowed, yet he was still up to his tricks – at that time, he was embroiled in an affair with a young actor from his new film *Written on the Wind* (1956), which had gotten Monty hot under the collar, because it happened to be based on Libby Holman's alleged murder of her much younger gay husband!

Because he had not anticipated Elizabeth's invitation, Monty had given his chauffeur the evening off, and as he had not driven for some time – he was terrified of 'doing a Jimmy Dean' – he asked Kevin McCarthy to lead the way in his car on the steep descent from Benedict Canyon to Sunset Boulevard. On the way down, Monty suffered a blackout and crashed into a telegraph pole. He received the most appalling facial injuries – two fractured jaws, a smashed nose and sinus cavities, severe cuts and lacerations – yet, apart from a little whiplash, the rest of his body was remarkably unscathed. The ambulance took 45 minutes to reach the unlit stretch of road, but Monty's friends, alerted by McCarthy, were there in minutes. So too were the press, alerted by the police at a time when such pay-off arrangements were commonplace. The photographers were hoping for some sick but valuable exclusive on Monty's pulped, unrecognisable face – mindless of the stench of gasoline and the threat of the vehicle suddenly bursting into flames. Elizabeth warned them that if they took so much as one shot or repeated one word of her expletives-charged tirade, she would never pose for the press again. Someone did snap a picture of the car, which Monty carried around in his wallet for years to remind himself how lucky he had been.

The photographers backed off, whilst Rock Hudson, the strongest man there, tried to force open the front door of Monty's car, a total write-off. Because it was pitch black, it was at first assumed that Monty had been flung clear of the wreckage, but when Kevin McCarthy turned around his own car so that his headlights lit up the scene, they saw that he had ended up under the dashboard. Elizabeth crawled in through the back window and found Monty choking on two dislodged teeth – in pushing her fingers down his throat and extracting them, she saved his life. With her beautiful white dress drenched in his blood, she cradled his head in her lap all the way to the Cedars of Lebanon Hospital, whilst Phyllis Hudson rode along for support.

Astonishingly, Monty's injuries were almost entirely below the skin, and only light-to-medium plastic surgery was required to patch him up. At that stage, no one considered the possible psychological damage. The *Raintree County* set was shut down for nine weeks whilst he recovered from the operation to reconstruct his face and teeth. Monty spent much of this time with his jaws wired – reportedly gaining strength from sipping martinis through a straw – and in traction on account of the whiplash injuries to his back. After three weeks, the surgeons had to break and reset his jaws. Elizabeth – feeling guilty because she had persuaded Monty to attend her party – Libby Holman and Monty's father took it in turns to sit with him. He flatly refused to see his mother. Edward Dmytryk and Dore Schary were frequent visitors, though the latter was less concerned about Monty's well-being than he was about the $2 million that had been ploughed into the production thus far. Friends (but not Elizabeth) advised him to abandon the film and allow MGM to collect on the insurance (which they did anyhow), but Monty would not hear of this – privately he knew that if he did not finish this film, he might never find the courage to work again.

The Wildings' marriage floundered completely during the break in filming – partly because Monty was not there for Elizabeth to lean upon, but largely because she allowed herself to be hustled into a love affair with Mike Todd, the overtly brash Jewish entrepreneur. It was an association that would very nearly cost Elizabeth her friendship with Monty, who frowned upon adultery if there were children involved.

Born Avrom Goldbogen in Minneapolis in 1905 (he later knocked five years off his age), Mike Todd was arguably America's most flamboyant, headstrong and cocksure showman since Billy Rose. Life for him was one seemingly endless, no-expenses-spared sideshow. Like Elvis Presley with the 'Memphis Mafia', he was rarely seen in public unless flanked by flunkeys who kow-towed to his every command – which were frequently outrageous or illegal – without ever questioning his judgement. These people were not particularly well paid, and Mike Todd's women were treated shabbily and insulted in public, but the perks they enjoyed were substantial.

The son (one of eight children) of a Polish émigré rabbi, Todd started out selling newspapers and shining shoes, then changed his name and hit the vaudeville circuit, writing sketches for the comedy duo Olsen and Johnson. He next turned to producing – his *The Hot Mikado*, a jazz-take on the Gilbert and Sullivan operetta, had set Broadway alight in 1939. He followed this with Mae West's hugely controversial *Catherine the Great* and *The Naked Genius* with Joan Blondell, whom he had poached from her husband, Dick Powell. Standing in the way of them getting hitched was Todd's wife, Bertha – the mother of his son and heir, Mike Todd Jr.

Elizabeth was so besotted by her not-so-attractive middle-aged beau that she probably knew little or nothing of his personal history at this time. Obsessed with large-breasted women, shortly after the Second World War he made a big star of his mistress, actress-stripper Gypsy Rose Lee, before turning his attention to Blondell, whence he hit the headlines by being arrested on suspicion of murder. Bertha, who steadfastly refused to give him a divorce, was discovered in their kitchen with a large gash on her arm and subsequently died on the operating table whilst surgeons attempted to repair a severed artery. Todd got off the hook when Joan Blondell furnished him with an alibi, claiming that he had been with her on the night of the incident. Additionally, the autopsy concluded that Bertha had died of a heart attack.

Todd married Blondell in 1947. The union was doomed from the start, and for the rest of his life, Todd was suspected of having had some involvement in his wife's death: if not of inflicting the actual wound – which, given his character and temperament, he had been more than capable of – then in driving her to the point of self-harm with his brashness and multitude of extra-marital affairs.

According to Michael Todd Jr. in *A Valuable Property: The Life Story of Mike Todd* (Arbor House, 1983), Elizabeth and Todd were thrown together by way of an affair between Elizabeth and Todd's 30-something production assistant, Kevin McClory. He *apparently* told Todd's son – who was 21 when Elizabeth met his father – that they were *so* serious they had contemplated marriage. This seems unlikely, as McClory would never have been able to provide her with the seriously opulent lifestyle to which she had become accustomed. According to McClory, Todd got wind of the affair and instructed his assistant to arrange a meeting – not just with Elizabeth, but with Michael Wilding, too.

Todd's own version of events is slightly different. He claimed that he had been intrigued to read of the Wildings' ups and downs in the press, so he had added their names to the guest list for a dinner party, held aboard his yacht moored off the Californian coast on 29 June 1956, in honour of David Niven, who played eponymous hero Phineas Fogg in Todd's film *Around the World in Eighty Days* (1956), arguably the most colourful adventure film of the 1950s.

At that time, Todd was dating the actress Evelyn Keyes, a woman with a suitably colourful past. Her first husband had shot himself, and husbands two and three (directors King Vidor and John Huston) were legendary brawlers, boozers and womanisers. Artie Shaw, her fourth husband, who was married eight times, picked up the pieces after her split from Todd. Keyes was present at the party but might as well have been invisible as Todd, the lecherous wolf, encircled his prey and moved in for the kill. Moreover, Elizabeth was a willing victim. 'Their behaviour was outrageous,' Todd's best friend Eddie Fisher later recalled in his memoirs, *Been There, Done That* (Hutchinson, 1999), 'and they didn't care what anybody else thought. Mike called her "My little Jewish broad, Lizzie Schwartzkopf", or he would tell her in front of a group of friends, "Soon as I finish my dinner, I'm gonna fuck you."'

Todd made his mind up at once to woo Elizabeth away from her 'boring and elderly' husband, regardless of the fact that *he* was older than Wilding. Elizabeth fell for the ruse hook, line and sinker, whilst Wilding, preoccupied with his slipped disc, was initially oblivious to what was going on around him. Two weeks later, Todd threw a reception for 200 A-list celebrities at his rented mansion in Beverly Hills. The guests of honour were Édith Piaf, her best pal Marlene Dietrich and fellow entrepreneur Ed Murrow, who was hoping to coax 'The Little Sparrow' into permitting him to film her life story. Piaf performed 12 songs but made it clear that she would never consent to any biopic. And whilst she stole the show with her fabulous voice and famous little black dress, Elizabeth turned heads by swanning into the room in a low-cut white-satin creation and $50,000 worth of diamonds. Todd flirted with her openly, and Wilding left in a huff – enabling his rival to pounce.

A few days later, on 19 July, the Wildings issued a joint statement to the press: they had opted for amicable separation. The very next morning, Elizabeth – whom virtually no one could order around – obeyed the summons to Todd's office. Here, with the ubiquitous fat

Elizabeth, aged seven, in one of her first Hollywood publicity shots, long before she ever faced a movie camera. (© Archive Photos/ Getty Images)

In 1948 with Roddy McDowall, the first of many gay actors she supported and championed. (© Murray Garrett/Getty Images)

A publicity shot for
A Place in the Sun, with
Montgomery Clift, the man
she later said she loved more
than *all* of her husbands.
(© Peter Stackpole/Time Life
Pictures/Getty Images)

In November 1950,
with abusive first
husband Nicky Hilton
on the SS *Queen
Elizabeth*. The marriage
lasted just months.
(© Leroy Jakob/
NY Daily News
Archive/Getty Images)

With second
husband Michael
Wilding in 1951.
(© Michael Ochs
Archives/Getty
Images)

With Jimmy on the set
of *Giant* in 1955.
(© Keystone/Getty Images)

With Rock, whom she bravely helped through his final illness. (©API/Gamma/Gamma-Rapho/Getty Images)

In 1956 with third husband Mike Todd, the man whom she claimed taught her how to appreciate rough sex. (© Michael Ochs Archives/ Getty Images)

With Fernandel, the great French actor-comedian, at the time of *Around the World in Eighty Days*, 1956. (© Alain Benainous/Gamma-Rapho/Getty Images)

In 1960, on the eve of the *Cleopatra* 'Scandale', with womanising fourth husband Eddie Fisher. (© Paul Popper/Popperfoto/ Getty Images)

Richard ... so exciting she married him twice and never stopped mourning his death. (© Hulton Archive/Getty Images)

One of Hollywood's costliest flops but a beautiful film just the same:
Cleopatra, 1963. (© 20th Century Fox/Getty Images)

Arguably her only truly great film with Burton,
Who's Afraid of Virginia Woolf?, which they scrapped
through in 1966. (© Apic/Getty Images)

cigar wedged between his teeth, he *ordered* her not to even think of looking at another man now that Wilding had been removed from the picture, because *he* had decided that she now belonged to him! Elizabeth later added to the story, telling Hedda Hopper that Todd had announced, 'I'm going to marry you, and from now on you'll know nobody but me.' Hopper later observed in her autobiography, *The Whole Truth and Nothing But*, that Todd had actually said, 'From now on, you'll *fuck* nobody but me!'

Meanwhile, shooting was resumed on *Raintree County*. Montgomery Clift, who was self-injecting himself with cortisone because of the tremendous pain he was in, was filmed mostly from the right, his least damaged profile. The left side of his face would remain semi-frozen and immobile on account of a severed nerve in his cheek. To get through the agonies of sleeping and waking, he took so many uppers and downers that on one occasion he lapsed into a coma with a lighted cigarette in his hand. The set doctor brought him around without too much difficulty, but Clift had burned the flesh of two fingers down to the bone. To cope with the pain from this new injury, he simply doubled up on the cortisone shots.

There were problems with the locations: first in Natchez, Mississippi, then in Danville, Kentucky. Never once letting his grey bag out of his sight, Monty survived on a diet of barbiturates washed down with alcohol to counteract the after effects of the accident – and more of the same to help soothe his shattered nerves. In Natchez, a small Methodist town unused to visiting celebrities, he and Elizabeth were treated like freaks. Like George Stevens, Edward Dmytryk preferred working on an open lot, which meant that the whole town was allowed to follow the shoot from start to finish. As such, the locals were witness to frustrated outbreaks and foul language from all concerned, along with the odd technical hitch. One such saw Monty attempting to climb into a carriage only to fall out of the other side – an exercise he repeated a dozen times before passing out cold. A few days later, it was fortunate that there were few people around when he was found wandering around the streets, stark naked and in a trance, having emerged from a drugs-induced nightmare in the middle of the night.

In Natchez and Danville, Elizabeth and Monty stayed in the same hotel and shared a bed, but only because he could not cope with being alone. Stories naturally circulated once more that they were having an affair, particularly when neither denied the fact when asked.

Monty was unhappy about a scene in *Raintree County* in which he is seen taking a bath. He was paranoid about the dense carpet of black hair that completely covered his chest, abdomen, arms and shoulders. In the past, he had tried trimming, shaving, depilatories and monthly visits to an electrolysis centre, none of which had worked. He had appeared smooth in a stripped-to-the-waist scene in *From Here to Eternity* but since his accident had allowed nature to take its course. Monty asked for the scene to be cut, but producer David Lewis insisted on behalf of MGM that it stay put. In the naive days of the studio system, hirsute actors were presumed to be heterosexual – in much the same way as gay actors were presumed to be straight once they had taken a trip down the aisle. Robert Taylor, confronted in a London street whilst making *Conspirator* with Elizabeth, had been called a 'fairy' by a group of hecklers, only to prove them wrong by unbuttoning his shirt and revealing that he was as 'normal' as the next man!

By the time the *Raintree County* unit reached Danville, Edward Dmytryk had virtually washed his hands of the film, handing over the directorial reins to Monty – which turned out to be a viable move. Elizabeth, like Rock Hudson in his early films, was still regarded by many as little more than a decorative addition to whichever production she happened to be in – guaranteed box-office sales but still near the foot of the ladder so far as legitimate acting talent was concerned. Even the most cloying admirer could not have denied that she had so far proved herself an actress of merit in just two films – *A Place in the Sun* and *Giant* – though these had still been dominated by the Method techniques of their stars, Clift and Dean. As a highly strung then easily influenced and insecure individual, Elizabeth's precocious talent needed to be coaxed out of her, not bullied by the likes of Dmytryk, and this is what happened whilst she was being 'directed' by Monty.

Between self-directing, narcotic semi-comas and drunken escapades – the latter encouraged by Elizabeth, who would soon be able to drink most people under the table – and despite the fact that he loathed the man, Monty acted as go-between as the Taylor–Todd romance blossomed then spiralled out of control. It was Monty who arranged for Elizabeth to be driven out to Todd's private jet so that the pair could spend the occasional weekend together. It was he who delivered the huge baskets of roses with the $30,000 black-pearl ring that Todd boasted would act as an unofficial engagement ring until he found something better. Later, it was Monty who persuaded Libby Holman – who disliked Elizabeth for no other reason than she was jealous of her close friendship with Monty – to allow the couple to meet at Treetops, her country retreat, but only if she or Monty were present to chaperone. Here, aware of her fondness for 'big rocks', Todd presented Elizabeth with an inch-square $95,000 diamond ring – allegedly the one he had given to Evelyn Keyes, who had returned it after being told about Elizabeth. Elizabeth wore this whilst shooting a scene in *Raintree County* that called for a wedding ring. Rather than use the one provided by the props department, she turned Todd's ring around so that the cameraman could not see the diamond. Monty saw it and refused to continue with the scene until she had taken it off.

On account of its multitude of problems, the film was not premiered until December 1957. On its release, many critics went to inordinate lengths to point out scenes that had been shot after Monty's accident, invariably getting it wrong. Most agreed, too, that despite the extensive plastic surgery, Montgomery Clift was still a dazzlingly attractive man and a consummate actor more than capable of riding sky-high above any co-star.

For her part, Elizabeth's Susanna Drake was criticised for having quite possibly the *worst* Southern accent thus far in Hollywood history, made even worse by her high-pitched whining as she hovers much of the time between obnoxiousness and insanity – reflecting Elizabeth's behaviour much of the time towards those around her. Indeed, one wonders how such a creature could woo mild-mannered John Shawnessy (Monty) away from his long-time sweetheart and into her twisted world, which sees her dying face down in a swamp. Most men would have run a mile! Monty, however, was not most men: he accepted the fact that Elizabeth was no different from Susanna – in turns passionate and vulgar, and at times thoroughly vile towards everyone around her – and never stopped worshipping the ground she walked upon.

The locations had begun shooting on 23 July, which was Michael Wilding's 44th birthday. This offered the press the opportunity to 'officially' recognise him as middle-aged and make more snide comments about his being wed to a gorgeous goddess young enough to be his daughter. The film then wrapped on 17 October, which was Montgomery Clift's 36th birthday. The same reporters demanded to know why Elizabeth had not married Monty instead. There were few surprises, therefore, when the Wildings announced, in another reputedly amicable joint statement, that they were getting a divorce.

Whether this overt friendliness with her estranged husband, coming in the wake of so many heated, frequently public rows, was merely acted out for the benefit of the press is not known, but it seems more than likely. Elizabeth needed to be constantly in the headlines to believe that she was achieving anything out of life and persistently presented herself as the maligned heroine. Most of Michael Wilding's Hollywood films had bombed at the box office, and it was a foregone conclusion that matters would only deteriorate once he ceased to be 'Mr Taylor'. MGM offered him just one more film – *The Scarlet Coat* (1955), set during the American revolution – and informed him that they would not be renewing his contract. The press were told that Wilding and the studio had come to a 'mutual agreement'. Soon afterwards, Wilding returned to England, where his career amounted to little compared with his pre-Hollywood halcyon days. The divorce itself was handled by

Mike Todd, who felt obliged to have his finger in every pie where Elizabeth was concerned.

The premiere of *Around the World in Eighty Days* took place in the October and saw the mega-rich entrepreneur flying in just about everyone who had appeared in it, even those only featured in the film for a matter of seconds in cameo roles. David Niven, Cantinflas, Frank Sinatra, Marlene Dietrich, Noel Coward, Shirley MacLaine, Charles Boyer, Ava Gardner and Buster Keaton were but a few. Anyone of importance who happened to be in Hollywood at the time was also invited – around 200 celebrities, plus the hierarchy of the movie industry. At the post-screening party, chomping on his ubiquitous cigar, Todd announced that he and Elizabeth would be marrying early in the new year. Some journalists compared his 'I Must Have' stance with that of Howard Hughes, and, years later, Todd would be cited as a role model for the equally vulgar and grasping Aristotle Onassis in his pursuit of Maria Callas and Jackie Kennedy.

Next came the premiere of *Giant* at the New York Roxy. George Stevens had taken over a year to cut and edit the vast amount of footage into an acceptable 198 minutes. Elizabeth was supposed to have been Rock Hudson's 'date', because he had recently separated from Phyllis Gates after just 11 months of marriage. However, Mike Todd would not hear of Elizabeth being accompanied by a 'fagelah', so she stayed home, and Rock escorted Tallulah Bankhead, the undisputed queen of the one-liner, who told a bemused young woman reporter, 'This *divine* young man is a *giant* in every conceivable way!' Elizabeth then attended a second premiere a week later at Grauman's Chinese Theater, where earlier she and Rock had left their handprints in the famous cement. This time Rock *was* accompanied by his wife, thanks to Warner Brothers' insistence that the evening should remain scandal free. Elizabeth's 'date' was Michael Wilding. The guests included Clark Gable, Natalie Wood, Tab Hunter and Joan Crawford, who turned her back on the Wildings as they walked past her.

Soon afterwards, Mike Todd celebrated having Elizabeth all to himself by flying her to the Bahamas in his private jet. In the harbour, she slipped on wet cobbles and injured her back. Todd flew her to New York, where she was admitted to the Presbyterian Hospital and diagnosed with crushed vertebrae at the base of her spine. In the subsequent operation, these were repaired with pieces of bone extracted from her thigh, and she was in traction for three weeks. As it was inconceivable that Elizabeth Taylor should suffer from an ordinary malady, she instructed the hospital's director to issue a statement that there was every possibility of her ending up in a wheelchair. She was doubtless cheered considerably by Todd's visits and convinced that affection translated to dollars. For this particular patient, chocolates and flowers were eschewed for original works by Renoir and Monet, and when Elizabeth finally emerged from her sickbed, in January 1957, Todd presented her with a Rolls-Royce Silver Cloud so that she could 'travel home in style'. The press reported that she whooped with juvenile joy, and *Photoplay*'s Aline Mosby called her 'a troubled star . . . still a child struggling to grow up and find peace of mind, torn between the demands of the woman and the child'.

As soon as Elizabeth was back on her feet, Mike Todd began 'working' on her divorce. Michael Wilding was flown in first class from London, and the trio headed for Acapulco to finalise the proceedings and make arrangements for Elizabeth's wedding to Todd. However, there was one problem that could not be resolved by Todd's wallet. The local elections were taking place, and none of the candidates wished to offend the Catholic Church – or scupper their chances of winning votes – by being seen to be supporting quickie divorces. Eventually, Todd found a judge who was about to retire from office so would not be affected by public opinion, and a decree of mutual consent was obtained on 31 January.

The obscenely expensive nuptials took place on 2 February 1957 when Elizabeth became Mrs Avrom Goldbogen, surrounded by thousands of white gladioli and wearing a powder-blue Helen Rose creation. Crooner Eddie Fisher, Todd's best friend, was best man, and Debbie Reynolds, Fisher's actress–singer wife, was matron of honour. The ceremony was conducted by the mayor of Acapulco after Todd's money failed to tempt the local pastor and a rabbi, both of whom had been instructed by their superiors to stay well clear of the event. Sara, Francis and Howard Taylor were able to attend the wedding: unlike Michael Wilding, Mike Todd was rich, so Sara naturally wanted to get things off to a good start by not snubbing him.

The reception was dominated by the biggest and most expensive fireworks display in Mexico's history – a wedding present from Cantinflas – that ended with a vast heart containing the initials 'MT' and 'ETT' (Elizabeth Taylor Todd). According to the legend (almost certainly invented to complement the tragedy of the following year), Elizabeth screamed, 'Mike, don't leave me!' as the smouldering ashes hit the ground.

To keep out gatecrashers, Todd hired 50 armed Mexican soldiers to mingle with the hundreds of celebrity guests, each of whom had been given shirts or blouses with 'ET–MT' monogrammed on them. No one seemed sure what Elizabeth had given her husband for a wedding gift, but Todd had presented her with a $50,000 diamond bracelet, two cinemas in Chicago and a 40 per cent share in the proceeds from *Around the World in Eighty Days*. He made a point of showing the receipts to the press, who were also made aware of Elizabeth's 'revised' living arrangements. The Benedict Canyon house she had shared with Michael Wilding was to be sold and the spoils divided 50–50. The divorced couple, 'advised' by Todd's lawyers, would share their children less evenly: Elizabeth would have access to them nine months of the year, Wilding three. When not residing with Todd in their sumptuous New York penthouse, Elizabeth could be found with him at their house in Connecticut or holidaying in unabashed luxury at their 'little place' in Palm Springs – unless, of course, they were zipping around the world in Todd's jet, now renamed *Lucky Liz*.

At the end of February, the Todds were A-list guests at the Oscars ceremony. *Around the World in Eighty Days* had notched up eight nominations and was pitched against *Giant*'s ten, including best actor for Rock Hudson and best supporting actor for James Dean. Neither actor won, although Rock was subsequently voted number-one box-office draw – the awards went to Yul Brynner for *The King and I* (1956) and Anthony Quinn for *Lust for Life* (1956). Todd won the Oscar for best film, and his production scooped five additional awards.

The Todds' lengthy honeymoon, billed as an extension of the film they were promoting, took in New York, London, Paris, Rome and Moscow, with Todd presenting his wife with some 'special little gift' each time they checked into the best hotel in town – again, the receipts were shown to reporters, Todd's theory being that the more he spent, the more this proved how much he loved her. In the Paris Ritz, it was a Degas, purchased at a snip from Ali Khan for $30,000. At the Cannes Film Festival on 2 May, Todd hired the casino and commissioned a replica of the hot-air balloon used in his film to float above its roof. Within the building, he had installed a circus complete with lions and tigers. Surrounding their cages were 300 tables for journalists representing every major publication in Europe – each was treated to a sumptuous banquet on the proviso that they write only *good* things about their hosts.

There were no gifts for Elizabeth when the Todd–Taylor extravaganza hit London on 2 July. Todd had hired Battersea Funfair instead, along with a dozen orchestras from around the world and enough food to feed several armies. To add a little of the 'common touch', he commissioned several fishmongers from Billingsgate to supply 2,000 portions of 'traditionally served' fish and chips, wrapped in replica copies of *The Times*, dated 1893, the year Phineas Fogg had embarked on his journey around the world. Todd liked to believe that there was nothing he could not arrange. When Elizabeth expressed a desire to meet the Queen's cousin Princess Alexandra to determine if the reports in the press were true – that Alexandra was as beautiful as she was – Todd got her to the party along with her mother, Princess Marina. And in the midst of this overhyped melee, Elizabeth announced that she was pregnant.

The tour continued throughout the spring and summer, with Mike

Todd now known to have been spending the vast revenue from *Around the World in Eighty Days* as fast as it was coming in. And the rows between the newlyweds continued, enabling Elizabeth to deliver her legendary quote, 'Mike and I have more fun scrapping than most people have making love!' Yet with her predilection for seeking out life's dramas and complexities, near tragedy lay on the horizon. In the July of that year, during the sea crossing back to New York, Elizabeth went into premature labour and had to be anaesthetised to prevent her from giving birth until the ship docked. Since injuring her back, she had been wearing a support, and complications were anticipated that the ship's doctors felt they might not be able to handle.

There is a scene in *Raintree County* in which Eva Marie Saint's character, Nell, comments on Elizabeth's character's sham pregnancy, concluding that people are able to 'count up to nine'. Typically, the press then speculated that, like her character, Elizabeth might have fallen pregnant *before* marrying Mike Todd when they were told that her baby was not expected until October.

Elizabeth was rushed into a clinic, but not before posing for photographs and giving a speedy dockside press conference. Because of her back support, her baby had been pushed upwards under her ribcage. However, rather than deliver at that point, the doctors kept Elizabeth under observation for two weeks before sending her home to the twenty-five-room mansion Mike Todd had rented in Westport. On 6 October, she returned to the clinic, where her daughter Elizabeth Frances (Liza) was delivered by Caesarean section. According to the story that emerged – put about by Elizabeth, who of course could not possibly allow the world to believe that she had endured a normal delivery – the four-pounds infant was stillborn, but when she was placed in an incubator whilst the parents were being given the grim news, she suddenly and inexplicably came back to life. Both mother and child remained in the clinic for over a month. Elizabeth's doctors advised her that having another baby might kill her, so she had her fallopian tubes tied as a safety precaution.

Like a well-rehearsed Pirandello grotesque, the *Around the World in Eighty Days* whirligig resumed. On 17 October, Mike Todd hired Madison Square Garden for a publicity bash – celebrating, of all things, the film's first birthday. Once again, the situation was engineered to ensure that he and his wife ended up on the front pages. Elizabeth arrived, according to one report, 'looking like the Empress Josephine' in a red-velvet gown and tiara. Twenty thousand invitations had been dispatched worldwide, and the proceedings opened with a circus parade headed by veteran actor Cedric Hardwicke riding an elephant. Topping the cabaret bill was French comedy actor–singer Fernandel, to whom Todd had promised the lead in *Don Quixote*, his next multimillion-dollar epic, which, he boasted, would naturally feature Elizabeth as Dulcinella – and which was cancelled on account of the tragedy ahead.

The press were alerted to the fact that this was an 'anything goes' event, and it certainly was. Ten thousand gifts, donated by sponsors, were randomly doled out to the guests: cars, motorcycles, jewellery, cameras and a Cessna two-seater airplane! There were hundreds of gatecrashers – again invited by Todd and 'primed' how to misbehave – and they ran amok in the auditorium, scoffing most of the food. The crowning glory came when the 14-tier cake Elizabeth was cutting collapsed on top of her, covering her and those about her in cream and icing – it was a staged stunt. When she began flinging chunks around, there was a free for all, resulting in a clearing-up operation costing thousands of dollars – which Todd, of course, paid for.

From New York, trailed by the world's press, the tour took in Hawaii, England, Japan and Australasia, and the boasting never stopped. 'We like a simple life,' Todd told the British *Daily Mail*. 'My wife pours her own champagne, and I make my own caviar sandwiches.' In Tokyo, Elizabeth caused a fuss by collapsing with appendicitis and an even bigger one when she expressed her mistrust of foreign hospitals, insisting upon returning to America to have her appendix removed – again, ensuring herself only the maximum publicity.

Upon her recovery (although cynics reasoned that there would have been no time to fly Elizabeth home had the appendix really needed removing), it was back to self-promotion. The Todds decided that they wanted to visit Russia, even though they were unknown there. Todd arrogantly declared that he would soon rectify this and kill two birds with one stone by ending the Cold War in his and Elizabeth's unofficial capacity as American ambassadors!

While many of the less impressionable public regarded this announcement as just another facet of the already over-extended Todd–Taylor farce, the American government took it seriously. Todd was warned not to interfere in international politics, and although he listened for once, he refused to cancel the trip. After *Don Quixote*, he said, Elizabeth would be starring in either *War and Peace* or reprising Greta Garbo's role in *Anna Karenina*. One shudders to imagine what this would have been like, with Tolstoy's heroine shrieking in a Deep South accent, as opposed to Garbo's delicious drawl. Thankfully, neither project saw the light of day.

The Todds flew to Prague on 26 January 1958, not knowing whether they would be allowed into Russia. By then, Elizabeth was *demanding* a meeting with Krushchev! Three days later, they flew into Moscow, where they managed – by way of Todd's wallet – to worm their way into a reception at the Indian embassy. The Soviet leader *was* there, although whether he made time to talk to his gatecrasher guests is not clear. Elizabeth certainly made an impression, dressed like a member of a defunct imperialist family and dripping with diamonds. Outside the embassy, she found herself surrounded by autograph hunters – they were aware that they were in the presence of someone of importance, although none of them actually knew who she was until an irate Todd enlightened them.

SEVEN

PASS THE PARCEL, MIKE

PREDICTING THAT THE EXCESSIVE PUBLICITY SURROUNDING Montgomery Clift's accident would ensure huge box-office returns, as had happened with *Raintree County*, Warner Brothers attempted to team Elizabeth and Monty as loan-outs for their next big-budget production, *Marjorie Morningstar* (1958). In Herman Wouk's bestselling novel, the heroine is a wealthy Jewish girl who defies the edicts of her religion by having an affair with a considerably older man. The still powerful Hays Office censors warned studio head Jack Warner that he would never get such an 'outrageous' scenario past them and ordered the scriptwriters to eliminate the religious element, thus robbing the story of its central significance. Elizabeth did not mind this: all she wanted was to work with Monty again. Mike Todd, however, did not want her to work with anyone – his wife's place, he declared, was by his side, promoting the by now weary *Around the World in Eighty Days* project.

When Monty turned the film down because of the story change – and in any case, he was busy shooting Edward Dmytryk's *The Young Lions* (1958) with Marlon Brando and Dean Martin – Paul Newman was approached to take his place. Newman also said no: he was busy with another production, after which he had been singled out to star opposite Elizabeth in *Cat on a Hot Tin Roof* (1958). The part of Marjorie Morningstar was, therefore, given to Natalie Wood, and the Clift/Newman role went to the less charismatic Gene Kelly.

As had happened with Nicky Hilton (at that time dating and knocking around the newly cast lead of *Marjorie Morningstar*) and Michael Wilding, Elizabeth's marriage to the ebullient, fiercely overpossessive Mike Todd was reputedly on the rocks no sooner than the rice had settled. Passers-by in Schuyler Road, the couple's main residence in Beverly Hills, reported hearing them yelling at one another from a hundred yards away. According to the couple, fights were an essential and healthy component of their existence. 'When Elizabeth flies into a tantrum, I fly into a bigger one,' a full-of-himself Todd had told the *Chicago Tribune*'s Marilyn Kruse the previous November. 'She's been on a milk-toast diet all her life with men. But me, I'm red meat!'

Eddie Fisher recalled in his 1999 autobiography *Been There, Done That* the occasion when he and Debbie Reynolds witnessed one of the Todds' arguments, during which Todd had slapped Elizabeth and then dragged her by the hair into their bedroom to make love. 'She liked to be roughed up,' Fisher concluded, adding elsewhere in his memoirs that Elizabeth and Todd had also participated in telephone sex.

Absolutely no one could contact Elizabeth, unless through Mike Todd, who is said to have pulled enough strings to ensure her an Oscar nomination for *Raintree County*, though she scarcely merited the accolade for such a dreadfully over-the-top performance. Todd had stopped her from doing *Marjorie Morningstar* but insisted upon her accepting *Cat on a Hot Tin Roof*, because he planned to 'arrange' another Oscar nomination. Elizabeth was so awestruck by her latest spouse, by the power his wealth brought, that when Todd told her to jump, she asked him how high.

Cat on a Hot Tin Roof began shooting early in March 1958, around the time Mike Todd began putting together *Don Quixote*. He had also recently completed his (ghostwritten) autobiography

– the soon-to-be portentously titled *The Nine Lives of Mike Todd* (Hutchinson, 1959). Todd had also been voted Showman of the Year by The Friars Testimonial and was scheduled to pick up the award at the New York Astoria on Sunday, 24 March. Elizabeth had planned to travel with him, but a few days before the event she came down with bronchitis and a fever. On 21 March, Todd took off in *Lucky Liz* with just his crew and ghostwriter friend Art Cohn, but the plane never reached its destination. A few hours after a refuelling stop in Albuquerque, it plummeted into the Zuni Mountains, over New Mexico. Todd's charred wedding ring was found in the wreckage a few days later. He and his colleagues were identified only from dental records.

Elizabeth was inconsolable. This was the worst genuine tragedy of her life to date – two divorces and now widowhood at the age of just twenty-six would have sent anyone over the edge – but many people accused her of going overboard with the hysterics, rushing out into the middle of Schuyler Road and screaming at passers-by that she wished she had died with him. Her doctor – celebrity physician Rex Kennamer, who had supervised Montgomery Clift's post-accident ordeal and had, needless to say, earned a tidy fee – was summoned, and he administered a sedative. Within an hour, Debbie Reynolds arrived to look after Elizabeth's children, and Michael Wilding, allegedly more concerned for their welfare than that of his ex-wife, flew in from London.

Schuyler Road had, of course, been transformed into a media circus. Mingling with the crowd of pressmen and reporters outside the house were hundreds of fans armed with cameras and autograph books. Few cared about Mike Todd, and they paid little credence to Elizabeth's latest admission that he would remain the great love of her life. With her track record, observers were of the opinion that this marriage would have ended in divorce, just like all the others, had Todd lived. The onlookers merely wanted to catch a glimpse of the widow and whichever celebrities dropped in on her to offer their condolences.

These were surprisingly few: Rock Hudson, Natalie Wood,

Montgomery Clift and Nicky Hilton, wishing to avoid the mayhem of the situation, sent telegrams or called. Richard Brooks, the director of *Cat on a Hot Tin Roof*, did turn up – only to be seen off by Elizabeth's vituperative tongue. According to John Parker in *Five for Hollywood* (Macmillan, 1989), her exact words to him were, 'You bastard, you've just come to see when I'll be back at work. Well, screw you and your movie. I'm *never* coming back!'

Once she had calmed down, Elizabeth needed someone to blame for Mike Todd's death – which was an accident, pure and simple. She filed a $5-million claim against the owners of *Lucky Liz* (Todd had merely rented it), which took almost five years to reach the courts. The company was subsequently ordered to pay just $27,000 in compensation – not to Elizabeth, but to their daughter, Liza Todd.

The funeral, little more than another Todd extravaganza, took place on 25 March at the Jewish Waldheim Cemetery in Zurich, Illinois. Todd's son had suggested a private cremation – aside from a few bones that could have belonged to any or all of the victims, the casket was empty – believing that this would preserve the frail widow from the spectacle of a very public interment. Todd, however, seems to have once expressed his disapproval of crematoria, and Elizabeth was intent on honouring his wishes. For two days, she deliberated over whether to attend, which only drew more attention to the event, but the lure of the spectacle rivalled her grief. As much as the public wanted to ogle her, she just as much needed to entertain them, at whatever personal cost.

Her supposed loathing of Howard Hughes did not prevent her from hitching a free ride to Illinois on one of his private planes. Cynics commented that she put on an act of being helped down its steps by her brother Howard and Eddie Fisher in order to gain sympathy. Helen Rose, who had dressed her for her weddings, had done the honours for the closing chapter of this equally stormy marriage. More than 2,000 fans gathered on the tarmac, yelling her name as she was whisked from the airport to the Drake Hotel. As many as 20,000 more lined the funerary route – reports claimed it was the highest attendance at a funeral since that of the seven members of the Bugs Moran gang, following the 1929 St Valentine's Day Massacre. It was here that the real circus began. Every hundred yards or so there was a hot-dog seller or refreshment van. A chapter of the Eddie Fisher fan club turned up, chanting his songs and waving albums, whilst buskers entertained the crowd outside the cemetery gates, declaring that Mike Todd would have wanted it that way. High above, the scene was filmed by a press helicopter.

A small marquee had been erected over the Goldbogen plot. Elizabeth had requested that only her family and very closest friends attend the ceremony. Montgomery Clift, who had disliked Todd and found him coarse, had not been invited, but he turned up all the same; he and Rex Kennamer mingled with the crowd. A police cordon surrounded the marquee, but this gave way as the crowd pressed forward, forcing Elizabeth to make a dash back to her limousine. It took the car almost an hour to leave the cemetery as the lunatic fringe of her fan base rocked it from side to side, hoping to get her out of the vehicle or, at the least, to wind down the window. Some fans clambered onto the roof and began stamping their feet, causing Elizabeth to suffer a panic attack, but as unyielding police restored order, the cortège was eventually allowed to leave.

Elizabeth had been invited to the Oscars ceremony, two evenings later, but wisely elected to stay home. She badly needed to be with Montgomery Clift, but as she had not wanted him at Mike Todd's funeral, he had returned to New York in a huff. Todd had been posthumously nominated for his Todd-AO cinematography, Elizabeth for *Raintree County*. Todd won, but Elizabeth lost out to Joanne Woodward, who was about to be married to Paul Newman and who won the Best Actress award for her superb performance in *The Three Faces of Eve* (1957).

Elizabeth might have threatened to walk out of *Cat on a Hot Tin Roof*, but to do so would have resulted in immediate suspension. Shooting was resumed in the middle of April, less than a month after Mike Todd's death. The film is so monopolised by ex-footballer Brick (Paul Newman) and cantankerous, larger-than-life but dying patriarch Big Daddy (53-year-old Burl Ives, reprising his acclaimed Broadway role) and his noisy, dysfunctional relatives that Elizabeth is hard put to keep up with them. It is an excellent piece and very typically Tennessee Williams: tantrums and mayhem, obligatory homosexuality, madness, drunkenness, protracted speeches and ever-present 'mendacity'.

'Skipper is the only thing I got left to believe in, and you're dragging it through the gutter. You are making it shameful and filthy!' Brick yells, referring to his footballer lover who killed himself after being confronted by Maggie. Being gay, he is oblivious to her attempts to turn him on, flashing her legs and adjusting her suspenders – the same tactics, some alleged, that she had used to attempt to seduce Monty Clift.

There is also a thinly veiled and much-discussed reference to Mike Todd when Maggie screams at Brick in desperation, 'Skipper is dead, and I'm alive!' Then comes *the* line adopted by the closeted Hollywood gay community of 1958 when, referring to Brick's never having a glass out of his hand, she says, 'Your hand was made for holding something *better* than that!' Of course, Maggie cures Brick of his 'affliction' – for as had happened with Rock Hudson in *Giant*, it was inconceivable that any man could remain gay having been subjected to the charms of Elizabeth Taylor!

By the time shooting wrapped on the film, Elizabeth was involved with theatre-chain entrepreneur Arthur Loew, Joan Collins's escort since divorcing British actor Maxwell Reed. According to Ketti Fringe, the wife of Elizabeth's agent, Elizabeth also had her eye on her late husband's 21-year-old son. 'She tried Mike Todd Jr first, but his wife said no and put a stop to it before it could develop,' Fringe told biographer Kitty Kelley. 'She got young Mike out of town before Elizabeth could move in on him.' Elizabeth was also enjoying secret trysts with Eddie Fisher, and Loew might well have been the scapegoat to throw the press off their scent.

It now emerged that Mike Todd had not been the multimillionaire everyone had assumed. His estate amounted to a little over $300,000, out of which debts had to be settled. Neither would there be much future revenue from *Around the World in Eighty Days* – Todd had borrowed heavily against the profits to fund his global gallivanting. Most of his cars and houses had been rented, including the property on Schuyler Road. Whilst looking for somewhere else to live, Elizabeth moved into a bungalow at the Beverly Hills Hotel complex, leaving her children with Arthur Loew. Both he and Elizabeth denied romantic involvement, but when the press refused to believe this, she pulled a publicity stunt by choosing Hedda Hopper to accompany her on her first 'official engagement' since Mike Todd's death. The pair went to Romanoff's, where, according to the columnist, Elizabeth wore 'as many diamonds as a grieving widow could get away with'. She was there, she told the press, to bid a temporary farewell to Hollywood because she had arranged to take the children on an extended tour of Europe.

In the August, having apparently changed her mind, Elizabeth flew to New York to spend a few days with Montgomery Clift – and, it appears, to enjoy a prearranged sojourn with Eddie Fisher, in town filming his top-rating television show. Though Debbie Reynolds had been left in Hollywood with the Fishers' two children, the pair dined several times without raising too much suspicion: to the casual onlooker, here was Todd's best buddy consoling his widow and weaning her back into society. However, when the couple slipped off for the weekend to Grossinger's Hotel, the Catskills resort, the press immediately jumped to the conclusion that the relationship had progressed beyond the platonic.

Discovered by Eddie Cantor and promoted by Mike Todd, Fisher had begun his career at Grossinger's Hotel. He and Debbie Reynolds had married there in September 1955, designating it as their 'special' place. In turn, its proprietors had revered them, and they had since held the reputation as the most perfect couple in American show business.

The first report went out on 9 September, when the *Los Angeles Examiner* ran the headline 'Eddie Fisher Romance with Liz Taylor Denied'. This was a clever ploy frequently used by the press. News papers would run a 'denial' of a story, along the lines of the Fisher-

Taylor one, as a means of bringing a scandal to the attention of the public without having the necessary evidence, in the hope that such evidence would then be forthcoming to enable the story to develop. The vociferous manner in which both parties denied the affair was interpreted by most of the tabloids as a confession of guilt; as a result, they did not feel the need to exercise caution. Elizabeth would reverse this ploy in later years, 'leaking' news to the papers that she was ill again, only to then deny it!

Debbie Reynolds' biggest hit, taking the American and British charts by storm in August 1957, was 'Tammy', the closing line of which was 'Tammy's in love'. Now, the headline ran 'Eddie's in Love – With Liz!' A photograph of the pair leaving The Blue Angel nightclub appeared in *Life* magazine, and the *New York Daily News* ribbed, 'The storybook marriage of Eddie Fisher and Debbie Reynolds skidded on a series of curves yesterday – Elizabeth Taylor's.'

Initially, Debbie refused to believe that her husband and Elizabeth were more than just good friends. However, Elizabeth soon put the record straight upon her return to Hollywood. Leaving Fisher to deal with the barrage of reporters camped outside his house, she unwisely granted an interview to Hedda Hopper, who claimed in her memoirs *The Whole Truth and Nothing But* that upon being accused of being a home wrecker, Elizabeth had responded, 'Mike's dead, and I'm alive! What do you expect me to do? Sleep alone?'

Elizabeth later declared that Hopper had fabricated the quote – whilst some believed Hopper had lifted the 'Skipper's dead!' speech from *Cat on a Hot Tin Roof* and changed the names – and insisted that what she had *really* said was, 'You know how much I loved Mike? I loved him more than my life. But Mike is dead now, and I'm alive, and the one person who would want me to try and live and be happy is Mike.' Elizabeth also denied Hopper's claim that she had remarked of Debbie Reynolds, 'Eddie's not in love with her and never has been.' True or not, she had helped bring down the curtain on the Fishers' fairytale marriage, *severely* blackening her own reputation in the process.

Hedda Hopper's unedited story ran on the front page of the *Los Angeles Times* and was quickly syndicated around the world, followed by news of the Fishers' split. Debbie Reynolds was the nation's favourite; along with Doris Day, she was everyone's idea of the archetypal girl next door who could do no wrong. She too played to the press, as she was entitled to do as the injured party. Whilst Elizabeth was photographed in her jewels and her Helen Rose creations, Debbie posed on her front porch with her hair in curlers, embracing her children and looking glum. The captions invariably alluded to 'Daddy' no longer being around. Though it was widely rumoured that her marriage had been on the rocks *before* Elizabeth's arrival on the scene, Debbie was still portrayed as the hapless victim of a scarlet woman and a philanderer.

Eddie Fisher had idolised Mike Todd to such an extent that once he began emulating Todd's spendthrift, high-flying ways, he was unable to stop. Splashing money around like water, prior to his marriage to Reynolds he had impressed and seduced – in full glare of the media spotlight – Marlene Dietrich, Merle Oberon, Hope Lange and any number of other starlets and Las Vegas hoofers, many of whom boasted to friends how 'hung' he was. For Elizabeth, such bravado and chutzpah must have been akin to Todd returning from the grave. Years later, Fisher pulled no punches when he wrote about his hundreds of alleged conquests. He dismissed his marriage to Debbie Reynolds as 'a charade for the media', claimed that she had not enjoyed sex and concluded, 'Mount Virgin. The real challenge was getting to the summit.'

Elizabeth, who had ridden high on a wave of global sympathy since Mike Todd's death, was now portrayed as the brazen hussy who had inflicted misery on his two dearest friends. Not even 15-month-old Liza's hospitalisation with double pneumonia in the middle of November changed attitudes towards Elizabeth. The child remained on the critical list for several days, yet the press ignored this and followed Robert Ruark's syndicated lead: 'This Monument to Busting Up Other People's Homes'. At the height of the scandal, she and Eddie Fisher attracted 5,000 letters of complaint a week, and there were even threats from the Ku Klux Klan. Many stores refused to stock Fisher's records, and newspapers warned the parents of teenagers that they ran the risk of turning them into 'immoral delinquents' by allowing them to watch him on television.

In his memoirs, Eddie Fisher frequently comes across as a deeply unpleasant individual: brash, boastful and big-headed. However, he is also extremely honest – to a cringe-making degree, one imagines, if any of his wives ever got around to reading what he wrote about them. But they, of course, would have been conditioned by their time with him so that they would be hard edged enough to bear the brunt of any attack. Whilst Debbie is painted as the proverbial ice maiden – the astonishingly naive, perennial virgin, as portrayed in her films, who was placed on a pedestal by Middle America – Elizabeth is the ultimate seductress, the Lorelei who set out to ensnare him mindless of scathing public opinion and the threat to all of their careers. Fisher makes no secret of the fact that *he* was a willing victim, declaring of Elizabeth's voracious sexual appetite, 'She was uninhibited, wild, so totally free with her body. We couldn't get enough of each other.' And recalling how they made love up to five times a day, he added, 'Sexually, she was every man's dream; she had the face of an angel and the morals of a truck driver.'

Fisher also claimed that Elizabeth liked her sex rough and probably only truly respected a man after he had belted her one. 'She hit me all the time, too, and tried to goad me into hitting her back,' he wrote. 'She'd force me to pin her down to stop her, and that inevitably led to sex.'

In December 1958, Debbie Reynolds filed for divorce, but in taking the first step towards granting Fisher his freedom, she failed to release Elizabeth from her position of society-clique pariah. The Theater Owners Association had presented Elizabeth with their prestigious Star of the Year award for *Cat on a Hot Tin Roof* and now promptly took it back. This led to many of her so-called friends and acquaintances – some of whom had behaved no less irresponsibly in their own private lives – turning their backs on her. The stalwarts remained loyal: Rock Hudson, now divorced from Phyllis Gates, Robert Wagner and Natalie Wood – who since marrying in 1957 had inherited the 'perfect couple' tag from Debbie Reynolds and Eddie Fisher – and, of course, Montgomery Clift.

Monty's confidence in his abilities, which had plummeted towards the end of *Raintree County*, had been bolstered by working with Marlon Brando in *The Young Lions*. Directed by Edward Dmytryk, Monty had played kindly Jew Noah Ackerman, who becomes a victim of anti-Semitism when drafted into the army. The reviews had been favourable, and he had successfully portrayed an agony uncle in *Lonelyhearts* (1958) opposite Myrna Loy. The filming of this movie had seen him reverting to his usual irrational behaviour, on and off the set, and resulted in the studios finally deeming him an uninsurable risk. Ostensibly, he was now rescued by Elizabeth, who insisted that Monty be given the male lead when she was approached to play another mad-woman role in the screen adaptation of Tennessee Williams' hysterics-fest, *Suddenly, Last Summer* (1959). However, with shooting not scheduled to begin until the late spring, Elizabeth channelled all her energy into planning wedding number four – but only after spending a short time with Monty in New York to confer with her best friend as to whether Eddie Fisher was suitable husband material. The same consultation had occurred before she had married Nicky Hilton and Michael Wilding.

Mike Todd had referred to her as his 'Jewish broad', but Elizabeth went one step further for Eddie Fisher by actually embracing the Jewish faith. This was almost certainly a ploy to gain public approval and sympathy, as was the case with Marilyn Monroe before she married Jewish playwright Arthur Miller. However, to be fair, Elizabeth had been seeking guidance from Rabbi Max Nussbaum since Mike Todd's death.

Eddie Fisher later confirmed that he had been indifferent towards her conversion and that Elizabeth had wanted to convert for Mike Todd, who had forbidden the move. Fisher even said that with so much anti-Semitism in Hollywood, becoming a Jew would only make those who hated her hate her more.

Her conversion was conducted by Rabbi Nussbaum in April 1959 and was attended by her parents with the same enthusiasm, according to Fisher, that they would have mustered watching their own home burn down. She chose the name Elisheba Rachel, learned several payers in Hebrew and at the few parties she was not excluded from casually slipped Yiddish expressions into the conversation. She did herself few favours by comparing her own tribulations with the persecution of Jews during the Second World War, telling a press conference, 'I was attracted to their heritage. I guess I identified with them as underdogs.' On an even more serious note, Muslim governments across the Middle East slapped a total ban on her films when she pledged $100,000 to the Israeli war effort to 'recompense' for her conversion.

The conversion, for which Elizabeth never subsequently supplied factual evidence, cut her no slack with the media or the disgruntled public. The press still used terms such as 'home wrecker', and Debbie Reynolds fans meeting Elizabeth in public certainly voiced their opinions. Not since Ingrid Bergman's desertion of her husband to move in with director Roberto Rossellini and bear his children a decade earlier had there been such a national outcry.

Debbie also had the last laugh on her adulterous husband when granted her divorce in February 1959. The judge awarded her full custody of her children, $10,000 alimony a year for 20 years (a vast amount in those days) and the Fishers' homes in Hollywood and Palm Springs. If this was not enough to sting him, and just in case he planned on marrying Elizabeth straightaway, Fisher was told that the divorce would not become absolute until February 1960. And to round off the proceedings, NBC cancelled his television series on account of the scandal.

Debbie, of course, could not prevent the couple from living together or from getting engaged. They rented a house in Las Vegas, where Fisher was due to open a season at the Tropicana Hotel, and threw a party for the few close friends they still had: the Wagners, Rock Hudson, Tony Curtis, Ronald and Nancy Reagan, and Peter Lawson. Monty Clift declined his invitation: he disapproved of

Liza Todd, his favourite child in all the world, being caught up in the middle of a messy divorce whilst trying to come to terms with her new stepfather. Fisher had presented his fiancée with a $50,000 diamond bracelet and an evening bag encrusted with twenty-seven diamonds (one for each year of her life) that spelled out 'LIZ'. As with his predecessors, his theory was that love was far better expressed in dollars than with heartfelt words.

Eddie Fisher's opening night at the Tropicana was a media-fest, with most of the audience less interested in the on-stage performance than the fact that Elizabeth would be braving the wrath of public opinion by having the gall to show her face. When she arrived, not very sensibly via the front entrance, she was greeted with hisses and 'LIZ GO HOME' banners. Between numbers hand-picked to milk the occasion – 'It Happens Every Day', 'Making Whoopee' and Dorothy Squires' 'I'm Walking Behind You on Your Wedding Day' – Fisher wisecracked with the audience, playing the cynics at their own game, and by the end of the evening had won over even the hardest of them. After the show, he and Elizabeth met the press and for the first time gained a little sympathy – not much, but it was a step in the right direction. At one time, the fans had clamoured to see Fisher the crooner-par-excellence, but from that point on audiences felt cheated unless Elizabeth was on full bejewelled display next to the stage at every performance, especially when the curious who had frequently *disliked* his singing began pushing out the genuine aficionados in the rush for tickets.

It is not known whether Debbie Reynolds had really intended to make her ex-husband sweat it out for a whole year before being allowed to marry Elizabeth, but neither is it clear why she changed her mind, granting him his freedom after less than three months. Whatever the case, Fisher obtained a Nevada divorce during the morning of 12 May 1959 (although the original stipulation of a one-year gap would have stood had he been in California), and within the hour the couple were wed in a civil ceremony. A blessing followed at the Temple Beth Shalom, and Elizabeth became Mrs

Edwin Jack Fisher. Mike Todd Jr was best man, and Elizabeth's sister-in-law, Mara (Howard's wife), was matron of honour. The bride wore an 'unlucky' green Jean-Louis gown recommended by Marlene Dietrich, who told me, 'She'd spent her whole life crying wolf most of the time. To my way of thinking, she deserved a little *genuine* bad luck for a change!'

Elizabeth told the press a variation of her usual stock statement, which was already starting to wear thin: 'This honeymoon is going to last 30 or 40 years. From now on, I want to devote my time to being a devoted wife and mother.' Few took her or the marriage seriously, particularly when she insisted on still wearing Mike Todd's wedding ring on her right hand.

The honeymoon, compared to its predecessors, was reasonably frugal, part-financed by Columbia Pictures. The couple flew to Spain to shoot the exteriors of *Suddenly, Last Summer*. Whilst there, Elizabeth also made an unbilled cameo appearance in Mike Todd Jr's 'Smell-O-Vision' curiosity *Holiday in Spain* (1960), something of a non-event starring Peter Lorre and Denholm Elliott. Naturally, with such a gimmick at its centre, it had a limited release and, fortunately, was soon forgotten. Fans had to wait until near the end to see Elizabeth – and almost choke on the stench of the perfume accompanying the scene as it was pumped through the cinema's air-conditioning system.

When shooting wound up, the Fishers borrowed producer Sam Spiegel's yacht and 'explored' the Mediterranean, attracting large crowds at each 'impromptu' anchorage – all arranged by the studio publicity department, of course. They then headed for London, where the interiors for *Suddenly, Last Summer* were shot at Shepperton Studios.

Upon hearing of director Joe Mankiewicz's Lothario reputation – arguably no worse than his own – Eddie Fisher took no chances and made a point of visiting the set every day. Though he might not have known it at the time, he was starting to ditch the crooner tag and take up the role of Mr Taylor. 'My real job was keeping Elizabeth happy,' he wrote in his memoirs. 'My own career was disappearing. My singing, which had once been the thing I lived for, was becoming more of a well-paid hobby.'

At Shepperton, Elizabeth walked in on a dispute that for once did not concern her. Katharine Hepburn, a fighter for a lost cause – like Elizabeth with Monty – had been coaxed by producer Sam Spiegel into playing wealthy widow Violet Venable, whose son Sebastian died 'Suddenly, Last Summer' in mysterious circumstances. Hepburn had read the script, and although she had understood that Sebastian was attracted to men, she had apparently been unaware of what homosexuals did in bed until being enlightened on the subject by gay scriptwriter Gore Vidal. Matters were made infinitely worse by a change in the script that resulted in Sebastian's interest turning to teenage boys. 'Ah, the perils of cruising for chicken!' Paul Roen later observed in *High Camp* (Leyland Publications, 1993), an essential guide to such films, published four decades later, which, surprisingly, contains just one Elizabeth Taylor movie. Hepburn tried to get out of her contract, but by then it was too late.

Claimed by Tennessee Williams to be semi-autobiographical, *Suddenly, Last Summer* was promoted behind the scenes as 'a film about homosexuality, cannibalism and frontal lobotomies'. It possesses all the elements of the classic camp spectacular, guaranteeing it will never being taken seriously: Grand Guignol settings, sadistic nuns, lesbian nurses and lunatics, all aided and abetted by masters of the genre, Elizabeth and Monty, and Mercedes McCambridge and Albert Dekker.

Elizabeth's gay fans hated the slur against them in the film's publicity poster, which depicted her wearing a swimsuit alongside the caption 'Suddenly, last summer, Cathy knew she was being used for evil!' The 'evil' refers to the men Elizabeth's character, Cathy, procured for her cousin, Sebastian, during his annual visit to the Med, once his mother, Violet Venable (Hepburn), had grown too old for the job. (Those in the know scoffed that Sebastian would have used another man to attract his pick-ups had he been so shy.) Sebastian has died in mysterious circumstances, and in order to protect her son's memory, Violet offers to donate $1 million to surgeon John

Cukrowiz's (Monty) decrepit asylum if he lobotomises Cathy, who seems to have flipped her lid, and stops her from revealing the truth about her son's homosexuality. The operation never takes place, of course – with so much character-actress confusion, it would be inconceivable that Elizabeth Taylor be thought of as insane. Instead, we get a hysterical speech akin to some of those Elizabeth gave during her later political rallies, in which we learn the true circumstances of Sebastian's death: that he was stripped and cannibalised by a group of angry young men, performing the ultimate parody of a blow job, all of which was witnessed by Cathy.

Montgomery Clift's health had deteriorated badly since *Raintree County*, though the magic of his performances had remained intact. During *Suddenly, Last Summer*, however, he experienced such difficulty remembering his lines that Joe Mankiewicz wanted to put shooting on hold until a replacement was found. Elizabeth defended him virulently, warning Mankiewicz that if her friend left the production, so would she. Katharine Hepburn, purely on a professional level, could not condone the way the director kept abusing Monty every time he fluffed a scene. On the last day of shooting, having been assured that she would not be required for retakes, she strode up to Mankiewicz and spat in his face.

Elizabeth's performance in *Suddenly, Last Summer* was exemplary, effortlessly matching Montgomery Clift's – she even held her own against Katharine Hepburn's stilted, over-the-top delivery, especially during the gut-wrenching denouement scene. The *New York Herald Tribune*, critical of much of Elizabeth's past work, observed, 'If there were ever any doubts about the ability of Miss Taylor to express complex and devious emotions, to deliver a flexible and deep performance, this film ought to remove them.'

It is, however, chiefly for its inadvertent ultra-camp value that the film will be remembered. Back then, it catapulted Elizabeth into the top-ten box-office stars list, along with her friend Rock Hudson and Doris Day, who had taken America by storm with *Pillow Talk* (1959). Before its release, Elizabeth had again talked of retirement, but the prospect of earning up to $500,000 per picture now put this thought out of her head. However, it would appear that even this was insufficient. When approached by producer Walter Wanger and Spyros Skouras, the head of Twentieth Century Fox, to consider the lead in *Cleopatra* (1963), a project that had already been on the stocks for two years, Elizabeth upped her demands. Skouras had spent over $500,000 on the production, planned to save cash by using some of the leftover sets from the 1917 production starring Theda Bara and had pencilled in Joan Collins for the title role. However, he believed Elizabeth would be better. She read the script and denounced it as appalling but agreed to do it all the same so long as the studio paid her $1 million! Skouras's lack of respect for her and her demands was only too evident by his quote to the press: 'Any hundred-dollars-a-week girl can play Cleopatra.' He nonetheless swallowed the bait and increased the budget to $3 million.

In the meantime, MGM informed Elizabeth that her final film in their about-to-expire contract would be *Butterfield 8* (1960) with Laurence Harvey and David Janssen. Her salary was a non-negotiable $125,000. 'It was the story of a nymphomaniac who falls in love with a married man and almost breaks up his marriage,' Eddie Fisher later observed. 'Hmm, now where did that concept come from?' Elizabeth attacked the storyline as 'pornographic' and initially refused to play a character described as 'a non-charging hooker'. MGM, she added, had only offered her such a role because they wanted to exact their revenge on her for leaving them.

Elizabeth's producer friend Pandro Berman, who had purchased the rights to John O'Hara's novella some years before but until then had failed to get the project off the ground, tried to talk her into doing the film. Berman quietly pointed out that owing to a 'technicality', MGM could legally hang on to her for another two years and prevent her from working for another studio. However, if she refused to cooperate, she would simply be suspended and not work at all during those two years, which would mean her giving up on *Cleopatra*. What the canny Berman did not let on was that he owned a huge share of the *Butterfield 8* movie rights – a share which would bring in 40 per cent of the profits, providing the film earned $2 million at the box office, no problem at all given the publicity attached to the star's private life.

Elizabeth still refused to do the film and was promptly suspended – a stalemate that ended one week later when she capitulated, doubtless swallowing a huge wedge of humble pie, although she was no less demanding, particularly when David Janssen dropped out of the production. She asked Berman to give Janssen's part to Eddie Fisher! MGM readily agreed to this: having the new husband around, they figured, might just keep their feisty star in check. Also, although the Fishers would never be regarded as being as lucrative or personable as Eddie and Debbie or the Wagners, MGM hoped that pairing them on the screen would fill cinemas – providing, of course, they were still together by the time the film was released.

No sooner had Elizabeth been placated than she fell ill again. Eddie Fisher's hype-inspired success at the Tropicana had brought in more offers, including a season at Las Vegas's Desert Inn and New York's Waldorf Astoria. It was while performing in New York that *Time* magazine declared him 'an absolute smash', though there would be few hit records for a while. Halfway through the run, Elizabeth began to experience breathing difficulties. When she collapsed and was rushed into the Presbyterian Hospital, doctors diagnosed viral pneumonia.

There seems little wonder, given certain aspects of what happened next, that some sections of the media found it hard to distinguish when Elizabeth was genuinely ailing or attention seeking. Neither did Fisher help by subsequently claiming that she had asked for her lip gloss whilst in the ambulance. But for almost a week she was confined to an oxygen tent and her condition described as critical. Then, as she started to rally, she attempted to obtain some sort of bonus from her indisposition by asking a specialist at the hospital if he could reverse her earlier operation to tie off the fallopian tubes. There were already rumours of a rift in her marriage, and Elizabeth believed that having a baby with Fisher might help the situation. She was advised that surgery would be risky in her current state of health – and she had only had the procedure in the first place because doctors had warned that having another child might kill her. Once again, searching for a way to remedy a situation she had created affected her capacity for reason.

This stubborn reluctance to see sense applied to her demands for Eddie Fisher to be in the new film. It was a hopeless attempt to hold on to him – not that he was going anywhere. She was obsessed with losing him to the point of making life merry hell for everyone around her. Fisher might have been one of the finest singers of his generation, but he had no proven acting ability, a fact he himself readily confirmed. In 1958, he had appeared with Debbie Reynolds in *Bundle of Joy*. The film was 65 per cent self-financed and slated by the *New York Times* as 'No bundle of joy . . . sadly deficient entertainment.' Elizabeth even attempted to transform her husband into a legitimate movie star by getting Montgomery Clift to give him acting lessons. This did not work. According to Fisher, the ever-bombed Monty flaked out during the initial reading with a lighted cigarette in his hand, setting fire to the script whilst Fisher was out of the room! Despite all this, he does exceptionally well in *Butterfield 8*.

Shooting on the film got under way in January 1960. Still weak, Elizabeth was laid low by influenza, though by now MGM were allegedly so tired of trying to work out which of her indispositions were real and which were invented that she would have been forced to work, come what may, had it not been for an impromptu strike at the studio. Elizabeth always professed to hating *Butterfield 8*, the plot of which was based on the real-life story of Starr Faithful, a Palm Beach call girl who had been murdered in 1931. By the time it reached the screen, of course, O'Hara's work had been so heavily censored that it bore little resemblance to the original. All that was important to MGM was that Elizabeth's character, good-time-girl Gloria Wandrous – who has the audacity to confess that she was sexually abused as a child and *enjoyed* the experience

– would have to die, to reassure moralists that 'divine' justice had been dispensed.

On the positive side, Elizabeth loved working with Lithuanian-born British actor Laurence Harvey. The fact that Harvey was another tormented soul fighting the twin demons of drink and homosexuality (though married three times) drew Elizabeth towards him like a magnet, just as it had to Montgomery Clift. The pair would remain good friends until the end of Harvey's life, which came prematurely at the age of just 45. His portrayal of arrogant Northerner Joe Lampton in *Room at the Top* (1958) had opened the door to Hollywood, and he had recently completed *The Alamo* (1960) with John Wayne. In *Butterfield 8*, Harvey excels as 'low-down rotten heel' Wes Liggett, though, like Elizabeth, he believed that he could have given more of himself with a better script. To this end, during the studio's strike, Elizabeth brought in pals Tennessee Williams, Truman Capote and Christopher Isherwood to liven up the proceedings. Between them they wrote some 'pretty explicit' love scenes for the Taylor and Fisher characters. Fisher later claimed that one of these had been filmed and that they actually had sex on the set. 'I didn't have an orgasm, but we did everything else,' he recalled, adding that being in front of the camera had been a tremendous turn-on. Of course, had such a scene survived it would have been worth a fortune on the black market. It ended up on the cutting-room floor, and the revised script was 'binned' by Pandro Berman and a new one commissioned from John Michael Hayes, the man responsible for getting *Peyton Place* past the censors.

Providing one is not put off by Laurence Harvey's 'fidgety toupee', it is a good film with none of the usual Tennessee Williams-style histrionics and raucous vocals. In one memorable scene, the barman at Gloria's local could be describing Elizabeth when he says, 'You don't have to describe her to me. I'd know her with my eyes closed, down the bottom of a coalmine, during an eclipse of the sun . . . She's like catnip to every cat in town!' Art also reflects life as the actress and character merge: the man Gloria loves is incapable of leaving his wealthy wife, because she is the one holding the purse strings, whilst the man is a thorough creep who drinks heavily and is physically violent, traits that – as with Elizabeth – only excite her and make her love him more. However, as with so many events in Elizabeth's personal life, all must end badly for Gloria.

By the time *Butterfield 8* was released, with rumours rife that Elizabeth's marriage to Fisher was well and truly on the rocks, the critics would be making inevitable comparisons between what they had watched on the screen and what was actually happening within the Taylor-Fisher camps.

EIGHT

THE LAUNCH OF THE
$40 MILLION BOMB

WITH *BUTTERFIELD 8* IN THE CAN, IT WAS TIME FOR THE *Cleopatra* fiasco to roll into action – a lengthy process that would be fraught with bust-ups of escalating virulence, threats of lawsuits and financial ruin, and for its star a maelstrom of tantrums, indispositions and more attention seeking than most people could sensibly handle. For starters, Elizabeth was not the only contender for the role that Spyros Skouras hoped would make the film Hollywood's biggest smash since *Gone with the Wind* (1939) had saved Twentieth Century Fox from the receiver, although her personal and financial demands had been met and she had been told that *Cleopatra* was hers for the taking.

Skouras worked his way up the Hollywood ladder the hard way. The son of a Greek shepherd, he and his brothers Charles and George arrived penniless in the United States in 1910. Settling in St Louis, they bought up every cinema in the city by the mid-1920s. When these were later snapped up by Warner Brothers, Skouras was appointed head of distribution. In 1932, after a brief spell with Paramount, Skouras took over Fox's movie theatres in New York. In 1942, he was appointed their president, investing in the

CinemaScope widescreen process, which, for a while, successfully fought off competition from television, the 'newfangled' craze that had hammered the final nail into the coffin of the all-powerful studio system. Skouras's debut film in this media, *The Robe* (1953), was a big hit worldwide.

Producer Walter Wanger had a no less illustrious pedigree. A graduate of Dartmouth College, he worked for Columbia, most notably on Greta Garbo's *Queen Christina* (1933), before becoming an independent producer, releasing such gems as *Stagecoach* (1939) and *The Reckless Moment* (1949), with his wife, Joan Bennett. In the early 1950s, he spent time in prison for shooting her agent/ lover but emerged from the scandal virtually unscathed to make *Invasion of the Body Snatchers* (1956). Both Wanger and Skouras boasted at the time that *Cleopatra* would prove to be their greatest achievement, though it would actually turn out to be their biggest nightmare.

In recent years, Fox had endured some of the lowest returns of any of the major studios. Aside from *The King and I* and *The Seven Year Itch* (1955), there had been no massive box-office hits, and a series of turkeys had lost the company $100 million.

In June 1960, Elizabeth was yet to sign her contract. One of the reasons for this was that her films were banned in Egypt, where the film was set, and in the rest of the Arab world because of her conversion to Judaism and links with Israel. Still sitting in the wings, but no longer clear favourite, was Joan Collins – who, in retrospect, would have been just as good in the role – along with Susan Hayward, Gina Lollobrigida and, more ridiculously, Marilyn Monroe and Brigitte Bardot, either of whom would have turned the production into a joke. Marilyn had just been assigned to *The Misfits* with Montgomery Clift and Clark Gable, and would cause them untold problems, turning up late every day, more often than not high on barbiturates and spreading the rumour that she and Monty were an item. Elizabeth detested her. During a confrontation at The Polo Lounge in Beverly Hills (quoted in Norman Mailer's biography of Monroe), Elizabeth is reputed to have exclaimed, in front of witnesses, 'Get that dyke away from me!'

All of the above-mentioned actresses were contract players and therefore cheaper to employ than Elizabeth. Aside from Monroe and Bardot, all were more talented. Elizabeth, however, was media manna from heaven – albeit an indiscriminate liability on account of health and personality issues – so much so that Wanger and Skouras were willing to stake their reputations in acquiring her, regardless of the cost. Any problems, they declared, would be ironed out along the way.

Like Rock Hudson and the Wagners, Elizabeth had founded her own company, the first of several – based in Switzerland for tax purposes, MCL was named after her children's initials – and she was proving to be a surprisingly shrewd businesswoman. When the Fox executives decided that a $1-million salary was too steep, she and her agents negotiated a deal whereby she would be paid a flat rate of $125,000 to be followed by $50,000 for each additional week she was asked to work after a to-be-fixed shooting period. Fox were clearly expecting the production to run pretty much to schedule and could not have foreseen any of the dilemmas of the near future. Additionally, the studio would pick up her expenses tab. This included $3,000 per week in personal expenses, the salaries for her entourage, a suite at the Dorchester in London, first-class air and rail travel, and a Rolls-Royce to be laid on around the clock. It was as if Elizabeth had actually seen into the future or had even planned to take Fox for a ride. Though all of these terms combined came to less than the original $1 million she had demanded, by the time *Cleopatra* hit the screens the tally would be almost double this amount.

To make money, Spyros Skouras avowed, money would have to be spent, and vast amounts were dispensed with in getting the project off the ground. In Italy, a rival company were about to begin shooting their version of *Cleopatra*, with a more sensible budget. Skouras bought them out to the tune of $500,000. He then gave the go-ahead for the sets to be constructed – recreations of Alexandria and Rome, spread across several acres at Pinewood Studios. By the time he had signed the supporting actors, the sets alone had cost Spyros $750,000. Stephen Boyd was hired to play Mark Antony, and Peter Finch was signed for the role of Caesar. Belfast-born Boyd, ethereally handsome and at the prime of his career, had recently triumphed as Massala in *Ben-Hur* (1959). Finch, a hell-raiser much admired by Elizabeth, had already worked with her in *Elephant Walk*. Welsh actor Stanley Baker was signed up to play Mark Antony's favourite, Rufio. Shooting was scheduled to begin at the end of September, with director Rouben Mamoulian confident that a typical British autumn would provide an exact climate to the one enjoyed by ancient Egypt.

By then, Eddie Fisher had all but been relegated to the role of Mr Taylor – the press reported him as her factotum/secretary, on Fox's payroll to the tune of $1,500 a week just to ensure that she got to work on time and sober each day. It was suggested that all they ever had in common was a mutual love for one man – Mike Todd – one passionately, the other platonically, and that neither had ever stopped mourning him.

The first major crisis occurred days into shooting when the studio coiffeurs staged a strike because Elizabeth had brought her personal stylist onto the set. When word got around that she must therefore consider British hairdressers to be useless, which was not the case, the technicians took a sympathy vote and downed tools, forcing the studio to shut for several days until the dispute was resolved. This apparently had an effect on Elizabeth's health, and soon afterwards one of her 'aides' – almost certainly Eddie Fisher – informed Mamoulian that she would be unavailable for work because of a high fever. The director was concerned enough, having been forewarned of his star's foibles, to cable Spyros Skouras in Hollywood – and for Skouras to be on the next plane to London. The press then learned that the production was costing the studio over $100,000 a day.

Eddie Fisher, by his own admission, found it necessary to get away from his wife from time to time. 'I was caught in a magnificent trap, and even though I was madly in love with her, it was still a trap,' he recalled, adding that his career had evaporated and that the only singing he was now doing was around the house. Taking a leaf out of Mike Todd's book, Fisher had decided to produce Elizabeth's films himself, which would mean jetting back and forth to Hollywood to strike up various deals and hopefully salvage their flagging marriage by putting some distance between them, thus applying the 'absence makes the heart grow fonder' technique used earlier by Louis B. Mayer to patch up the marriage of Elizabeth's parents. She was reputedly interested in playing the outrageous American dancer Isadora Duncan (later immortalised on the screen by Vanessa Redgrave), mindless of the fact that she could not dance, and the great French tragic actress Sarah Bernhardt, mindless of the fact, some sniped, that she could not act. George Stevens, who had directed her in *Giant*, was also assembling the cast for *The Greatest Story Ever Told* (1965) and wanted Elizabeth to play Mary Magdalene, a move that would have seen her torn to shreds by the moralists. Other projects lined up by Fisher included Harold Robbins's *The Carpetbaggers* and *L'affaire gouffre*, a French drama co-starring Charlie Chaplin.

In what now appears to have been a trial separation, Fisher put his heart into these projects. 'The truth was, I just wanted to breathe on my own,' he observes in his memoirs, describing the tantrum Elizabeth had thrown when he had bid her au revoir. The nearest he came to signing a deal was when Warner Brothers wanted to team her up again with Paul Newman in *Two for the Seesaw* (1962). When the studio president learned that she would not work for less than her now statutory $1 million, the deal was off, and Fisher returned to London and inevitably more drama, for his wife was ill again.

Never one to do things by halves, Elizabeth had gained a valuable ally during Fisher's absence: Lord Evans, the Queen's personal physician. When she was suddenly declared seriously ill at the end of October, it was he who booked her into the London Clinic. She also flew in her personal doctor from Los Angeles, and despite the gravity of her condition, insisted on being stretchered out of the *front* entrance of the Dorchester – but not until the press had been informed.

For two weeks, all the public were told was that Elizabeth Taylor was very ill, possibly dying. Sara and Francis Taylor, declaring that her illness was 'connected to the spirit', breezed into town, accompanied by a Christian Scientist practitioner. The trio spent several nights at Elizabeth's bedside, taking it in turn to read aloud passages from Mary Baker Eddy's 1875 tome *Science and Health with Key to the Scriptures*. The main thesis of this book is that 'disease is of an illusory nature, curable without medication'. Whilst the cynics scoffed, Elizabeth accredited it with helping her towards her recovery, whilst her husband more realistically suspected that the true cause of her malady was her fondness for painkillers. Recalling how she popped pills prescribed by several different doctors, each with no knowledge of the other, he explained how one day he experimented by taking one of the more unfamiliar medications from Elizabeth's nightstand – before then he had never knowingly taken anything addictive. 'I couldn't stand up until the next morning,' he wrote, adding that he feared that she might overdose. 'The most I could do was be there in case – just in case.'

Fisher claimed, just as others have, that Elizabeth knew more about these drugs than most doctors, that she was constantly passing out and that the situation became so bad that he had to be prescribed Librium to get a good night's sleep. In fact, he had been addicted to drugs for years, something he might not have been consciously aware of. One of his mentors was alternative physician Max Jacobson, the infamous Dr Feelgood, whose celebrity clients included neurotics Margaret Leighton and Tennessee Williams. Both relied on his notorious 'vitamin' injections and, like Fisher, might not have known of their amphetamine content. Also, because these were not yet illegal in the United States, patients might have interpreted the unpleasant cold-turkey experience that followed once their effect wore off as merely being part of the condition for which the injections had been prescribed. Jacobson usually administered the shots himself, but once a client was hooked, he taught them to self-inject. According to Fisher, whoever was treating Elizabeth also allowed him to inject her with morphine. 'She needed it more than she needed a husband,' he recalled. 'Ah, the things we do for love.' Then it emerged that the cause of her mystery illness was nothing more than an abscessed tooth. This was removed and the patient given the all-clear, much to everyone's relief.

During Elizabeth's indisposition, Rouben Mamoulian had worked around her, shooting crowd scenes and scenes with Stephen Boyd that did not involve Cleopatra. No sooner had she returned to the set than she collapsed with severe headaches and had to be rushed back to the London Clinic. Lord Evans and his colleagues now diagnosed something much more serious: inflammation of the spinal cord and brain, possibly meningitis. On 18 November 1960, she was declared 'unfit to work for the foreseeable future'.

For Twentieth Century Fox, this spelled disaster. Spyros Skouras had luckily, but with some difficulty, taken out a $3-million insurance policy in the event of such a catastrophe befalling the studio, and when it was decided that filming would have to be postponed, not just on account of Elizabeth but because of the fast-approaching winter – the cameras were getting steamed up due to the cold and there was steam coming from the actors' nostrils and mouths, hardly appropriate for Egypt! – Lloyds of London suggested that Skouras find himself another Cleopatra and begin shooting elsewhere. Susan Hayward, Joan Collins and Joanne Woodward (a late contender) were no longer available, but Marilyn Monroe – a hopeless wreck after *The Misfits* – was still interested, and so too now were Kim Novak and Shirley MacLaine. Skouras would not hear of this. He announced that he was closing down the production until the new year, by which time he hoped Elizabeth would be fit.

The tabloids, meanwhile, were having a field day, fuelled by Elizabeth's own passion for the dramatic. The *Daily Mail* suggested she had been faking it – keeping away from the set because she had put on weight. Insiders, who were effectively little more than idle speculators, leaked snippets to the American trash mags. One such rumour was that Elizabeth was cheating on Eddie Fisher with gay actor Stephen Boyd and that the Fishers' marriage – founded solely on their joint grief for Mike Todd – was all but over. Boyd was enjoying a discreet relationship with the British boxer Freddie Mills, who later left him for singer Michael Holliday, but the press refused to believe that a man even reputed to be involved with Elizabeth Taylor could be anything but red-blooded and did not 'out' him.

Whilst Boyd breathed a sigh of relief, the Fishers sued various tabloids for a collective $8 million. Not that this did much good. A few years earlier, the *Daily Mirror* had been taken to the cleaners by the flamboyantly homosexual Liberace for suggesting that he was effeminate, since which time the press had been meticulous in checking their sources. No doubt the newspapers would have supplied proof of where their stories had come from had the matter gone to the high court – and no doubt released more details of the Fishers' troubled marriage. The couple were therefore compelled to settle out of court for smaller amounts than they had anticipated, amounts which have never been disclosed.

Shooting on *Cleopatra* resumed on 3 January 1961, but ground to a halt days later when Rouben Mamoulian denounced the script rewrites as 'tosh'. Acting on a whim, he flew in writer-cum-producer-cum-director Nunnally Johnson from Hollywood, an exercise which did not come cheap. Johnson had worked on *Tobacco Road* (1941), *The Grapes of Wrath* (1940) and, more recently, Elvis Presley's *Flaming Star* (1960). His fee for *Cleopatra* was a non-negotiable $100,000, and his on-set presence only added to the general mayhem, forcing Mamoulian to confess that he had made an almighty mistake and throw in the towel. Through no fault of his own, he had ended up with just 15 minutes of usable film, which, he told reporters, had cost Twentieth Century Fox around $500,000 a minute!

It was Elizabeth who suggested that Mamoulian's replacement should be Joe Mankiewicz, much as she loathed him for his treatment of Montgomery Clift during *Suddenly, Last Summer*. Riding high on the crest of a wave of popularity following the success of the film, Mankiewicz upped his fee in a deal that very nearly catapulted the studio irretrievably into the red. Mankiewicz joint-owned a production company with NBC that Spyros Skouras had been after for some time. Part of the deal was that Fox should buy him out for $3 million – and pay him a salary way above the norm, as well as 'executives' expenses. As such, he became the highest-paid director in Hollywood history up to that point.

Mankiewicz hit Pinewood like a tidal wave. To pacify the film's backers, who were threatening to pull out, he dismissed Nunnally Johnson and the lesser scriptwriters, sacked most of the bit-parts and extras, and gave instructions for the sets to be trashed and rebuilt. Within a month of taking the helm, he had sent the *Cleopatra* budget soaring to over $12 million. Then he announced a target date: 3 April 1961. By then, he vowed, he would have come up with a script that would not have cinemagoers cringing and a movie with actors worth watching. Until this date, production would be suspended.

Elizabeth, now on the $50,000-a-week part of her deal with Fox – currently being paid just to hang around waiting for the studio call – accompanied Eddie Fisher to Munich's pre-Lenten carnival. No sooner had they arrived than Fisher was taken ill with suspected appendicitis. Elizabeth insisted upon him being flown back to London – again suggesting that the condition cannot have been serious. Fisher subsequently confessed that he had invented the illness in order to draw attention to himself for once and thus prevent Elizabeth from self-destructing completely. Some people might think it incredible that he should actually undergo surgery in order to assuage his wife's acute selfishness rather than 'kick her into touch' as some husbands might have done. Such was her power over him.

Fisher had barely recovered from his ordeal when Elizabeth's lungs became congested and she almost choked to death during the night of 3 March 1961. Her life was ostensibly saved by one

J. Middleton Price, an anaesthetist attending a party at a nearby suite at the Dorchester who performed an emergency tracheotomy. Rushed into the London Clinic, she was diagnosed with pneumonia and placed on the critical list, with a 40 per cent chance of survival. The headline in the next day's *Evening Standard* read, 'Liz Fights for Her Life'.

Outside the London Clinic, hundreds of fans kept a round-the-clock vigil, mingling with the curious and reporters eager to relay news of her death to their editors who would vie for the best exclusives on her busy love life once she was deceased and incapable of suing. Some of those religious organisation that had previously denounced her held prayer meetings for her recovery – they were unashamed to admit that they wanted her well so that they would not feel guilty about attacking her. Some even delivered bottles of Lourdes water to the hospital.

London had not witnessed such an emotional scene since June 1939, when Gracie Fields had been placed on the danger list after being admitted to the Chelsea Hospital with ovarian cancer. Photographers were offered huge amounts of cash to infiltrate the tight security for an exclusive of Elizabeth's corpse should the worst befall her. Just over a year earlier, the same incentive had been put forward when French heart-throb actor Gérard Philipe had died in Paris. Elizabeth's parents flew in to be with her, this time without their Christian Science miracle worker. Montgomery Clift called every day; John Wayne and Tennessee Williams, working in the capital, dropped in to see her. Every hour on the hour there was a bulletin: these either declared her to be slightly on the mend or sinking fast.

On 10 March 1961, Elizabeth was taken off the critical list, though she would remain hospitalised until the end of the month. There was absolutely no hope of her returning to the *Cleopatra* set for the time being, but the showbiz wheel had to keep turning, even if the star was out of action. Upon her discharge, Elizabeth was driven to Heathrow, looking pale under her make-up but still every inch the movie legend in her furs and jewels. On a specially equipped plane, she was flown back to Los Angeles to pick up a Best Actress Oscar for *Butterfield 8*. Many critics believed that the award was given to her not on account of her acting abilities, but out of pity – others suggested that this was the Academy's way of apologising for their harsh treatment of her during the Fisher-Reynolds split, though she had, of course, brought this upon herself. 'They always gave you an Academy Award when they thought you were going to die,' Marlene Dietrich told me. 'It was their way of salving their conscience – "The Deathbed Oscar" – and many believe that Elizabeth Taylor died a death every time she stepped in front of a camera.' Elizabeth was presented with the award by Yul Brynner. Her chief rival had been Shirley MacLaine, nominated for *The Apartment* (1960), who later observed, 'I lost to a tracheotomy.'

Elizabeth embarked on a strange and most mysterious relationship during this period with Max Lerner, the 59-year-old ex-Harvard and Brandeis University professor and columnist with the *New York Post* who had penned a glowing review of her performance in *Suddenly, Last Summer*. Lerner had also defended her against some of the vitriolic comments that had appeared in the press following her marriage to Eddie Fisher, particularly those made by Robert Ruark, who had denounced her as 'a monument to busting up other people's homes'. Praising Elizabeth and Eddie for their frank expression of their feelings for one another, despite the hurt this had caused, Lerner observed, 'This is a case where joyous candour is far better than a hysterical show of virtue. Where so many people have been desensitised in our world, I welcome this forthright celebration of the life of the senses.'

Biographer Kitty Kelley later compared Elizabeth and Max Lerner with Marilyn Monroe and Arthur Miller: 'The perfect complement of "The Brain" and "The Body", a melding of the cerebral and sexual.' It is unlikely Lerner would have bothered watching a film such as *Suddenly, Last Summer* had it not been for an impromptu meeting with Elizabeth in June 1959, when he had been covering the summit talks between Prime Minister Macmillan and President Eisenhower. It was obviously love – or lust – at first sight on his part, and now that her fourth marriage was crumbling, Elizabeth welcomed the attention of a worldly wise, super-intelligent man as an antidote to the inarticulate braggarts she had been involved with in the past.

Speaking to *McCall's* magazine in September 1974, Lerner retrospectively confirmed their relationship: 'It strengthened Elizabeth's self-respect, her index of self-worth.' Certainly, her confidence needed a boost after one violent husband, one who was pathologically docile and two more who believed that true love was expressed by way of the wallet, not the heart. According to Lerner, their affair was sufficiently serious for them to contemplate marriage, though with a 32-year age gap, and with both parties still married, this would have created an even bigger scandal than the one involving Eddie Fisher. Elizabeth also trusted Lerner enough to confide her innermost secrets, which she now wanted to share with the world, no doubt wishing to set the record straight should she fall ill again and not survive. She announced that this project would be called *Elizabeth Taylor: Between Life and Death*, and an undisclosed publisher paid her $250,000 for the privilege of opening her heart. The exercise produced some 200 pages of transcripts from the taped interviews given when she was feeling up to it. Her friend Roddy McDowall compiled a collection 50 never-before-seen photographs for use in the book, an exercise he would later repeat for his famous *Double Exposure* (William Morrow and Company, 1993) tome. Though the project was subsequently abandoned, some of these confidences are believed to have been incorporated into *An Informal Memoir by Elizabeth Taylor* (Harper & Row, 1965). Elizabeth's relationship with Lerner, like all the others, quickly fizzled out, though the journalist would remain a close friend until his death, aged 89, in 1992.

Spyros Skouras, meanwhile, announced that *Cleopatra* would resume shooting in Hollywood in June, and the hardly used Pinewood sets were dismantled and crated up. They were halfway across the Atlantic when a Twentieth Century Fox executive reminded Spyros of the clause in Elizabeth's contract stipulating that MCL had insisted upon the film being made outside the United States for tax purposes. Skouras spent $400,000 creating a huge artificial lake for the film's battle scenes but now had to have this filled in, selling the land at a loss to a real-estate company. Then he began searching for what he considered would be the next best thing to ancient Egypt and Rome: a location in Italy.

To acquire his director, Skouras had been compelled to buy some of Joe Mankiewicz's holdings. Now, to raise additional funds for what was already being labelled 'Hollywood's costliest turkey', he found himself selling 250 acres of Twentieth Century Fox's studio lots in Beverly Hills. Instructions were given to reconstruct Rome's Forum on a 12-acre back-lot, whilst the Alexandria site sprung up across 19 more, with the studio conveniently forgetting the stipulation in Elizabeth's contract that filming should be done outside the USA for tax purposes. Skouras then commissioned an exact replica of Cleopatra's barge – at a cost of $100,000. Replicas were made of 200 statues, 30,000 ancient weapons and 25,000 costumes. This done, he summoned his leading lady to work – only to be informed by her doctors that she would require another three months to recuperate. She was, however, apparently well enough for socialising and attending official functions. On 8 July 1961, Elizabeth and Attorney General Robert Kennedy spearheaded a fund-raising event for the Cedars-Sinai Hospital, with guests paying up to $3,000 to hear her open her heart about her near-death experiences in an 'off the cuff' speech, actually scripted by Joe Mankiewicz:

> Dying is many things, but most of all it is wanting to live. Throughout many critical hours in the operating theatre it was as if every nerve, every muscle were being strained to the last ounce of my strength. Gradually and inevitably, that last ounce was drawn, and there was no more breath. I remember I had focused desperately on the hospital light hanging directly above me. It had become something I needed almost fanatically to continue to see, the vision of light itself. Slowly it faded and

dimmed like a well-done theatrical effect to blackness. I died. Shall I tell you what it was like? Being down a long, dark tunnel, and there was a small light at the end. I had to keep looking at that light. It was painful, but beautiful too. It was like childbirth: painful but *so* beautiful.

Cynics were not slow in pointing out that Elizabeth had never *experienced* childbirth, having undergone three Caesarean sections. The full speech, syndicated to newspaper columns around the world and frequently dipped into by Elizabeth for future interviews and press conferences, might have been contrived, but the sentiment, linked to her need to reach out and help others, was heartfelt and genuine. When she and Eddie Fisher chipped in with $100,000 for the cause, the well-heeled guests reached for their chequebooks, and the evening raised over $8 million! The world's press had spent years detailing every last moment of her complicated private life; now they were witnessing the birth of Elizabeth Taylor the great humanitarian. What a tremendous pity, then, that over the next decade this quality would be overshadowed by her mania for spending vast amounts of cash on what some people considered to be trivialities.

Three days later, the Fishers flew to Russia for the Moscow Film Festival. This time, everyone knew who she was. The couple and their entourage, which included Rex Kennamer, stayed at the Sovietskaya Hotel. Again, the subject of *Anna Karenina* was brought up. Elizabeth now wanted the film to be shot on location in Leningrad, but, again, nothing came of it. There was also a minor incident of sorts when Eddie Fisher was invited to sing at the Kremlin – the first American to do so since Paul Robeson. Elizabeth and Gina Lollobrigida turned up wearing identical Yves St Laurent dresses.

By early September, Elizabeth and her court had temporarily relocated to Rome: an assortment of servants and animals that decamped, at Fox's expense, to the 20-room Villa Papa near the Cinecittà studios, where the *Cleopatra* sets had been reconstructed to the tune of $1 million. Stephen Boyd, Peter Finch and Stanley Baker had moved on to new projects by this time. Because they had had no part in the delays, they retained their combined salaries of over $350,000, and Elizabeth had a new Caesar and Mark Antony – Rex Harrison and Welsh actor Richard Burton. Playing Rufio was Martin Landau. And the so-called 'Roman Scandal' was set to begin.

NINE

THAT INTEMPERATE VAMP

ICHARD BURTON HAD RECENTLY WON A TONY AWARD for his interpretation of King Arthur in the stage musical *Camelot* – a role later reprised by Rock Hudson. Because this was still playing to packed audiences on Broadway, Spyros Skouras paid the producers $50,000 to release the actor from his contract. Bearing in mind that the production had only a few months to run, and the fact that Burton would be kept hanging around because of Elizabeth's indisposition, this money could have been saved, though, of course, the studio did not know this at the time.

Initially, Burton was reluctant to play opposite Elizabeth, who he did not rate as much of an actress. The $250,000 fee offered by Fox, along with a villa and all its trappings for the proposed three-month shoot, convinced him to change his mind. His one condition was that his friend and *Camelot* co-star (and alleged lover) Roddy McDowall be given the part of Octavian. In the film, McDowall plays him as an amalgamation of his past and future roles: camp, sexually ambiguous and slightly unhinged. Burton further insisted that McDowall and his current boyfriend also be allowed to stay at the villa.

When asked about his new role at a subsequent press conference, he let out an enforced sigh and pronounced, 'Ah, well, I suppose I've got to put on my breastplate and play opposite Miss Tits!' When reminded by Hedda Hopper that such an expression was impolite, he barked, 'Then I shall call her MGM's Miss Mammary – good at getting sick and acquiring husbands!'

On the first day of shooting, as if on cue, the heavens opened, and it poured almost every day for a month, delaying production and sending the already sky-high costs soaring even further. Walter Wanger reported that the film was costing him over $60,000 a day. There were further delays when workmen extending the Alexandria site unearthed a large number of unexploded mines – it emerged that the area had been a minefield during the Second World War. Richard Burton, who does not appear much in the first half of the film, spent his time doing what he was best at – drinking, hell-raising, womanising and being generally unpleasant – leaving his wife Sybil at the villa. Joe Mankiewicz, still rewriting the script and making drastic changes on a daily basis, only added to the mayhem. When he asked Skouras to postpone shooting for a whole month until he had completed the script, Skouras announced that there would be *two* films – the first, *Caesar and Cleopatra*, would end with a cliffhanger and would be released whilst a sequel was being completed, perhaps in six months' time. Upon hearing that he might be 'laid off', Burton threatened to sue. By then, he had Elizabeth firmly on side, having decided that he did like 'Miss Tits' and very much so!

The 'moment of truth' occurred on 22 January 1962 when Elizabeth and Burton filmed their first love scene. Later, she would recall, 'I kind of resented him, and I was certainly determined not to become another notch on his belt.' Eddie Fisher also had his reservations. 'Even if he hadn't destroyed my marriage, I would have disliked him,' he wrote in his memoirs. 'From the first moment I met him, I thought him an arrogant slob.'

On the 20th anniversary of Richard Burton's death in 2004, the *Daily Mail* ran a feature in which Glenys Roberts, writing about the actor's homosexual conquests, observed, 'Some claim he first tried to seduce Liz's then husband Eddie Fisher and turned to her only when he was rebuffed.' True or not, she fell for him the way she had other gay or bisexual men: Glenn Davis, Nicky Hilton, Montgomery Clift and Michael Wilding. Like them, she said, he positively oozed sensitivity and roguish charm, and his 'poetic voice' sent shivers down her spine. Clearly, her marriage problems had compelled her to search for a scapegoat, an excuse to ditch Eddie Fisher, following the familiar pattern of her previous marriages to Hilton and Wilding. With Stephen Boyd out of the picture, it might well be that she subconsciously plumped for the best that was on offer and allowed nature to take its course.

Elizabeth claimed that the crunch came one morning when Burton was hung-over and suffering from the shakes. He asked her to hold his coffee cup to his lips whilst he drank, playing to her maternal instincts, just as the older Jimmy, Rock and Monty had done in the past. Even so, although he obviously found her sexually attractive, Burton was still able to criticise what he interpreted as her lack of professionalism – her 'useless' acting and 'inaudible' voice – until Joe Mankiewicz informed him that her speaking voice could be captured on film with specialised sound techniques just as effectively as everyone else's, as happened with Marilyn Monroe and Marlon Brando.

With Burton, this was a classic case of the pot calling the kettle black. Although he excelled at Shakespeare, with his booming voice and mellifluous accent, his movie roles alternated between the sublime and the downright abominable. That he used Elizabeth as a ladder to scale the summit of the global publicity machine goes without saying – though this did not add much to his prestige, and once he began working with her, there were many people, including most critics, who regarded him as little more than an ebullient, bother-causing, drink-addled buffoon.

Neither was Richard Burton particularly good-looking once he reached 40, something which did not sit well with his acute narcissism. A severe case of acne during his late teens had left him with a face covered in pockmarks. Before shooting a scene, these had to be filled in with heavy layers of make-up – in some later close-ups, he resembles a hammy, over-painted villain from a silent movie. Burton was also less than fastidious when it came to personal hygiene: during drunken binges he would go for days, sometimes weeks on end, without washing or taking a shower. Confidence in his own abilities, however, was not lacking. Like Mike Todd before him, he genuinely believed himself to be God's gift to mankind, and this chutzpah gave him the hard edge and courage to brave whatever insults the critics flung his way – and in his later years there were considerably more of these than accolades.

Like Elizabeth, despite his seven Oscar nominations (but no actual winners), Richard Burton had a phenomenal knack of choosing turkeys. Born Richard Walter Jenkins on 10 November 1925, the 12th of a Pontrhydyfen coalminer's 13 children, he liked to boast that he had been raised in abject poverty. This is untrue. After their mother's death, when Burton was about two, the Jenkins brood was farmed out to various relatives. He was the first in his family to attend secondary school, and as an impressionable teenager he was unofficially adopted by a local schoolteacher called Philip Burton, who recognised his budding acting talents, became his legal guardian and gave him his name.

Philip Burton's extra-curricular activities included writing, directing and acting in radio plays, and he had important contacts in London. The relationship between the boy and his mentor, whose earlier schoolboy protégé-lover was killed in the Second World War, is believed to have progressed beyond the platonic. Encouraged by this kindly man, albeit one who might have been breaking the law, the young Burton finished school, joined the ATC cadets and as part of their training programme was assigned to a six-month stint in Oxford, where he read classics and joined the university dramatic society. In 1944, he was befriended by fellow miner's son Emlyn Williams, believed by many people to be the greatest Welsh actor, writer and director of his generation.

Again, Burton and Williams were almost certainly lovers for a time, and it was Williams, something of a matinee idol with lean features and a shock of dark, unruly hair, who gave Burton his first professional stage role, in *The Druid's Rest*. Like Philip Burton, he was unable to control his headstrong pupil: Burton the younger was a heavy beer drinker from the age of 14, and he now took up womanising with a vengeance – the handful of men he had slept with had been offered a good time solely with the purpose of furthering his acting career.

Burton met 19-year-old Sybil Williams whilst shooting his first film, *The Last Days of Dolwyn* , directed (in the Welsh language) by Emlyn Williams, and they married soon after its release in 1949. Their first daughter, Kate, was born in 1957 and was followed two years later by Jessica, who was born severely autistic and placed in an institution, where she remained for the whole of Burton's life.

On the stage, with his booming voice, perfect pronunciation and commanding presence, Burton quickly established himself as an actor almost in the same class as Sir Laurence Olivier. His greatest triumph was in *Hamlet* at the Old Vic, where he was perfectly at ease with the largely gay clique headed by John Gielgud. His first British films – notably *My Cousin Rachel* (1952) and a stunning contribution to *The Robe* – should have set Burton in good stead for celluloid greatness. Meeting Elizabeth Taylor, however, and his insistence on constantly appearing with her on the screen – attempting but failing to emulate the legendary stage partnership of Alfred Lunt and Lynn Fontanne – would ultimately result in critical ridicule.

By the time of his involvement with Elizabeth, Burton's finest screen performances were behind him. To a certain extent, she taught him how to become a better film actor – as *Cleopatra* progresses, we witness the annoyingly over-the-top Burton boom gradually giving way to a more controlled tone, along with a decrease in the histrionics, a development that was welcomed by theatre audiences. Sadly, these traits returned once *Cleopatra* was in the can, especially in the films he made with his future wife. Harry and Michael Medford, in their famous book *The Golden Turkey Awards* (Angus & Robertson, 1980), polled a dozen films in which Burton and Taylor appeared, separately or together, amongst the worst movies of all time, and awarded him the gong for Worst Actor of All Time. Speaking of Burton's 'conscientious hard work to ruin nearly ever film in which he appeared', the Medfords concluded:

> When he is good, he is very, very good, but when he is bad – well, he's just the pits. Anyone can make a bad film when working with hack directors and inane scripts, but it takes a true genius like Burton to come up with garbage when teamed with serious artists like Vincente Minnelli, Peter Ustinov, Vittorio de Sica and Joseph Losey. King Richard has developed a sort of Midas syndrome in reverse: everything he touches turns to trash. In forms of wasted opportunities, of promising projects soured through his personal efforts, no one in Hollywood can equal him.

The first hint of a relationship between Elizabeth and Burton appeared in the Italian tabloids in late January 1962, causing concern for Twentieth Century Fox, who, of course, should not have been surprised. Burton had already told Joe Mankiewicz that he had slept with all of his leading ladies except Julie Andrews, because they had been incapable of resisting his Welsh charms, which had apparently compensated – until they had grown fed up of him – for his coarseness and almost permanent drunken state. Burton was also currently involved with a Copacabana chorus girl named Patricia Tunder, who had been promised a small part in *Cleopatra* in exchange for the usual favours. Now, she was sent packing.

Eddie Fisher witnessed Richard Burton at his worst. They were in the same room when Burton called Elizabeth and audaciously reproached her for being unfair to her husband! 'I don't know what she said to him,' Fisher revealed in his autobiography, 'but he screamed at her, "You fucking sagging-titted, no-talent Hollywood cunt. This man loves you so much . . . Elizabeth, if you're not careful, I'm going to take him upstairs, and *I'm* going to fuck him!"' This admission adds credence to the later rumour that Burton tried to seduce Fisher first, resurrected by the aforementioned Glenys

Roberts in her anniversary tribute in the *Daily Mail*. Fisher and others have also maintained that Elizabeth derived sadistic pleasure from such vulgarity, just as she enjoyed being knocked around by her men; indeed, she could out-vulgar the best of them. One gets a pretty accurate indication of how the Taylor-Burton relationship was, even in its early days, by watching one of the key scenes from *Cleopatra*, after Mark Antony's defeat at Actium. When they argue and she slaps him three times, he gives her such a backhander (reputedly for real), before going completely off his head, that she is sent sprawling – yet this only makes her want him more.

Elizabeth's volatile, extremely public relationship with Burton completed her transition from femme fatale to gay icon. Like many of her predecessors and contemporaries, she perceived suffering and self-destruction to be the key to a happiness that was never found; in fact, were it to be found, this would have defeated the whole objective. One thinks of Judy Garland, Édith Piaf, Joan Crawford and Billie Holiday as being others who genuinely believed that the path to true love was paved with pain and that no man was worthy of their love until he had displayed an ability to use his fists. Piaf and Crawford sported their black eyes and bruises with immeasurable pride, and stunned the world by disclosing every intimate, angry moment with uncompromising honesty. Nicky Hilton had knocked Elizabeth around, but this had been abuse. Sexually, Michael Wilding and Eddie Fisher had been less exciting, perhaps because they had been too mild-mannered and gentlemanly – from the point of view of the femme fatale, weak. Richard Burton was like Mike Todd: verbal abuse and physical violence were perceived as essential foreplay. 'I adore fighting with him,' Elizabeth told *Life* magazine in December 1964. 'It's rather like a small atom bomb going off. Sparks fly, walls shake, floors reverberate!'

The truth surrounding the Fishers' collapsed marriage was relayed to the US public by the ever-reliable Louella Parsons, whose report appeared on the front page of the *Los Angeles Herald-Examiner* on 14 January 1964. Louella was keeping her cards close to her chest regarding her sources, and it was widely

rumoured that Twentieth Century Fox had used her as a 'plant'
– a paid informant to bolster public interest in the forthcoming
film the studio were promoting, and about which people were
probably already sick of reading. Copies of Louella's feature were
wired to news agencies all over Europe, where they were often
badly translated, causing a heavy increase in paparazzi following
the 'guilty' couple around.

With the costs of *Cleopatra* escalating way beyond reason, the
last thing the studio needed was another Elizabeth Taylor sex
scandal. Walter Wanger expressed genuine remorse that his first
Mark Antony, Stephen Boyd, was no longer around, as she would
never have met Burton and the affair would never have happened.
The Italian newspapers reported a suicide attempt when Elizabeth
passed out after washing down too many barbiturates with alcohol
following a confrontation with Eddie Fisher. There were further
rumours of a marriage rift when Sybil Burton unexpectedly returned
to New York, claiming that she was visiting Philip Burton, who
was sick.

Richard Burton temporarily evaded this mass-media intrusion by
flying to Paris to shoot a cameo for *The Longest Day* (1962). He was
still absent on 18 February 1962 when the press reported Elizabeth's
latest indisposition – variously described as food poisoning, nervous
anxiety and a recurrence of her earlier meningitis but most likely
another attention-seeking suicide bid following another bust-up
with Eddie Fisher. He later confirmed this in his memoirs. 'She
grabbed a bottle of Seconal that was sitting on her night table and
poured a handful of pills down her throat,' he wrote, adding that
Elizabeth had hit him when he had tried to shove his hand in her
mouth to make her vomit. She then rushed into the bathroom to
down more sedatives and started foaming at the mouth. According
to Fisher, rather than take her to hospital, Elizabeth was given a
life-saving injection by an elderly German doctor, who was paid
$1,000 in the hope of keeping the incident out of the papers. It
was another example of Elizabeth trying to make Fisher, the hapless
witness to her selfish folly, feel responsible for her actions. 'She

trusted me enough to make a suicide attempt from which only I could save her,' Fisher concluded.

The scandal this time around was far worse than the Taylor, Fisher and Reynolds fiasco, and over the next few years would give rise to more mad scenes than all of Elizabeth's Tennessee Williams tantrums put together. The Cinecittà lot was besieged by reporters from all corners of the globe, whilst Richard Burton was flushed out of his Parisian bolthole. It was around this time that he uttered the famous statement to friends that has since entered Hollywood folklore: 'I've just fucked Elizabeth Taylor in the back of my car.' Yet in a press statement he fervently denied 'La Scandale', as he haughtily called it. Not that anyone believed him. Most of the reporters present had already acquired titbits from supposedly reliable on-set sources, and these confirmed the fact that the pair *were* an item. And when Burton swore on his own life, delivering a boisterous speech that would have done the Old Vic proud, that there was absolutely no truth in any of the rumours, the press believed him less. There was just the one exception when an Italian tabloid swallowed the story that Joe Mankiewicz fed them to cover up his own affair with Elizabeth, which had begun during the filming of *Suddenly, Last Summer*. Mankiewicz only inflamed the situation by grabbing Burton, kissing him on the lips and announcing to the stunned journalist, 'There you are. I'm the one having the affair with Richard Burton!'

In a desperate last bid to salvage what remained of his marriage, Eddie Fisher did what he and his predecessor, Mike Todd, were best at: he attempted to buy Elizabeth's affection, and the press, of course, were kept informed of the tally. He paid around $300,000 for the Chateau Ariel, a luxurious chalet in the soon-to-be-fashionable Swiss ski resort of Gstaad. The Aga Khan lived nearby. Elizabeth would retain the property once Fisher was out of the picture, and in the future her neighbours would include Julie Andrews, Peter Sellers and the Robert Wagners.

On 27 February 1962, Elizabeth's 30th birthday, Fisher threw a party in the Hostaria dell'Orso's very exclusive Borgia Suite, inviting all the leading lights from *Cleopatra*, except Richard Burton, and representatives from every major newspaper and magazine in Europe. As the flashbulbs popped, Elizabeth squealed with delight as she unwrapped the 'little gifts' her estranged husband had bought her: a ten-carat diamond ring and the £100,000 'Cleopatra' mirror, a commissioned Bulgari creation that opened out into an emerald encrusted asp. Richard Burton later retorted that he had given her the best present of all: the 'ruby-tipped snake' he kept inside his trousers.

By the end of March, Elizabeth and Burton cast their fate to the winds by openly socialising. In America a few weeks earlier, Hedda Hopper had let the cat out of the bag, penning a feature for the *Los Angeles Herald-Examiner* entitled 'Row Over Actor Ends Liz and Eddie's Marriage'. Hedda did not feel the need to name the actor – by then, everyone knew who he was. She blamed Elizabeth for the break-up but criticised both parties for leaving their offspring behind. 'I only hope Eddie's children will recognise him when he gets home,' she sniped. Fisher would neither see nor speak to Elizabeth for almost two years.

When Fisher returned to the United States, public opinion was very firmly on his side, despite Hedda Hopper's acid comments. On both sides of the Atlantic, those who had attacked *him* for cheating on Debbie Reynolds now levelled their spite against Elizabeth. Italy's *Il Tempo* called her 'that intemperate vamp who devours husbands'. The Pope denounced her as immoral, and the Vatican's official publication, *L'Osservatore Della Dominica*, declared her 'an erotic vagrant' and attacked her for her latest 'foible', which was a desire to adopt a baby:

> Do not such institutions consider the facts before handing out these children? Do they not request moral references? Would it not be better to entrust this little girl to an honest bricklayer or modest housewife than to you, dear lady, and your *fourth* husband? The bricklayer and housewife will have worked harder and made serious sacrifices for the child – but not you, dear lady, who have other things to do!

Before separating from Eddie Fisher, the couple had made plans to adopt, as they were unable to have children of their own. Negotiations with a Greek orphanage run by Catholic nuns had broken down because of the Fishers' Jewish faith. Instead, they had advertised anonymously for a baby in the German press, with the help of their actress friend Maria Schell. They had subsequently been offered a nine-month-old girl called Petra Heisig, whom they had named Maria, after Schell. The baby had been born with a deformed hip, and her birth parents had been told by doctors that she might not walk unless operated on.

Because her birth parents were extremely poor, they had put Maria up for adoption, an act which today might attract adverse criticism. Similarly, any would-be adoptive parent, not least of all a millionairess, might today receive short shrift from society for being seen to have taken advantage of a sensitive situation, in this case by removing a child from its mother, as opposed to paying for the operation. In 1962, however, attitudes were different, and in any case the press were not made aware of the full story. They saw only an 'immoral' woman, denounced by the Holy See, embroiled in a messy love triangle and now intent on adopting as a single parent. She was allowing her heart to rule her head, it is true, but what must be remembered is that she was not being entirely selfish. Her caring side was also demonstrated many years later when she nursed Rock Hudson through the final days of his agonising and often messy illness. Elizabeth was like a child in a candy store, grabbing everything in sight, but, ultimately, in her diminished way of reasoning, she genuinely believed she was acting in Maria's best interests by giving her a life beyond her wildest dreams. The biased media were unable, or unwilling, to see this.

In America, House of Representatives member Iris Blitch proposed a motion that, had it been passed, would have resulted in Elizabeth's passport being confiscated. She was, Mrs Blitch declared, an 'undesirable with no respect for the name of decent American womanhood'. Elizabeth even considered suing the *Daily Mirror* when it picked up on this, their columnist Cassandra observing, 'The lady is one long eruption of matrimonial agitation.' This was not nearly as offensive as some of the other comments printed about her, but Elizabeth thought about taking legal action for no other reason than Liberace had successfully sued Cassandra a few years earlier for denouncing him as 'an unmanly man'. The fact that he was speaking the truth on both occasions prevented Elizabeth from taking the matter further. The backlash from the other tabloids who were saying more or less the same thing would have been merciless.

There was also mass condemnation from most of the 30 million viewers who tuned in to *The Ed Sullivan Show* on a regular basis. Six years earlier, Sullivan's condemnation of Elvis Presley's on-stage gyrations had resulted in the singer being filmed only from the waist upwards. Now, he announced, 'I do hope youngsters will not be persuaded that the sanctity of marriage has been invalidated by the appalling example of Mrs Taylor-Fisher and married man Burton.'

On a lighter note, but no less explosive, a *Cleopatra* sketch featured in *The Perry Como Show*, depicting the Queen of the Nile with a slave named Eddie. Even Fisher himself partook in the mickey-taking. Back in demand as a singer, he began his act with 'Arrividerci Roma' and at New York's Winter Garden did a duet with Juliet Prowse of 'I'm Cleo, the Nymph of the Nile'. Meanwhile, Elizabeth did not mind Decca re-releasing Joan Regan and Dickie Valentine's 'Cleo And Meo', which had been recorded in 1954 and really had nothing to do with La Scandale, but she did take exception to Prowse singing, 'She uses her pelvis/Just like Elvis/There wasn't a man she couldn't get/Such was Cleo's problem on and off the set!'

Things started to get really out of hand when Twentieth Century Fox began receiving death threats from religious and moral fanatics. The studio drafted in two dozen armed policemen, who mingled amongst the *Cleopatra* extras dressed as Roman soldiers. The mockery and defamation, deserved or not, would have far-reaching effects on Elizabeth. Henceforth, all of her employees would be compelled to sign confidentiality agreements. Eddie Fisher, too, was made to sign an affidavit promising not to rubbish her in the future. This prevented him from publishing an autobiography begun around this time – he had to wait until 1981 before bringing out *My Life, My Loves*, though the real kiss-and-tell *Been There, Done That* came out in 1999, long after the dust had settled.

The trade press in Hollywood blamed Spyros Skouras for the Taylor-Burton scandal, claiming that he was sufficiently aware of the character of each and should never have cast them together in the first place. Skouras rushed off to Rome to offer them an ultimatum – cool it, or else. Their response to this was that unless Skouras and his 'monkeys' let them be, they would drop out of the film, regardless of the personal cost to themselves. Skouras retreated.

Meanwhile, as Sybil withdrew to the rented villa in Rome and waited with Roddy McDowall for La Scandale to die down, as always happened with her husband's affairs, news came in of Eddie Fisher's nervous breakdown. Hooked on Max Jacobson's amphetamine shots and a total wreck, he had been approached by Mafia boss Frank Costello. Fisher, who had recently taken to carrying a gun, recalled how Costello had told him, 'Anything you need, you come to me,' which the jilted husband had interpreted as an offer to remove Burton from the scene. Naturally, he declined, believing that if Burton stayed with Elizabeth, he would suffer soon enough!

Assuming Eddie and Sybil to be out of the picture, Burton rented a villa overlooking the sea, where he hoped that he and Elizabeth might spend their weekends away from the paparazzi. No sooner had they settled in for their first sojourn than he received an impassioned call from Sybil: she was anxious for him to return to Rome and give their marriage another go. Burton acquiesced, and when Elizabeth threatened to kill herself if he left, he simply shrugged his shoulders and told her to go ahead. As had happened during the row with Eddie Fisher, she swallowed a fistful of pills and had to be rushed to hospital to have her stomach pumped.

Again, the studio saved face by announcing that she had food poisoning.

Four days later, Elizabeth returned to the set. The bruises around her eyes and nose, she said, were on account of the oxygen mask she had been compelled to wear – they had actually been inflicted by Burton, whilst in a drunken rage, though Elizabeth had given as good as she had got. When the make-up department was unable to conceal them, an exasperated Joe Mankiewicz halted production for two weeks. There was a second incident around the same time, reported by *Time* magazine, when shooting was put on hold after Burton gave her another good hiding.

Sybil Burton suddenly found herself facing more reporters than she had seen in her life after her husband, interviewed by columnist Sheilah Graham, maintained that his affair with Elizabeth had been a 'nine-day wonder', and insisted upon her printing the statement, 'By the time the film's released, everyone will have forgotten about it – unless something new happens, like my divorcing my wife to marry Elizabeth, and there's no chance of *that* happening!'

By that point, Twentieth Century Fox had had enough. At the beginning of June, the studio's chief executives flew to Rome, summarily dismissed Walter Wanger and ordered drastic cuts to the script to curb future expenditure. Elizabeth's salary was stopped to make up for all the time she had not worked but still been paid. Richard Burton's salary had trebled for some reason and Rex Harrison's had quadrupled, but through no fault of their own, so the increases were allowed to ride. By the end of the month, Spyros Skouras's tenure as Fox's president was terminated, and Darryl F. Zanuck was welcomed back into the fold to replace him. Skouras later commented that the move had prevented him from suffering a stroke or worse.

At once, the mogul who had made Twentieth Century Fox in the first place went for Elizabeth's jugular, blaming her for much of the *Cleopatra* fiasco – by now the budget had surpassed the $30-million mark. When Joe Mankiewicz attempted to defend her, Zanuck fired him and declared that he would not be permitted to take part in editing the finished footage of the film he had struggled so hard to complete – over eight hours so far. Zanuck then rubbed salt into his wounds by issuing a press statement: 'After spending two years on Fox's prized project – and around $35 million of our shareholders' money – Mr Mankiewicz is now taking a well-earned rest.'

Elizabeth complained loudly about the wretched treatment that she and Mankiewicz had to endure and promptly ended up with egg on her face when Zanuck called another press conference and granted the public access to 'privileged' information about his leading lady's greed. Elizabeth had demanded $1 million for the picture, he said, but she'd effectively been paid twice this amount and would earn even more when the film was released, because she had negotiated a deal, kept under wraps until then, that would reap a whopping 35 per cent of the profits. What the press were not told was that Fox had every intention of offsetting a large portion of these earnings to meet the exorbitant cost of the production. Zanuck subsequently issued Elizabeth and Burton with writs totalling $50 million – for tardiness and for impeding the film's future commerciality with their shocking off-set conduct. Zanuck later dropped his demands to $44 million. Elizabeth and Burton filed a counter-suit, and the matter was settled out of court.

The *Cleopatra* treadmill ground to a complete stop in July 1962. One of the last scenes to be shot was that aboard the golden barge, which had meant the whole production relocating to Ischia off the coast of Naples. The studio facetiously arranged for a boat-ambulance to be on standby – just in case Elizabeth collapsed due to 'post-production stress' and had to be ferried across to the nearby city. She did not, and for the time being she and Burton went their separate ways – he to Pays de Galles, his villa on the shores of Lake Geneva, and she to her Gstaad chalet, one of the four homes she had bought with Eddie Fisher, the others being in Las Vegas, Westchester and Jamaica. Here she was joined by her parents, who, of course, believed the story that she had been the unwilling victim these last few months.

Cleopatra was released in June 1963, a $40-million, beautifully filmed exercise in Hollywood folly, although some critics believed it was overlong. The movie was a glorious soap opera, with the ancient precursor of *Dynasty*'s Alexis Carrington (marvellously portrayed by Joan Collins, who many people still think should have played Cleopatra) given plenty of opportunity to show off. Right up to the cutting and editing stage, for which Joe Mankiewicz had been rehired, Fox had been hoping to issue two films: *Caesar and Cleopatra* and *Antony and Cleopatra*. Darryl F. Zanuck, however, had the last word. He wanted the saga to hit the cinemas whilst Elizabeth and Burton were still making headlines. However, Richard Burton appeared for a matter of mere minutes in the first half of the six-hour production, so the film was trimmed to a little over four.

Elizabeth is perfection itself in the role of the celebrity harlot, who history tells us once fellated a hundred Roman soldiers in a single night and who, like Elizabeth, had an especial fondness for gay and bisexual men, Caesar and Mark Antony being at the top of her list. Several scenes were cut from the finished print for fear that they might be misconstrued, notably the one where Rufio (Martin Landau), Mark Antony's favourite, bursts into tears upon mistakenly hearing that his love-hero is dead. 'Someone said that generals don't cry,' Landau later said of the cut (in an interview included on a French special edition DVD of *Cleopatra*), 'but that's not the case where there's this kind of love between two men.' Similarly, Burton was told to 'bite his lip' in the scene in which he discovers Rufio's body and holds him in his arms. And when Mark Antony is about to fall upon his sword and begs Appolodorus (Cesare Danova), Rufio's successor, to lend a helping hand, the emotion is again forcibly suppressed.

The critics had a field day over Elizabeth's personal appearance in the film – the fluctuation in her weight over the two-year shooting schedule is very much apparent. She looks chubby and double-chinned dressed as Venus, greeting Mark Antony on their golden barge and when they meet up again after the battle of Actium.

'Overweight, overbosomed, overpaid and undertalented, she sets the acting profession back a decade,' sniped television critic David Susskind – whilst *Time* magazine, erroneously for once, drew attention to 'her screeching like a ward-healer's wife at a block party'.

The other leads, particularly Rex Harrison as the cynical, epileptic Caesar, are mostly remarkable. Only the occasionally wooden Richard Burton lets the side down. Instinctively, one feels that the more charismatic and much more handsome Stephen Boyd would have brought depth and sincerity to the role. Burton also fluffs some of his lines, depending upon which print one views, most notoriously during Cleopatra's entry into Rome when she is swathed in a $7,000, 24-carat gold dress, riding atop a giant sphinx with her son, who was fathered by Caesar. Commenting on the ceremony, a hung-over Mark Antony quips, 'Nothing like this has come into Rome since Romulus and Romulus,' meaning, of course, Romulus and Remus!

TEN

THE BIG HANGOVER:
WHO'S AFRAID
OF VIRGINIA WOOLF?

OR A WHILE, THE TAYLOR-BURTON AFFAIR HAD BEEN KEPT off the front pages by the death in August 1962 of Marilyn Monroe. Suicide was given as the official cause, but, then as now, there was much speculation over whether she might have been murdered. Cynics have suggested that with her greed for hogging the limelight, Elizabeth deliberately maintained a low profile until the Monroe scandal had abated. But if she and Richard Burton were trying to kid their respective circles that their 'romance' was over, those who stood to gain financially from their liaison – for example, the studios, who hypocritically were more than eager to rake in any profits from La Scandale they had openly condemned – were delighted when, at the end of the month, they read in the press that it had resurfaced with a vengeance. When news leaked that the pair had met for lunch 'somewhere in Switzerland', MGM were the first to monopolise on the tidings – and Elizabeth's 'scandalous' comment that rather than marry Burton she had no objections to becoming his mistress – by persuading them to appear in Terence Rattigan's *The VIPs*.

Shooting began early in 1963, with Elizabeth and Burton travelling separately from the Victoria boat-train to the Dorchester, where they took up residence in separate suites. Burton feigned the dutiful husband, ping-ponging back and forth to see Sybil at their house in Hampstead's Squire's Mount. Needless to say, the press were not fooled because neither Burton nor Elizabeth stopped boasting about how much they missed one other whilst apart, even for a few hours. So that he would always be thinking of her whilst alone in his suite, Elizabeth forked out a cool $250,000 for a Van Gogh landscape, along with $10,000 for several hundred leather-bound books that Burton never found time to open. If he was not with Elizabeth – indeed, most of the time that he *was* with her – he was in too much of a stupor to be aware of his surroundings.

Occasionally, Burton sobered up sufficiently to bellow a few good lines in *The VIPs*, not that this made the film any better. Pathologically boring, it comprises a series of *Grand Hotel*-style vignettes set in and around the VIP lounge of a London airport. The flights have been delayed by fog, allowing an assortment of odd-bod characters to meet and fling around a few home truths. On account of the leads' salaries, it was MGM's costliest production in years: Elizabeth demanded and received $500,000, along with half this amount against a percentage of the box-office receipts. Upon her insistence, Burton was paid the same, and the money was deposited in bank accounts in Bermuda for tax purposes. The rest of the cast received considerably less than $1 million among them, despite being comprised of the cream of the British acting crop, including Maggie Smith, Rod Taylor, Michael Hordern, Richard Briers and the wonderful Margaret Rutherford, who ran rings around everyone else as an eccentric duchess and who was rewarded with a Best Supporting Actress Oscar.

Despite its mediocrity, *The VIPs* did tremendously well at the box office, earning Elizabeth and Burton a collective $5 million over the next two years. Without doubt, they had become the world's premier couple, and from then on they would go to inordinate lengths to ensure that they maintained the position.

Burton was on his best behaviour during a break in shooting when he took Elizabeth home to Wales to meet his family. Surprisingly, considering their affection for Sybil, they took to Elizabeth very well. In the not too distant future, she would begin sending them clothing parcels – original creations by Fath, Dior and Balmain that she had grown tired of. She would also fly some of them over to New York to watch their famous relative murder the classics on the stage.

On other days off, for a whopping $500,000 fee, Elizabeth made her first television documentary. *Elizabeth Taylor in London* was financed by CBS, and for 60 minutes she escorted viewers around her favourite 'home town' haunts and recited a little Elizabeth Barrett Browning for good measure. This was essentially her way of showing how good she looked in the latest fashion trends. *Variety* observed, 'Miss Taylor, pompous and so very, *very* cultured, got in the way of the cameras – for nearly two-thirds of the programme,' but gallantly concluded, 'she was in competition with London – *and she won!*'

At around this time, the inevitable exclusives from the 'extras' in the Taylor-Burton soap opera also surfaced – Eddie Fisher and Sybil Burton. Fisher had moved to Nevada for residency purposes in preparation for his divorce, and despite his wealth, demanded a $1-million settlement. He is also thought to have asked for his jewellery back. What he did not get was access to Maria, the baby he had adopted with Elizabeth. Although few details were made public, it was revealed that Fisher had relinquished any claims on Maria and that if Elizabeth married Burton, the child would be legally adopted by him and take his name.

Sybil Burton, the only one of the quartet whose behaviour had been exemplary, now let off a little steam, telling reporters, 'I've no intention of allowing the father of my children to become Elizabeth Taylor's fifth husband.' She subsequently changed her mind when informed by him that there was no hope of their ever being reconciled. After their divorce, Sybil married pop singer Jordan Christopher of The Wild Ones, who at the age of 24 was 14 years her junior. The union proved successful and only ended with Christopher's death in 1997. Burton was generous with his divorce settlement. Sybil was assigned one half of his personal fortune, reputed to be in the region of $1 million, with the promise of a decent percentage of his future earnings, whether he married or not.

Towards the end of September 1963, having played the title role in *Becket* (1964), Burton flew to Puerto Vallarta in Mexico to shoot *The Night of the Iguana* (1964). The production company was hoping that Elizabeth might not tag along, though by now the couple were inseparable. Indeed, there were clauses in their contracts that if they were not appearing in the same film, they should not work more than one hour's travelling distance from one another. Elizabeth flew into Mexico with Burton because she did not trust him – suspicious that he might make a play for one of his co-stars, as had happened in the past. This time there were three to choose from: *Lolita* (1962) babe Sue Lyon, Deborah Kerr and the man-eating Ava Gardner. Elizabeth and Burton were mobbed at Mexico City Airport – courtesy of a studio publicist, who was instructed to put out a 'Liz and Dick' alert to ensure them maximum media coverage – and did not disappoint by bawling each other out over some trifle whilst leaving the plane.

Elizabeth conducted herself in Puerto Vallarta as if it was her film, invading the set every day and exercising her hold over Burton, who as per usual spent most of his time bombed. In fact, this was virtually an 'everybody's had everybody else' production. Director John Huston – whom Elizabeth hated for his shoddy treatment of Montgomery Clift whilst shooting *The Misfits* and *Freud* – had formerly been the lover of Ava Gardner. So too had scriptwriter Peter Viertel, now married to Deborah Kerr. Huston's ex-wife – the woman Mike Todd had dumped to be with Elizabeth – was now married to Ava's ex-husband, bandleader Artie Shaw. Bringing so many exes together only added to the tension of Elizabeth's presence, and matters were exacerbated by the unexpected arrival of Michael Wilding in his new capacity as assistant to Burton's agent, Hugh French. Huston, who loved nothing more than a brawl – he and

Errol Flynn had famously engaged in a scrap that had not ended until both men had sustained an equal number of broken ribs! – added spice to the occasion by presenting all the protagonists with tiny gold-plated Derringers, along with bullets inscribed with everyone's names. He is said to have been disappointed that none of these had been used by the time the production wrapped.

In Puerto Vallarta, acting typically on impulse, Elizabeth fell in love with Casa Kimberley, the villa provided by the studio for Burton's stay in the town. She promptly bought it, and a little later Burton acquired a property across the street – he had a connecting footbridge constructed so that if they argued, he would be able to escape to his 'pad' with the minimum of effort.

After *The Night of the Iguana*, Burton took a sabbatical and returned to what he had formerly been best at – the legitimate stage – appearing in John Gielgud's production of *Hamlet*. This kicked off in Toronto, where he and Elizabeth rented the most expensive suite at the King Edward Hotel. And on an 'unlucky' 15 March in Montreal, ten days after Eddie Fisher had obtained his Mexican divorce on grounds of abandonment, Elizabeth and Richard Burton were married. 'Beware the Ides of March!' at least one headline read.

Elizabeth had wanted them to be married in Ontario by a rabbi, but the state refused to recognise the validity of Mexican divorces, so they had to 'make do' in Quebec Province with a Unitarian minister, the only clergyman available who was not against marrying a woman of scandalous repute for the fifth time in less than 15 years. According to Hollis Alpert, Burton's biographer, the bride arrived late at their hotel suite (where they had booked in as Rosamund Sutherland and Walter Rule), and the groom, blind drunk, exploded, 'Isn't that fat little tart here yet? She'll be late for the last bloody judgement!' Looking lovely in yellow chiffon, dripping with diamonds and emeralds, and with $650 worth of Roman-style extensions decorated with hyacinth petals in her hair, Elizabeth reeled off her usual spiel: she had never been happier, and this time the marriage was for real. Again, few people believed her.

On 22 March 1964, *Hamlet* hit Boston. The Taylor-Burton publicity machine had gone into overdrive, and the newly weds were manhandled by a vast crowd outside the Sheraton Plaza Hotel. Crying wolf, Elizabeth collapsed and was taken to her suite, where a doctor gave her a sedative. Just hours later, she was back in the spotlight, looking hale and hearty for a press conference. By that stage in the *Hamlet* tour, Burton had gone beyond testing his co-stars' patience. Wandering around backstage, almost always with a glass or bottle in his hand, he would suddenly stop some unfortunate in their tracks and assault them with an ear-shattering rendition of a Federico García Lorca poem or some obscure quote from Oscar Wilde or Rabelais. The booze reacted with the painkillers he was taking for alcohol-related arthritis, though much of the time his behaviour was just down to his binge drinking. More than once he is reported to have pushed his fingers down his throat and vomited in the wings, simply in order to guzzle more. Colleagues and co-stars put up with this thoroughly reprehensible behaviour, of course – the longer the play ran, the more there was in it for them.

Montgomery Clift, who had not seen Elizabeth in a while and who was yet to express a personal opinion of her new husband, attended the Broadway premiere of *Hamlet* at the Lunt–Fontanne Theater, where it would play to packed houses until August with just one break (22 June) when Burton took the evening off for a poetry reading with Elizabeth for an American Musical and Dramatic Academy benefit event. Monty's brother Brooks recalled in several interviews that Monty had said of Burton, 'He's turned Shakespeare and serious theatre into a freak show.' Monty was right. Every performance might have been a sell-out, but theatregoers were less interested in Burton's now hammy acting than they were in witnessing what was termed the 'Liz and Dick Roadshow'. And the more Burton performed, the more mediocre he became, until, in desperation, Elizabeth flew in Philip Burton and Emlyn Williams to give him a few 'pointers'. Neither ventured the truth – that he was drinking himself senseless and was too full of his own self-importance for any self-respecting critic to even take him half-seriously. Monty never repeated his comments about Burton to Elizabeth for fear of hurting her feelings; he liked Burton as a person and later said that he was his favourite amongst her husbands after Michael Wilding.

Over the previous couple of years, whilst Elizabeth had been hogging the spotlight, Monty had been going through a tough patch. On the plus side, *Judgment at Nuremberg* (1961) had seen him working alongside Spencer Tracy, Marlene Dietrich and a very washed-out Judy Garland. Playing a Jew castrated by the Nazis, he had been given just seven minutes of screen time, but his stunning performance had earned him an Oscar nomination. In *Freud*, directed by John Huston, several scenes had necessitated endless retakes, because the sadistically gung-ho Huston refused to pander to Monty's sensitive side – on one occasion he had beaten him up and trashed his dressing-room.

During the first summer of their marriage, Elizabeth and Burton were offered *The Owl and the Pussycat*, but it was shelved when Burton refused to do comedy – some years later it would be a huge hit for Barbra Streisand and George Segal. Next, they were offered three films: *The Sandpiper* (1965), *Who's Afraid of Virginia Woolf?* (1966) and *Reflections of a Golden Eye* (1967). Burton accepted the first two but had reservations about portraying the latently homosexual army officer in *Reflections of a Golden Eye*, in which Elizabeth would play his nymphomaniac wife. She therefore took it upon herself to 'offer' the role to Monty – without consulting Warner Brothers. When the studio objected, claiming that Monty was completely uninsurable, Elizabeth was able to sympathise. She herself had encountered insurance problems since *Cleopatra*. She had paid her own insurance for *The VIPs* and declared that she would do the same for Monty when the time came. Additionally, she is alleged to have agreed to forfeit her $1-million fee, should Monty not make it to the end of the picture, which would go into production as soon as she had completed her two films with Burton – possibly in the summer of 1966. Warners, meanwhile, put Monty into *The Defector* (1966).

Another visitor to New York during the *Hamlet* season was Eddie Fisher, there to iron out differences in his and Elizabeth's divorce settlement. Burton was later quoted by John Cottrell and Fergus Cashin in *Richard Burton* (Coronet Books, 1974) as saying, 'Elizabeth may not have been legally married to Mike Todd after the Wilding divorce. So that means no one was ever married to anyone . . . we might as well start again and get married and divorced on the Koran.' No such comments hit the press at the time. According to the wronged ex-husband, Burton was civil, and there were none of the anticipated run-ins. Fisher was even permitted to watch *Hamlet* from the wings and was later 'amused' to see how Elizabeth had 'domesticated' his rival and converted him to her factotum. 'Maybe he was doing Hamlet on the stage,' Fisher recalled, 'but in real life he was playing my role.'

Not long afterwards, as his career picked up, at least for a little while, Eddie Fisher took up with Swedish sexpot Ann-Margret, Edie Adams, a German model named Renata Boeck – he boasted in his memoirs that he had once made love to her nine times in a single night – Juliet Prowse, Stephanie Powers and several others, before finally becoming involved with the actress Connie Stevens, whom he wed in 1967 after the birth of their daughter. This union proved to be even more ill-fated than the one with Elizabeth: it lasted less than a year.

In October 1965, the Burtons flew to Paris to film *The Sandpiper*. Here, Elizabeth gathered her brood about her for the first time in years, only to be severely criticised for the way she went about it. She had demanded her usual $1 million, plus a share of the profits, and successfully negotiated a five-day ten-till-six schedule so that she would have her evenings and weekends free to spend with her family. However, *Paris-Match* reported that the Burtons' occupancy of twenty-one rooms at the Hotel Lancaster on the rue de Berri, for themselves and their ten-strong entourage, was costing them the equivalent of $10,000 a week, and such was the couple's imperiousness that the children, staying on a different floor, would often go several days between being 'summonsed' to their parents' suite. Other publications observed that they had to bow or curtsy when meeting them and other important 'dignitaries'.

The press were astonished that four-year-old Maria – now welcomed 'full-time' into the family fold following the last of her hip operations – had not been taught to speak English, and that seven-year-old Liza Todd could barely read or write. The Wilding boys were also reported to be hyperactive and hard to handle due to lack of parental control. None had enjoyed an even half-decent education, being dragged from one school to the next in the wake of their mother's divorces and remarriages. There was also a humiliating confrontation when Maria's birth parents, the Heisigs, turned up at the Hotel Lancaster with a lawyer and several journalists, claiming that Elizabeth owed them money for the 'sale' of their daughter. The mystery surrounding Maria's adoption deepened when Elizabeth instructed her own lawyers to pay them.

Next, Elizabeth announced that she wanted to renounce her American citizenship and become British. 'I was born there,' she told French reporters. 'It isn't that all of a sudden I love America less – it's just that I love my husband more!' The move had considerably more to do with the wealthy 'Briton' being able to enjoy lower taxation rates if she resided overseas than any sense of patriotism. It was avarice, pure and simple, from a woman who already had more money than she could sensibly handle. She was summoned to the American embassy to sign the papers, refused to comply and managed to coerce the embassy lawyers into visiting her so that negotiations could be concluded in the comfort of her hotel suite.

The entire family uprooted in February 1965, when Richard Burton left for Dublin to shoot *The Spy Who Came in from the Cold* (1965). There was no question of Elizabeth allowing him to travel alone, because his co-star was Claire Bloom, with whom he had had a passionate affair seven years before. Elizabeth had the pair watched like hawks, though Bloom was happily married to Rod Steiger and was no longer interested in the crumbling, liquor-addled Lothario. Then, Elizabeth's insurmountable pride took a bashing when it was announced from Hollywood that Burton had broken into the top-ten-box-office-stars list, on account of his success in *The Night of the Iguana*, which saw him ranked alongside the arguably far more charismatic Cary Grant, Rock Hudson and Elvis Presley. What might have upset Elizabeth most was the fact that Burton could not help boasting that she had entered the running at number 11 and declaring that her acting was marginally inferior to his. Time has, of course, proved otherwise; nowadays, Richard Burton is arguably known more for his relationship with Elizabeth Taylor and for the generally mediocre films they made together, than for anything he did on his own.

Almost as successful, and as dreary, as *The VIPs*, *The Sandpiper* was directed by Vincente Minnelli and co-starred Eva Marie Saint and Charles Bronson. Today it is remembered mostly for Johnny Mandel and Paul Francis Webster's haunting theme song 'The Shadow of Your Smile'. This won them an Academy Award and was a big hit for Peggy Lee and Matt Monro. Wearing a succession of kaftans to disguise her 'fuller' figure, Elizabeth played Laura Reynolds, a Bohemian beach-dweller artist with an illegitimate son who when not working spends much of her time saving wounded birds. With echoes of Somerset Maugham's *Rain* (1932), Burton was Hewitt, the spineless, hypocritical married clergyman who falls in love with her. Most of the critics recognised the scenario as the Taylor-Burton story in disguise, with Hewitt's long-suffering wife representing Sybil Burton. The only difference was this was not the real world, with Hewitt having to renounce his illicit ways and go back to his wife.

The Golden Turkey Awards called the film 'another tour de force by Liz and Dick, the uncrowned King and Queen of boredom'. The film critic Judith Crist, writing in her syndicated column, came straight to the point: 'Miss Taylor and Mr Burton were paid $1,750,000 for performing in *The Sandpiper* – and *I* wouldn't settle for less for watching them.' Elizabeth always claimed to have detested the film (though not the $3 million-plus it earned her) and later threatened to sue one critic for libel – for giving it a good review!

Elizabeth and Burton had read the script of *Who's Afraid of Virginia Woolf?* shortly after he had finished *Hamlet*. Scripted and eventually produced by Ernest Lehman from Edward Albee's smash-hit Broadway play, the film describes a single evening in the marital upheaval of a middle-aged couple called Martha and George, and delves deep into their impossible-to-live-with, impossible-to-live-without situation. Elizabeth found the character fascinating: foul-mouthed, corpulent, blousy but seductive, tyrannical. The character was hugely reminiscent of the part the great Italian actress Anna Magnani had played opposite Burt Lancaster in *The Rose Tattoo* (1955). Elizabeth instinctively knew that if she accepted the role, she would rid herself in one fell swoop of the tacky B-actress tag foisted upon her by *The Sandpiper*.

Whose idea it was to reach a compromise over Martha's age is not known: in Albee's play she is 55, Elizabeth was 33 and in the film the character is 45. Elizabeth was certainly not afraid of applying Method principles to the way she looked, something she also had in common with the not unattractive Magnani, and must be admired for the potential risk she took: she reached 155 pounds, donned the most horrendous wig and dropped her voice to a throaty baritone that must have been uncomfortable if not painful to maintain. Likewise, Burton ruffled his hair, wore old-fashioned clothes and sported horn-rimmed glasses in order to portray the lethargic George. The only difference between him and Elizabeth was that whereas she shrugged off the Martha image once the film had been canned, much of George's self-pity was retained by Burton. Just as *Cleopatra* had ignited the spark then fanned the flames for his passion for Elizabeth, so *Who's Afraid of Virginia Woolf?* reaffirmed his fears that he might be passing his sell-by date. Henceforth, it would be mostly downhill for the Burtons.

Burton, initially, did not want to play George. As the washed-up, weakling, henpecked husband, he was afraid that the critics would make too many comparisons between the character and the actor. Amongst the contenders for the part were Jack Lemmon, Glenn Ford and Arthur Hill, who had played George on Broadway. It was only when Elizabeth agreed to do the film and when Ernest Lehman, in vogue after recently completing *The Sound of Music* (1965), began looking for someone else that Burton changed his mind. The contracts were duly signed – Elizabeth on £1.1 million plus 10 per cent of the gross, Burton on $750,000 – and Elizabeth was asked to choose the supports and crew.

She wanted John Frankenheimer to direct, having admired his film *Seconds* (1966) with Rock Hudson – a Kafkaesque piece, photographed through fish-eye lenses, about clapped-out old men being surgically reconstructed to become younger, lustier specimens. Frankenheimer would not work with Burton, so Elizabeth chose 34-year-old German-born Mike Nichols instead. She particularly admired him because he had done a number of ad-hoc jobs to pay for his education after arriving in America as a seven-year-old Jewish refugee: he worked as a cabaret comic (with Elaine May), joined Lee Strasberg's Actors Studio and enjoyed success as a director on Broadway. *Who's Afraid of Virginia Woolf?* would be his first film; equally famously, he would go on to direct *The Graduate* (1967) and *Catch-22* (1970).

The director of photography should have been Harry Stradling, whose impressionistic work Elizabeth had liked in *My Fair Lady*. Stradling's *truc*, picked up whilst working in Europe, was to attempt to recapture the quality of Flemish paintings in key scenes – not easy in monochrome. His mistake was to sit through a showing of Fellini's *Otto e mezzo* (*81/2* in the UK) with Mike Nichols – the director's favourite film – only to dismiss it as 'a piece of shit'. Nichols refused to work with him, so Warner Brothers approached Haskell Wexler, currently shooting *A Fine Madness* with Sean Connery. For reasons known only to the 'must be obeyed' Jack Warner, Wexler, famed for his documentary approach to cinematography, was pulled from the Connery film, assigned to *Who's Afraid of Virginia Woolf?* and threatened with ostracism from Hollywood should he refuse to comply.

For the supports, who would play two young party guests who early in the scenario probably wish they had stayed at home,

Elizabeth chose Sandy Dennis and George Segal. She had admired
Dennis in her first film, *Splendour in the Grass* (1961). According
to Haskell Wexler (*Who's Afraid of Virginia Woolf?*, DVD, audio-
commentary), throughout shooting Dennis and Elizabeth infuriated
everyone with their belching contests – with Dennis always winning.
Thirty-one-year-old George Segal had met Richard Burton on the set
of *The Longest Day*. Both Segal and Dennis were wry, natural but
inadvertent comedians, perfect stooges for the sparring Burtons.

Shooting began in September 1965 at Smith College, Northampton,
Massachusetts, and wound up two weeks before Christmas. At a
cost of over $7 million, it proved the most expensive black-and-
white movie ever made – so filmed, it is alleged, because Heskell
Wexler believed that the make-up to conceal Burton's pockmarks
would not have to be as 'critical' for the extreme close-ups as it
might have been had he been filming in colour. It was also the
first American film to use profane language, though today words
such as 'goddam', 'crap', 'screw' and 'bastard' are pretty tame and
commonplace – the stage play featured worse. Even so, the fuss
this caused resulted in the introduction of the Motion Picture
Association of America rating system, which declared that no one
under the age of 18 could see the film unless accompanied by an
adult. And for those not wishing to be seen entering a cinema
in these overtly moral times, Warner Brothers released a special-
edition, 'uncensored' double LP of the soundtrack.

'I'm loud and I'm vulgar and I wear the pants in the house because
somebody's got to! But I'm not a monster!' So Elizabeth pronounces
in what is generally regarded as her most accomplished role since
Suddenly, Last Summer, and perhaps the only one which puts her
on a par with Garbo, Hepburn, Davis and Crawford at *their* best.
It was also the best thing she ever did with Richard Burton (back
to being a great actor in this one), though considering some of the
tosh they made, it would be unfair to make comparisons. The film
opens with George and Martha (effectively a bickering, *La Cage
aux Folles*-style homosexual couple in flimsy disguise) arriving home
after a New Carthage University faculty party hosted by her father,

who is its principal. What happens over the course of the next two hours is told in near-real time and so mirrors the Taylor-Burton relationship that it is not difficult to imagine how hellish it must have been to live in close proximity to these tyrants, whose minds and bodies were so addled by liquor and feuding that they could no longer differentiate between fact and fantasy.

Martha, aka Taylor, the mighty star, never lets George, aka Burton, the ham, forget that she is a well-connected somebody, whilst he is a mere nonentity whose career is at a standstill. One is hard put to determine which of these two is the more despicable when entertaining the guests – college-jock Nick and his fruit-loop-wife Honey – they have asked over for the evening. One can imagine Burton yelling at Elizabeth when George says to Martha that she must make an impression by keeping her clothes *on*, and adds, 'There aren't many more sickening sights in this world than you with a couple of drinks inside you and your skirt up over your head.' According to contemporary reports, Martha and George's little drinks party was no different from most Taylor-Burton soirées, in that everyone gets plastered and the home truths come tumbling out, along with a number of incidents that, although tame today, genuinely shocked American audiences back then. George refers to his deceased imaginary son as a 'little bugger', a British euphemism for 'handful' that many people misinterpreted for 'sexual deviant'. Then George infers that Nick might be gay, a situation that Martha 'rectifies', just as Elizabeth had done for her gay co-stars in the past, by displaying her ample cleavage and having him thrust his crotch inches from her face as she pronounces, 'You're right at the meat of things!' Martha further humiliates George when he gets grumpy and fetches his rifle. When he pulls the trigger, an umbrella pops out of the barrel. Using this as an opportunity to mock his – and Burton's – occasional impotence, she coos to the younger man, '*You* don't need any props, do you, baby? No fake guns for *you*!'

When the two men discuss their recipe for success, which involves being with well-heeled wives, it parallels the way in which Burton ensured his own swift elevation to the top of the show-business ladder:

NICK: Take over a few courses from the older men. Plough a few impertinent wives!

GEORGE: Now, that's it . . . you can shove aside all the older men you can find, but until you start ploughing pertinent wives, you're not really working. That's the way to power. Plough 'em all! The way to a man's heart – the wide, inviting avenue to his job is through his wife, and don't you forget it!

NICK: And I bet your wife's got the most inviting avenue on the whole damn campus! I just better get her off into the bushes straight away!

The two couples end up playing the jukebox at a roadhouse in a scene choreographed by the then little-known Herbert Ross, who later worked with Barbra Streisand in *Funny Girl* (1968) and with her and Segal in the film Elizabeth and Burton should have made, *The Owl and the Pussycat* (1970). George flirts with Honey, calling her 'monkey nipples', but when Martha fake copulates with Nick, George tries to throttle her and thus begins what Haskell Wexler later described as a carbon copy of a Taylor-Burton fight, made more dramatic, at Elizabeth's request, by being filmed with a hand-held camera.

Martha then goes off with Nick, though they are too drunk to later remember of they had sex – she just needed to determine if he was gay or straight. This he interprets as a slur on his manhood, until she explains that in this respect he is no different from the other men she has known, which is again true to life. Adding to the character-actress similarities she concludes that only one man has ever made her happy, one whom she now reviles and who must be punished because he has made the mistake of loving her. Finally, she confesses that she and George invented a son, and that the charade has got them through a dreadful marriage. Now, the pretence must end, and Martha's closing monologue is so utterly heart-rending and convincing that we actually feel sorry for her. As happened with Elizabeth herself, we are witnessing a sad, disillusioned woman starting off on the path towards a Calvary of her own making. A masterpiece!

ELEVEN

DUDS AND DIAMONDS

IN FEBRUARY 1966, THE BURTONS FLEW TO ENGLAND TO appear in an Oxford University production of Christopher Marlowe's *Dr Faustus* – a week-long practice run for the film version that would be directed by Burton later in the year. The couple insisted upon performing for free, which was just as well, critics observed, for under any other circumstances they would have been paid up. Whilst Burton ranted, flung his arms about and made little sense of the script, Elizabeth merely postured in the middle of the stage and uttered not one word.

The film version was little better. Filmed in Rome with students from the university dramatic society (with everyone, including the Burtons, on a daily rate of £18), it was funded to the tune of $1 million out of Burton's pocket, and it earned the celebrity couple some of their worst critical reviews ever. The *New York Times* denounced it as 'an awfulness that bends the mind'. *Time* magazine went out of its way to praise co-director Nevill Coghill (who had directed the play) for keeping Elizabeth 'mercifully' mute throughout the production and said of her appearance, 'When she welcomes Burton to an eternity of damnation, her eyeballs and teeth are dripping pink in a hellish combination of conjunctivitis and trench mouth.' Ouch!

Richard Burton, the former thespian, was accused of selling out for the sake of the almighty dollar when he and Elizabeth returned to Oxford for the film's premiere on 15 October 1967. The presenter who interviewed them from a local television news magazine made the mistake of comparing the Faust legend – the magician who sells his soul to the devil in exchange for material possessions and is dragged down to hell by the women he loves – with that of the Burtons' relationship. Burton was unable to get a word in edgeways as Elizabeth went for the jugular:

INTERVIEWER: You must have sometimes, Richard Burton, faced the question as to whether you should have continued as an imposing and even in the view of many people great stage actor, and moved into the world of films, which is more commercially rewarding but not perhaps so rewarding artistically. Do you ever regret moving into the commercial cinema?

ELIZABETH (narrowing her eyes, pointing accursedly): That makes me so angry because he has *not* left the stage. That's absolute bloody rubbish, when last year he just got through doing a thing here for Oxford on the stage. The year before that, what was he doing on Broadway? How can you say he's left the stage?

INTERVIEWER: But that is not a continuous stage career in the sense that, for example, Paul Schofield and Laurence Olivier . . .

ELIZABETH: He's not continuous, either. He still does films for money, and so does Paul Schofield.

INTERVIEWER: But Schofield has made one film in ten or fourteen years, and Richard was one time potentially the greatest stage actor that England had ever produced. I wondered whether in a way your making of *Faustus*, which is the story of a man who sells out to a dream, almost, is perhaps comparable with your decision? I want to ask, Elizabeth Taylor, if your irritation was because you felt that the cinema was not the creative medium that the theatre was. I don't know why you got so cross . . .

ELIZABETH (cutting the interview short): Because you said the exact phrase that I knew you were working up to – 'sold out' – and it offends me to the soul!

It was possibly also the interviewer's phrase 'potentially the greatest actor' and the fact that he was no longer recognised as such, probably because of her, that rankled Elizabeth. *Dr Faustus* was the first of Elizabeth's films not to recover its production costs, grossing less than $500,000 at the box office on *both* sides of the Atlantic.

Meanwhile, in the spring of 1966, the Burtons drove overland, via Switzerland, to Rome to appear in Franco Zeffirelli's *The Taming of the Shrew* (1967), described by film critic Alexander Walker as 'a *Tom and Jerry* cartoon in costume'. Instead of salaries, they opted for a hefty share of the profits, which earned them in excess of $3 million, despite the mediocrity of the film – Burton performs drunk throughout.

Since leaving America, Elizabeth had spoken to Montgomery Clift every day on the telephone. He had had a tough time shooting *The Defector* in Germany, but with Warner Brothers there was no let-up: on 15 July the studio contracted both parties to inform them that *Reflections in a Golden Eye* would begin shooting in the September. Until then, there had been some talk that Burton might direct, but Monty dismissed the idea – even though it meant handing the reins to John Huston, whom he hated. Elizabeth promised to keep an eye on the bad-tempered director to ensure there would be no repetition of the violence that had accompanied *Freud*.

Elizabeth had just been offered the film adaptation of *This Property Is Condemned* (1966) opposite newcomer Robert Redford, but this role now went to Natalie Wood – for half the fee Paramount had offered Elizabeth. She was still reeling from this when Richard Burton received a call from Roddy McDowall: on the morning of 23 July 1966, Monty had been found dead in his bed, the victim of heart failure. This proved to be Elizabeth's biggest loss since Mike Todd, a grief she would carry with her to the grave. The man she often claimed to be more important to her than all of her husbands was just 45. She did not attend his funeral, three days later in Brooklyn's Quaker Cemetery, using work commitments as an excuse, although it is believed she stayed away to avoid turning the ceremony into a media event. Her wreath of white chrysanthemums was inscribed 'Rest, perturbed spirit'.

As she had been given contractual approval of her co-stars, and feeling that only he could step into his shoes, Elizabeth contacted Marlon Brando, Monty's nearest rival, and asked him to replace Clift in *Reflections in a Golden Eye*. When asked by reporters if he had accepted the role as a tribute to Monty, Brando responded, 'Nope. I need the $750,000.'

It was by no means a poor film: minus the encumbrance of Richard Burton's booming, drunken histrionics, it was a distinct improvement on anything that Elizabeth had done since *Who's Afraid of Virginia Woolf?* The story was based on a 1961 novella by Carson McCullers, a complex individual whose work was labelled by critics and admirers as 'Southern Gothic'. She described her work and the frequently grotesque array of characters who populated her books as, 'The hungry search of people for an escape from individual loneliness, for self-expression and for identification with what each most idealises in human living.' McCullers certainly practised what she preached: she had a lifelong unfulfilled sexual obsession with Greta Garbo and shared a lover with her homosexual husband Reeves, whom she married and divorced twice and who subsequently committed suicide. Who better then to have inadvertently provided a vehicle for Elizabeth Taylor and Montgomery Clift, now replaced by the equally offbeat Marlon Brando?

In the film, set in an army post in the Deep South (but filmed in Rome for tax purposes), Elizabeth plays Leonora, the sex-starved wife of the latently homosexual, self-loathing Major Weldon Penderton (Brando), who, in a replica of the Reeves McCullers situation, has the hots for the younger, lustier Private Williams (Robert Forster), who is similarly obsessed with Leonora. And this being rarely-to-the-point Southern Gothic, and as had been the case with the homosexual references in *Suddenly, Last Summer*, Penderton 'outs' himself to cinemagoers in an inarticulately roundabout manner during a lecture to his men when he asks, 'Is it morally honourable for the square peg to keep scraping around in the round hole, rather than to discover and use the orthodox one that would fit?' Add to this Leonora's penchant for bashing her husband in public, Private Williams' acute narcissism and underwear fetish, and Brando's Method acting and persistent mumbling of his lines, and the end result is either fascinating or downright boring, depending upon how one is 'tuned in' to these complicated, high-charged scenarios.

Even so, working with an actor of Brando's calibre was a step in the right direction for Elizabeth. Her performances were starting to gain more depth with roles such as Leonora Penderton, and had there been more of these in her middle years – instead of lending herself to mostly trash in order to placate Richard Burton – she might have developed into an American Anna Magnani. Indeed, to save her unsalvageable marriage from sinking, she signed up for two more productions that might have proved worthwhile with another leading man but with Burton dragging her down ended up as stinkers.

The Comedians (1967) was especially scripted for the Burtons by Graham Greene from his novel of the same name. Set in Haiti during the 'Papa Doc' Duvalier regime, it had at its helm Peter Glenville, who had more patience with Burton than most: he had directed him in *Becket* but would rue doing so again. Also, possibly owing to the success of the other film, Burton had top billing – the only time this happened when he appeared with Elizabeth – which was reflected in his salary. Shooting was a miserable experience for all. As Papa Doc had refused to allow a film unit in Haiti, the locations were filmed in the African republic of Dahomey (now the Republic of Benin), where the heat was intolerable and everyone was plagued by mosquitoes. Elizabeth played another sex-starved siren, ambassador's wife Martha Pineda, with an accent only marginally less atrocious than the one in the later *Divorce His, Divorce Hers*

(1973). Throughout the overlong (160 minutes) production, she alternates between German, French and Spanish, with a dash of the Queen's English thrown in for good measure. Suffering nobly alongside the Burtons were Alec Guinness and Peter Ustinov, who trounced them in every scene. Declaring that he had to fight to get even a half-decent performance out of his stars, Peter Glenville told *Vogue*, 'She was bored by her own fame and obsessed with his.'

Shooting on *The Comedians* had almost wrapped when the Burtons received a call from Jack Warner, urging them to return to Hollywood to attend the Oscars ceremony. Both had been nominated for *Who's Afraid of Virginia Woolf?*, as had the film itself, but three of its numerous nominations. These were the days when stars were expected to show up for the event – unless seriously indisposed – or risk being frowned upon by their peers and the media. Elizabeth finished working on the *The Comedians* first and told Warner that she would be there. Burton threw a fit, announcing that as soon as he had canned his scenes he would be flying to the south of France and that Elizabeth should be by his side as his dutiful wife. She initially fought against this, relenting only when Burton fabricated the story that he had seen her plane crash into the Atlantic in a dream.

Elizabeth was widely tipped as favourite for the Best Actress award, having already won the New York Film Critics Circle Award and a British BAFTA. Also nominated were George Segal and Sandy Dennis (Best Supporting Actor/Actress), Mike Nichols (Best Director), Richard Stybert (art direction), James Hopkins (sets), Haskell Wexler (cinematography) and Irene Sharaff (costumes). Elizabeth's only serious rival, the critics believed, was Anouk Aimée for *Un homme et une femme*, whilst Burton was pitched against Paul Schofield (the mention of whose name had caused Elizabeth to see red in Oxford) for *A Man for All Seasons*. Schofield had already won numerous awards for his brilliant portrayal of Sir Thomas More, and he picked up the Oscar, as did the film and its director, Fred Zinneman. Elizabeth won her category, becoming only the fifth actress (after Ingrid Bergman, Louise Rainer, Olivia de Havilland and Vivien Leigh) to win two Oscars. Her award was collected by Anne Bancroft. For the rest of his life, Burton was plagued by the fact that Elizabeth had achieved something (twice) that he had not.

On 29 September 1967, the Burtons flew to Paris, attracting a vast crowd in the Place de l'Opéra when they turned up for the premiere of *The Taming of the Shrew*. Unable to attend, even though Burton is said to have summoned him, President de Gaulle sent a small delegation and armed guard to escort them from an airfield on the outskirts of the city, and Elizabeth posed for photographs wearing a hired Van Cleef & Arpels tiara that cost almost $2 million. And when she commented on how comfortable the flight had been in the private jet that had conveyed them to France, Burton made arrangements to buy it – for a cool $850,000.

The Burtons' next venture was *Boom!* (1968), based on Tennessee Williams' *The Milk Train Doesn't Stop Here Anymore*. Rumour had it that Elizabeth had been suggested for the central role of Flora Goforth, the world's richest woman, by Tallulah Bankhead, who had played the part on the stage a few years earlier. 'She's a promiscuous, pill-ravaged rip, born in a Georgia swamp,' Tallulah had said at the time, 'so she could only be played by me!' Now, she declared, who better to portray Goforth on the big screen than Elizabeth Taylor, who as 'the world's biggest joke' would only have to be herself? The setting was not far removed from Williams' earlier *The Roman Spring of Mrs Stone* (1961), with Vivien Leigh and Warren Beatty in the main roles, although Lotte Lenya had received all the praise and been Oscar nominated playing the contessa.

Tallulah's co-star on the stage was the 32-year-old Tab Hunter, ethereally handsome and perfectly cast as Chris Sanders, the hunky beach-boy poet who has fashioned a career out of consoling rich, moribund ladies – and on one occasion an elderly man he helped to commit suicide – on Italy's 'Divina Costiera' (though the locations were shot in Sardinia), earning himself the nickname 'Angel of Death'. Tennessee Williams observed in his 1975 autobiography, *Memoirs*:

The death of Miss Flora Goforth is essentially the death of a clown. There is hardly a bit of nobility, nor even dignity, in her fiercely resistant approach to life's most awful adventure – dying. But you will find it very possible to pity this female clown even while her absurd pretensions and her panicky last effort to hide from her final destruction make you laugh at her.

At 35, Elizabeth was far too young to play Flora (Tallulah had been 61), but, as always, when she stepped into the shoes of a Tennessee Williams heroine-madwoman, her interpretation was exemplary, and she looked stunning in her all-white Annalisa Nasalli-Rocca creations. Burton, on the other hand, was no Tab Hunter – bloated and bucolic, much of the time he resembled a badly made-up fourth-rate ham from a cheap medieval drama. Noel Coward, as the Witch of Capri (a female character in the play), is embarrassing to watch, and Joanna Shimkus, who plays the long-suffering secretary Blackie, is totally wooden. And surely director Joseph Losey was playing a joke on cinemagoers by casting a dwarf (Michael Dunn) in the role of Flora's bodyguard, Rudy?

Although much of Williams' original theatre script is incorporated into *Boom!*, he was forced to make a few changes to the screen adaptation to reflect the Taylor-Burton situation. The arguments between the two main characters are therefore more vociferous, bordering on the maniacal, and Burton insisted on being able to kiss both Flora and Blackie, which does not happen in the play. The Taylor-Burton diamond, along with a few of its companions, makes an obligatory appearance. Also upon Burton's request, Williams added a 'put-down' line to counteract Flora's domination of everyone around her. 'Tough as you are,' Chris pronounces, 'you're not so tough that one day, perhaps soon, you're gonna need someone or something that'll mean God to you, if it's only a human hand or a human voice.' The critics hated the film, but the lack of plaudits failed to affect the box office, despite the fact that the Burtons' marriage was starting to fall apart at the seams – hardly surprising given their volatile, complex relationship.

The rot appears to have set in early in 1968, after Elizabeth wanted to play Anne Boleyn opposite Burton's Henry VIII in *Anne of a Thousand Days*. He turned her down in favour of the younger, more appropriately sylph-like Canadian actress Geneviève Bujold – a role for which she was Oscar nominated. When Bujold politely requested that Burton's famous wife should not be allowed on the set because of the fuss this would cause, Elizabeth immediately suspected that the pair were having an affair. Almost certainly they were not, though Burton *was* playing around behind Elizabeth's back – a question of old habits dying hard. And matters were not helped in the September by the not unexpected death of Elizabeth's father at the age of 70. A few years earlier, Francis Taylor had suffered a stroke from which he had never really recovered. His demise reunited mother and daughter, with Elizabeth confiding in Sara about her marital problems.

As the rows escalated, time after time Burton reached for his chequebook in an increasingly futile attempt to keep their ship from sinking completely, just as Eddie Fisher had done before him. And the press, who trailed around the world after the couple, following the circus like devotees of some fanatical religious sect, delighted in relaying to their readers how every last dollar had been spent.

Towards the end of their second marriage, Richard Burton would boast to an astonished press conference, 'I've spent $20 million on Elizabeth, because she is my baby child.' In a modern, politically educated world, where poverty and starvation were rife, Burton's extravagances were nothing short of shameful. Not long after *Anne of a Thousand Days*, he bought the wife who already had everything and more the infamous 38.9-carat Krupp Diamond, hardly the sort of trinket one would have thought a Jewish convert would wear with pride, for it had originally been purchased with blood money by the Nazi industrialist Alfred Krupp. Shortly after the Second World War, Krupp had been convicted by an American tribunal for plundering occupied territories and employing slave labour in neo-concentration-camp conditions. Burton bragged that the bauble had been but a 'snip' at $305,000.

Next, Burton acquired an equally controversial piece for $37,000. This was La Peregrina, the fabulous pearl that Philip II of Spain had given to Henry VIII's daughter, Mary Tudor, in 1554 at the start of the union that had made 'Bloody Mary' the most hated woman in England. She is seen wearing it in her official portrait. By the time it ended up in Elizabeth's possession, it had been reset and suspended from a $100,000 diamond, ruby and pearl necklace. The fact that she owned two artefacts steeped in a history of bloodshed, extreme hardship, unpleasantness and evil did not perturb her unduly.

Then there was the even more staggering pear-shaped 69.42-carat Taylor-Burton Diamond, fashioned by Cartier – an inch-thick monster that set Burton back $1.1 million. Only the French music-hall stars Gaby Deslys (responsible for the downfall of the Portuguese monarchy) and Mistinguett had owned sparklers of such value, closely followed by the Duchess of Windsor, who was Elizabeth's only living rival and who always tried to outshine her whenever they crossed paths on the social circuit. Soon after acquiring this, Burton let Elizabeth in on the secret that one of the bidders had been Sophia Loren's director husband, Carlo Ponti. According to biographer Kitty Kelley, Elizabeth denounced Loren to friends as 'too piss-elegant for words', and the fact that the Italian beauty had almost ended up with her diamond rankled her. Though they would later socialise and pretend to like each other, behind her back Elizabeth would refer scathingly to Loren as 'Madama Ponti'.

Elizabeth herself doled out $100,000 for a diamond necklace from which her latest trinket could be suspended so as to conceal her tracheotomy scar. She then paid $80,000 to have it insured by Lloyds of London, when no other American or European company would touch it. There were, however, certain conditions. Elizabeth was only permitted to wear the piece 30 times a year and had to be accompanied by an armed guard, at her own expense, when doing so – otherwise it would have to remain locked in a bank vault.

The Burtons enabled the American public to ogle the Krupp

Diamond in May 1970 when they made an appearance on *The Lucy Show*, one of their truly great celluloid moments, if not their best since *Who's Afraid of Virginia Woolf?* The hostess naturally insisted upon trying on the ring, got it stuck on her finger and had it removed by Burton, using the best vintage champagne. Before this happened, however, the press turned up wanting to see the ring: the Burtons received them standing in front of a curtain, behind which hid Lucille Ball, her hand pushed through the gap and up Elizabeth's kimono sleeve. Burton explained that he found the diamond in a 'crackerjack barrel' whilst Elizabeth's 'spare hand' wreaked havoc, gesticulating to the press, stroking Burton's face, trying to strangle Elizabeth and forcing her to drink *two* glasses of champagne. 'And they call me a two-fisted drinker,' he pronounced, bringing the response from his wife, 'Of all the sinks in Los Angeles, you had to pick *her* faucet!'

Besides the jewels, there were the properties in Gstaad, Puerto Vallarta and Céligny, their walls festooned with Rembrandts, Picassos, Renoirs, Van Goghs and Monets. And there was the $420,000 yacht, the *Kalizma*, so named after their daughters Kate, Liza and Maria. Jessica Burton was still in the nursing home, conveniently out of the way and, it would appear, forgotten. With seven cabins and two staterooms, the vessel was filled with Chippendale furniture and other antiques. Then there was the $1-million customised private jet and the $500,00 helicopter. The list was apparently endless. As the film critic Alexander Walker observed, 'They lived on a scale few hereditary rulers except the despots of Africa or Arabia thought prudent for either their people to witness or their treasuries to support.' So much money was flying around, with even more coming in, that one story of Burton 'sorting out the clutter' atop his piano in the couple's Gstaad retreat reached the tabloids. While doing so, the actor 'chanced upon' an envelope containing a cheque for over $2 million in royalty payments!

It was not just the tabloids who were mercilessly critical of the couple's excess. *Look* magazine called Elizabeth 'a fading movie queen who has too much and wants more'. The *New York Times* observed of the Taylor-Burton Diamond, 'It would have been nice to wear in the tumbrel on the way to the guillotine. In this age of vulgarity marked by such "minor" matters as war and poverty, it gets harder every day to scale the heights of vulgarity.'

This Borgian extravagance extended towards Elizabeth's pets. In 1968, when she came to London to make *Secret Ceremony* (1968) – Burton had eschewed this one for *Where Eagles Dare* (1968) – the press were less interested in her latest hospitalisation (on 21 July for a hysterectomy) than they were in the arrangements she had made for her menagerie. Prohibited from bringing her dogs into the country because of British quarantine regulations, and with the *Kalizma* undergoing a refit, for a mere $10,000 a month, she hired a 200-ton yacht named the *Beatriz*, which was moored on the Thames. This was also used some evenings for private parties – and with Elizabeth's disdain for cleaning up after her animals, one can only imagine what the conditions must have been like for the guests. 'The World's Most Expensive Dog Kennel' was also debated in Parliament by Home Secretary James Callaghan, with MPs wanting to know if the British taxpayer would be footing the bill for the police, customs and RSPCA officers patrolling the Thames Embankment to ensure the Burtons didn't bring their pooches ashore. Mr Callaghan duly reassured them that they were not. Even so, there were far-reaching consequences. Burton had been put forward for a knighthood in that year's Queen's birthday honours list, not for his questionable acting abilities, but for his equally dubious charity work – donations brought about mostly by tax concessions. Prime Minister Harold Wilson, himself from a working-class background, faced a Cabinet backlash. They basically came to the conclusion that the only 'charities' Richard Burton were interested in were himself and his wife. The honour was revoked, though two years later he would be awarded a CBE.

Burton's greed was additionally highlighted when Elizabeth was assigned to *Secret Ceremony*, and he attempted to get her co-star, Robert Mitchum, fired from the production so that he could take his place. Such unprofessional conduct gave him a bad name in

With Burton at the Golden Mask Awards, 1966.
(© Keystone-France/Gamma-Keystone/Getty Images)

Elizabeth with her other 'rock' – her mother, Sara, in 1973.
(© Apic/Getty Images)

One queen plays another! In costume as a very bitchy Mary Queen of Scots in Agatha Christie's *The Mirror Crack'd*, one of her best later films, which also saw her working again with Rock Hudson, 1980. (© AFP/Getty Images)

In 1982, congratulated after a performance at London's Victoria
Palace Theatre by Princess Diana. (© Central Press/Getty Images)

Attending Richard
Burton's memorial service
at St Martin-in-the-
Fields in August 1984.
(© Keystone/Getty Images)

With George Hamilton in *Poker Alice*, 1987, which saw Elizabeth
engaged in a thrilling catfight! (© CBS Photo Archive/Getty Images)

At London's Mirabelle Restaurant for an AIDS benefit with last husband
Larry Fortensky, 1991. (© Gerry Penny/AFP/Getty Images)

At London's Dorchester Hotel, May 2000 – Dame Elizabeth Taylor!
(© Dave M. Benett/Getty Images)

An AIDS benefit
in Cannes, 2001
– still gorgeous!
(© J. Vespa/WireImage)

At Macy's Passport Gala
in 2009. The indefatigable
champion is fading,
but, frail and ill, she
still radiates a charisma
no other star has ever
possessed. (© Charley
Gallay/WireImage)

the trade. Tony Richardson, who had directed Tallulah Bankhead in *The Milk Train Doesn't Stop Here Anymore*, signed Burton for *Laughter in the Dark*, to be made immediately after *Where Eagles Dare*. Upon hearing of the Mitchum incident, Richardson tried but failed to get rid of Burton. Therefore, when Burton turned up for his first day's work late and drunk, the director seized the opportunity to give him his marching orders.

The Burtons' cinematic downfall was kick-started following the May 1968 New York premiere of *Boom!*, a mega-flop that would take 15 years to recover its production costs. The instigator of what many people believed to be their long-overdue demise was the 29 May issue of *Life* magazine. Having denounced the couple's arrogance, along with their audacity in expecting the public to accept 'anything they cared to shovel out', the editorial concluded:

> There is a slack, tired quality to most of their work that is by now a form of insult. There is neither dignity nor discipline in what they do. *She* is fat and will do nothing about her most glaring defect – an unpleasant voice which she cannot adequately control. *He*, conversely, acts with nothing *but* his voice, rolling out his lines with much elegance but with no feeling at all. Perhaps the Burtons are doing the very best they can, laden as they are by their celebrity. But if they are not cynics, overestimating their charisma and underestimating our intelligence, then they are guilty of a lack of aesthetic judgement and self-awareness that is just as threatening.

Despite this critical pummelling from one of America's premier publications, the couple were still in demand – but separately. This caused tremendous problems for anyone interested in offering them contracts, because they refused to work apart – as if aware that with some distance between them they might never reconcile. Elizabeth was signed to star opposite Frank Sinatra in the gambling comedy *The Only Game in Town* (1970) and demanded $1.25 million. What is astonishing is that the studio was Twentieth Century Fox, who had sued Burton and Taylor over the *Cleopatra* debacle and had vowed never to work with either again. Burton demanded, and received without argument, the same fee to play a gay hairdresser opposite Rex Harrison in *Staircase*. This pathetic horror, released in America on the eve of the Stonewall riots of 1969, dredged up every prejudice, religious reference and gay cliché in the bigot's book, and today makes for uncomfortable viewing. As Paul Roen observes in *High Camp*, 'If nothing else [this movie] vividly illustrates that the time for gay liberation was way past due.'

The budgets for both productions were bumped up by the Burtons' insistence – once the contracts had been signed – that they be filmed in the same place for tax purposes. This ruled out Las Vegas (for Elizabeth's film) and London (for Burton's). The settings were therefore recreated on adjacent lots at a studio on the outskirts of Paris. A further hitch occurred when Frank Sinatra dropped out of the production and was replaced by Warren Beatty, currently a white-hot property following his success in *Bonnie and Clyde* (1967). With Burton concerned that some of his fans might think him gay because he was playing 'an old queen' and, at the same time, worried that acknowledged Lothario Beatty might make a move on Elizabeth, he increased his already heavy drinking, ignoring doctors' warnings that he was slowly killing himself on account of an enlarged liver.

In *Secret Ceremony* – something of a poor man's McCullers/ Williams psycho-fest – Elizabeth played another Leonora, a middle-aged prostitute kidnapped by a mentally unbalanced girl (Mia Farrow) who thinks Leonora is her mother. For a while, she keeps her in a spooky Edwardian mansion filled with music boxes and junk – the pair are just starting to get along when the stepfather (Robert Mitchum) shows up with tragic consequences. The real tragedy, according to the critics, was the film itself. Rex Reed observed in his syndicated column (later collated in the 1977 volume *Valentines and Vitriol*, Delacorte Press, 1977), 'The disintegration of Elizabeth Taylor has been a very sad thing to stand by helplessly and watch . . . She had become a hideous parody of herself – a fat, sloppy, yelling, screaming banshee.'

Elizabeth worked little during the first half of 1970. She was hospitalised for a while with the anal bleeding spasms that, it was now revealed, had laid her low the previous summer. In the July, she accompanied Richard Burton to Mexico, where he filmed the exteriors for *Raid on Rommel* (1971). Then in the September they flew to London, where he made *Villain* (1971) and she *Zee and Co.* (1972). Whilst they were there, 17-year-old Michael Wilding Jr married 19-year-old Beth Clutter at Caxton Hall on 6 October, with every tabloid headline screaming a variation of 'Here Comes the Mother of the Bride'. Not to be outdone, the Burtons gave the couple a new Jaguar and a £70,000 townhouse, conveniently situated next door to Burton's own in Hampstead. It was a happy wedding in every sense: the groom wore shoulder-length hair, a purple kaftan, bell-bottom trousers and 'Jesus' sandals; his mother a knitted trouser suit and maxi coat. One wonders whether she would have attended the ceremony had she not been working in London at the time, bearing in mind that there had hardly ever been a full family gathering at her own weddings.

The following August, the Wildings presented Elizabeth – at 39 – with her first grandchild, Leyla, precipitating Marlene Dietrich to relinquish her 'World's Most Glamorous Grandmother' crown. 'I was being sarcastic, naturally,' she told me. 'With all her aches and pains, she was physically *older* than I was. She'd earned it!' Elizabeth would attempt to spoil the child by sending her Christian Dior layettes. She found young Michael work as a photographer's assistant on *Zee and Co.*, which he walked out on because of the unsocial hours. She then offered the couple financial support, which he despised. By the time of Leyla's birth, the London townhouse was transformed into a mini-hippy commune, with Michael the fully fledged flower child, in favour of self-sufficiency and decidedly anti-materialist in lieu of genuine maternal affection. 'My mother's life seems just as fantastic to me as it does everyone else,' he told *Time* magazine. 'I really don't want any part of it.'

To get away, the couple sold the London house, packed their bags – along with around $50,000 of musical equipment that Elizabeth seems to have paid for – and headed for Ponterwyd, a village in the Welsh mountains. Here they set up their own commune, with Beth appointing herself 'earth mother'. One month later, she left Michael and moved into the Dorchester with the Burtons, taking Leyla with her. When this arrangement failed to work, Beth returned home to her family in Portland, Ohio, and filed for divorce. According to Beth (speaking to Kitty Kelley), Elizabeth demanded not just access to her granddaughter, but that Leyla be *sent* to her when she wanted to see her. Not surprisingly, Beth refused to comply, and Elizabeth hit the roof. 'Nobody tells me whether I can see my own grandchild,' she is alleged to have exclaimed. 'I'll never help you again!' Beth was, however, adamant. She vowed that her child would have a stable upbringing and would never find herself torn between pillar and post, as had happened with Michael Jr and Elizabeth's other children.

As for *Zee and Co.*, the film was marginally better than its predecessor, but it was still categorised third-rate by most of the critics. It was based on a novel by Edna O'Brien, who later complained that the script had been amended to fit in with the Taylor-Burton story to such an extent that it barely resembled the original. Elizabeth, unsalaried but on a high box-office percentage, played Zee Blakely, and Michael Caine was cast as her husband who is having an affair with a young widow (Susannah York). When he leaves her, she bungles a suicide attempt – then gets the widow on side, so to speak, by raking up her lesbian past and seducing her!

Just as this film coincided with the Wildings' wedding, so the birth of Elizabeth's first grandchild was blessed with her presence only because the Burtons were working in the country – this time filming Dylan Thomas's *Under Milk Wood* (1972) in Wales. Directed by Andrew Sinclair, this was another hotchpotch of booming histrionics and bawdy giggles, and owes more to Russ Meyer than the legendary Welsh poet. Elizabeth was Rosie Prebert, the village harlot, and Burton portrayed 'First Voice', the narrator with whom she was once intimate.

In February 1972, Elizabeth celebrated her 40th birthday. For this one, Burton presented her with a heart-shaped pendant set with the $1-million yellow Shah Jahan Diamond, which the Indian mogul responsible for building the Taj Mahal had given his wife, circa 1650. On it were inscribed the Parsee words for everlasting love. Burton arrogantly told reporters, 'I would have preferred buying Elizabeth the Taj Mahal itself, but transporting it would have been far too costly.'

The weekend-long bash took place in Budapest, where Burton was filming *Bluebeard* (1972), a film that was mocked by the *Washington Post* as 'Burton announcing his availability for Vincent Price roles, [as] it would be difficult for him to sink below this credit'. The guests at Elizabeth's birthday celebrations included David Niven, Michael Caine, Princess Grace of Monaco, the Ringo Starrs and Susannah York. To show that there were no hard feelings, Elizabeth invited Michael Wilding and his new wife, Margaret Leighton. Liza Todd was there, and Christopher Wilding flew in from Hawaii, where he was attending university. Michael Wilding Jr was conspicuous by his absence, having made it clear what he thought of such squandering of money when there was so much poverty in the world. The guests were instructed what to wear for the various parties – and were advised to bring dark glasses for the hangovers in between. The Burtons seem to have overlooked that they were guests of a poor Communist country that had seen more than its share of political upheavals and which frowned upon ostentatious spending, such as when Elizabeth paid to have Princess Grace's suite at the Intercontinental Hotel redecorated *and* filled with borrowed antiques. Just as Mike Todd before him, Richard Burton seemed to be of the opinion that any problem could solved by whipping out his chequebook. Summoning a hasty press conference, he announced that whatever his wife's party had cost, he would donate an equal amount to UNICEF. Good to his word, five months later he presented its representative, Peter Ustinov, with $45,000, although this did not alleviate the ill-feeling harboured by the citizens of Budapest against the Burtons for holding the celebrations there in the first place.

At some stage of the festivities, the Burtons were interviewed for David Frost's television show, and they were not particularly friendly towards their host. Burton was bombed on bourbon, with Elizabeth not far behind him, and matters were made worse by the producer's insistence that there be as little editing as possible so that Frost's viewers – or at least the ones who did not already know – might see what the couple were really like under the influence of drink, which was, of course, most of the time.

By that stage in their marriage, Burton was totally out of control. Mood swings and tantrums saw him, time and again, walking out on Elizabeth and into drunken one-night stands. Their arguments spilled out into the public arena as they went at it hammer and tong in bars and restaurants. The press reported incidents in which Elizabeth would smack Burton in the mouth, employ language foul enough to make a docker blush then continue necking with him as if nothing had happened. 'I will accuse her of being ugly, and she will accuse me of being a talentless son of a bitch,' Burton told the *Daily Mirror*, claiming that they had frequently 'pitched' battles for the fun of it. He added coyly, 'I *love* arguing with Elizabeth, except when she is in the nude. It's impossible to take an argument seriously with her naked. She throws her fingers around so vigorously, she positively bruises herself!'

Such utterances were voiced at a time when the Burtons' films were absolutely trashed by the critics. *Hammersmith Is Out* (1972), directed by and co-starring Peter Ustinov (who had obviously not learned his lesson since starring with them in *The Comedians*), was regarded as their most dire so far. Supposedly set in the American southwest, it was filmed in Cuernavaca, Mexico, so that they would not have to travel far from Puerto Vallarta. Elizabeth played a rough-edged waitress at a greasy spoon, Burton the nutcase who is convinced that he is the devil and promises to get her away from her life of drudgery and turn her into a movie star! Woven into the hammy storyline is his relationship with another 'disciple', played by Beau Bridges. It was the kind of scenario that might have worked well three decades earlier with Joan Crawford and Zachary Scott, but here the leads are wishy-washy and embarrassing: Elizabeth appears bored, and Burton looks overweight, ill and old. *Variety* observed, 'Burton, as the lunatic Hammersmith, goes through the film with a single (the director told him never to close his eyes!) bored expression.'

Elizabeth's *Night Watch* (1973), filmed in June 1972, was little better. Alongside Laurence Harvey, now in the latter stages of cancer, she played yet another Tennessee Williams-style madwoman who gets to wear stunning Valentino creations whilst going out of her mind.

There were also overseas family problems. Burton's brother Ifor suffered a serious fall during a visit to the house in Céligny. Paralysed from the neck down and confined to a wheelchair, he died soon afterwards. Then Michael Wilding Jr was arrested when police raided his Welsh commune and discovered that he had been growing cannabis. By then, he had another 'earth mother', Johanne Lyke-Dahn, and a second daughter, Naomi. At least one of Elizabeth's offspring was turning out to be a chip off the old block. Burton was also cheating on her. There were reputed affairs with Princess Margaret and French actress Nathalie Delon, who also had a fling with Eddie Fisher (or so he claimed). Elizabeth would later suspect Burton of being involved with Sophie Loren in Rome whilst shooting *The Voyage* (1974). But the affair that caused her the most distress was that with Jackie Onassis.

Many people blamed Elizabeth's complex personality for her husband's straying from the unsettled marital nest. She had always been hopeless when it came to choosing men and seemed to go out of her way to bring out the worst in them. One Hollywood divorce was more or less accepted as the norm, two could just about be excused but a possible fourth meant that there must have been something radically wrong not just with her, but with every man who crossed her path, for they too had had a multitude of partners and acrimonious splits.

In Britain, Harlech Television (in which Burton had invested $250,000 so that he and Elizabeth could sit on the board) took the brave step of trying to monopolise on the ongoing Taylor-Burton saga by proposing a two-part television movie, *Divorce His, Divorce Hers*. This told the story of a couple's marriage break-up, each part told from one of the partner's point of view, and did not attract a single favourable review. *Time* magazine called the Burtons 'a matching pair of thudding disasters', whilst *Variety* observed, 'This film holds all the joy of standing by at an autopsy.'

Television movies rarely come tackier than this. Jane and Martin Reynolds *are* Taylor and Burton, the spoilt wife and philandering husband, whose mistress, portrayed by Carrie Nye, resembles a second-rate drag queen. 'I am permanently adrift,' Jane proclaims, and she is not kidding! In a flashback scene, 20 years before, she looks older than she does now. Her accent dithers between queen's English and a Bronx-honk, and there is the obligatory mad scene. She wears only the best Edith Head costumes and makes a point of showing off the $1-million-plus La Pelegrina necklace given to her by Burton, who stumbles through the picture so bombed out of his skull that most of his lines make no sense at all.

This dreadful production in the can, now remembered as 'Liz and Dick's Last Stand', Elizabeth and Burton spent the Christmas holidays in Switzerland. In February 1973, they flew to Italy, where she was to make *Ash Wednesday* (1973), whilst he worked on the aforementioned *The Voyage* with Sophia Loren, directed by Carlo Ponti. In her film, Elizabeth played Barbara Sawyer, a middle-aged woman who submits to plastic surgery in an attempt to prevent her husband (Henry Fonda) from divorcing her. In doing so she attracts the attention of Erich, a beautiful young gigolo – portrayed by Austrian heartthrob Helmut Berger. When asked by a reporter from *The Ladies Home Journal* if she would ever consider going under the knife for real, Elizabeth responded, 'We can't stop the inevitable, so why try? Plastic surgery isn't for me because I don't base my happiness on the physical aspects of life.'

In fact, with her marriage at breaking point, Elizabeth had probably never felt so miserable, and it shows on the screen. Even the combined attractiveness of Berger and the ski resort of

Cortina D'Ampezzo, where the locations were filmed, failed to put an authentic smile on her face. Upon her return to America, she announced that she and Burton were separating, though only long enough for them to iron out their differences. The exclusive was given to the *Los Angeles Herald-Examiner* and was deliberately timed to coincide with Independence Day:

> I am convinced it would be a good, constructive idea if Richard and I separated for a while. Maybe we loved each other too much. I never believed such a thing was possible, but we've been in each other's pockets constantly, never being apart but for matters of life and death . . . Wish us well during this difficult time. Pray for us!

Richard Burton responded to the statement and defended their volatile relationship by announcing, 'You can't keep clapping a couple of sticks of dynamite together without expecting them to blow up!' Many critics were surprised that with her track record and his womanising and boozing they had lasted as long as they had. Yet she appeared to be making a concerted effort to hang onto him. Within three weeks of her announcement, the first reconciliation took place in Rome. Naturally, the press were informed well in advance of the staged, very public event at the city's Fiumicino Airport. Some 200 police were drafted in to control the 2,000-strong crowd, which fought with reporters and photographers to get to Burton's car that was waiting for Elizabeth's privately hired aircraft. She arrived accompanied by two of her dogs and was suitably 'dressed down' for the occasion, wearing denims and T-shirt, but she still flashed the Taylor-Burton Diamond at the photographers. The police managed to get her into Burton's car, the rear door of which was left open just long enough for the press to catch a glimpse of them falling into one another's arms and shedding a few crocodile tears. They were then pursued throughout the 12 miles to the Pontis' villa in Marino.

By 30 July 1973, it was all over. Burton stayed on in Rome to finish his film; Elizabeth remained in the city for a week or so to complete the locations for her latest offering, *The Driver's Seat* (1974; also released as *Identikit*). This was a woeful tale, if ever there was one, to cheer her up after her second split from her husband. She played Lise, an unhinged nymphomaniac who wishes to right the wrongs of her shady past by finding a lover willing to kill her – whilst they are having sex! Her co-star and the man selected to do the deed was Guido Mannari. But if many observers expected her to turn to the young Italian stunner for comfort, the shoulder she instead leaned upon was that of arch weirdo Andy Warhol, playing himself in a cameo in the picture. This was a ploy on Warhol's part to get an exclusive for his monthly *Interview* magazine, which failed when she heard the tiny tape recorder whirring away in his coat pocket. Exit Andy Warhol, at least for the time being.

At the end of August, Elizabeth returned to Los Angeles, where press reports soon linked her with Christopher Lawford, the 18-year-old son of 'Rat Pack' actor Peter. Alarmed that his son was seeing a woman old enough to be his mother, not to mention one of the world's most infamous man-eaters, Lawford fixed Elizabeth up with a 40-year-old half-Jewish Dutch used-car salesman named Henry Wynberg. According to biographer Jane Ellen Wayne (*The Golden Girls of MGM*, Carroll & Graf Publishers, 2002), Lawford described Wynberg, who was divorced with a young son, as 'a great cocksman with the type of equipment that appealed to Elizabeth'.

Before long, Elizabeth and Wynberg were cruising the Mediterranean aboard the *Kalizma*. Burton, monitoring the situation from afar, could not resist quipping to a reporter, 'If he's a used-car salesman, a vital part of Wynberg's anatomy might fall off when he needs it the most!' It was Wynberg who escorted Elizabeth to a charity event, organised to raise funds for the families of Israelis killed in the Middle East war, in Amsterdam, where some of his family lived. She donated some of her jewellery and upped the takings by $200,000.

Whilst in Amsterdam, Elizabeth received word that her friend and former co-star Laurence Harvey was dying. It is evident from her memoirs (*One Tear Is Enough*, M. Joseph, 1975) that Paulene Stone, Harvey's wife, did not want Elizabeth there, but this was Elizabeth Taylor, accustomed to always having her own way, regardless of anyone else's feelings. There was also a 'family' connection: Harvey's first wife, Margaret Leighton, had married Michael Wilding. In her book, ex-model Paulene explained that she had tried to prevent Elizabeth from seeing Harvey because he had not wanted to see her: '"She went on and on about life and death – it seems to be her favourite subject after diamonds," Larry growled at me, after one of her calls.' But, Elizabeth being Elizabeth, she managed to slip into the sickroom – *and* to get into the dying actor's bed, telling him that she wanted to die with him.

Three weeks after this distressing, if not humiliating, display of exhibitionism, Laurence Harvey died, and Elizabeth vied with his widow to deliver the most fitting but rehearsed eulogy. 'He was part of the sun,' she told reporters, 'and for everyone, the sun is a little more dim.' And just as she had attempted to monopolise Laurence Harvey's deathbed, so she took over the memorial arrangements. With Peter Lawford, she organised an Episcopal service (for a Lithuanian Jew) and greeted mourners at the church door like she was his widow, clad in black, sparkling with the diamonds Harvey despised and handing out bunches of violets.

And this was not the only humiliation Elizabeth caused that year. Only the intervention of Maria Callas's entourage prevented the greatest operatic diva of her generation from 'committing grievous bodily harm' when Elizabeth turned up for her recital in Hamburg on 25 October 1973. The reason: Elizabeth, tired of Richard Burton's womanising in Budapest, had played him at his own game on 5 May the previous year by flying to Rome to have dinner with Aristotle Onassis. The pair had been snapped by the paparazzi – naturally, they had been tipped off beforehand – and most of the subsequent press reports drew the conclusion that they had spent the night together. Callas would carry a torch for Onassis until his death in 1975, and she despised Jackie Kennedy for stealing him from her. Just as there seemed to be a chance of them reuniting, with the Onassis's marriage reputedly on the rocks, Elizabeth had attempted to pull the rug from under her.

Feelings were still running high in September 1997 when I met up with what was left of Callas's entourage in London on the occasion of the 20th anniversary of her death. Her chauffeur from Hamburg told me:

> Such was Madame Taylor's massive self-esteem that she really expected Maria to welcome her with open arms. Maria had already hit the roof because someone had persuaded, shall we say, her secretary to appear in an Elizabeth Taylor film [Nadia Stancioff, *Ash Wednesday*]. In her dressing-room, Maria fumed, 'Just who does she think she is, flaunting her diamonds and love affairs in everybody's faces? I'll tear the fucking bitch to pieces and cratch out her eyes if she comes anywhere near me!' The ensuing scene, had it taken place, would have been more exciting than any Hollywood movie – *and* Maria would have won!

This was Maria Callas's farewell tour, a joint series of recitals with tenor Giuseppi Di Stefano. Her magnificent voice was starting to fail her, and she was a bag of nerves – a condition not helped by the start of the show being held up by ten minutes by the arrival of a woman she positively loathed. Elizabeth's secretary had demanded complimentary tickets, which Callas had refused, suspecting that if Elizabeth turned up at the theatre, she would only end up stealing her thunder. 'Tell her to take a hike along the Rieperbahn,' her chauffeur reported Callas as responding, referring to the city's infamous red-light district. Elizabeth, however, had instructed her secretary to purchase an entire row of top-priced tickets, and, as Callas had predicted, she entered the auditorium to thunderous applause and the popping of hundreds of flashbulbs. Callas, however, had the last laugh when one of Elizabeth's staff and a press photographer attempted to effect a backstage meeting after the recital. 'Elizabeth Taylor?' she spat out. 'Never heard of her!'

Richard Burton was still filming in Rome at the end of the year when Elizabeth collapsed and was rushed to the UCLA Medical Center. Doctors diagnosed an ovarian tumour, necessitating her 30th operation. Burton flew to Los Angeles to be with her, his press office announcing that this time they were together 'for keeps' and that he had given up the demon drink once and for all. The tumour fortunately proved to be benign, and after her discharge she and Burton spent a week in Puerto Vallarta before jetting back to Rome, where he added the finishing touches to *The Voyage*. They then flew to Oroville, California, where he was to make *The Klansman* (1974) with Lee Marvin. Here, in an alcoholic stupor, the Burtons celebrated their tenth wedding anniversary: he with the new Miss Pepsi Cola; Elizabeth alone. The film was another stinker, with Marvin playing the hero who takes on the might of the Ku Klux Klan, whilst Burton camps things up and bumps into the scenery. 'His grotesque performance turns a merely mediocre film into a full-blown baddie,' observed the Medved brothers in *The Golden Turkey Awards*.

Throwing together a pair of alcoholic rabble-rousers such as Richard Burton and Lee Marvin was always going to be problematic. Director Terence Young told the press halfway through shooting that there already had been moments when he had seriously considered flinging himself out of his hotel window. Another story circulated that each day began with Burton guzzling pre-breakfast cocktails – and ended with him bedding one of the waitresses who had served them. He took ill on the set, and Elizabeth had him flown to Los Angeles, where he was admitted to St John's Hospital. He had diseased kidneys, suspected irreversible liver damage, bronchitis and influenza. Of late, he had also taken to snorting cocaine. Doctors warned him that unless he curbed his drinking habits he would be dead within the year. From then on, Burton was living on borrowed time – and did absolutely nothing to help himself.

Elizabeth had had enough. On 25 April 1974, she instructed her lawyers to draw up the divorce papers.

TWELVE

FROM PLAYBOY'S MUSE
TO FARMER'S WIFE

O N 26 JUNE 1974, THE BURTONS' TEN-YEAR MARRIAGE ended in a courthouse in Saanen, the Swiss ski resort near Gstaad. Elizabeth told the judge that life with her husband had been intolerable – not exactly true, for there is more than sufficient evidence that the pair had been making life hell for one another since *before* their marriage. Some cynics remarked that making up – i.e. rough sex – had maybe lost its magic towards the end.

Burton, too sick to attend the hearing, excused himself with a physician's certificate. As had happened with Sybil, he was extremely generous with the divorce settlement. Elizabeth got to keep their yacht, which she transformed into a temporary floating holiday home. Additionally, she kept the $15-million worth of jewellery and personal effects – and adopted daughter Maria, who had been shunted around for the entirety of her short life. Burton also set up more than substantial trust funds for his and Elizabeth's children.

After the divorce, Elizabeth submitted to a handful of interviews in which she explained how sad she was that her favourite marriage had ended – she then returned to Henry Wynberg. Though Elizabeth had told the press that losing Burton had been the 'second-worst day' of her life (the worst being the day Mike Todd died, a point she was still putting forward as this book was being prepared), she was soon back to letting her heart rule her head, playing the tearful, disillusioned little girl who had mislaid one toy and then stumbled upon another that she did not really want but that would keep her occupied until something better came along. Neither had she severed her ties with Burton completely, having left a clause in her will instructing for them to be buried together, when the time came, next to his parents in a Welsh village cemetery – whether he wanted this or not.

The fact that Henry Wynberg only bought a pair of matching friendship rings should have given Elizabeth an inkling towards his intentions, even more so when he told reporters that he had made the mistake of marrying before and was not in any hurry to do so again. Elizabeth hoped to persuade him otherwise by getting him to move into a mini-mansion in the Hollywood hills, which she 'kinked up' by having the bedroom walls decorated with metallic wallpaper so that they could watch distorted images of one another whilst they were having sex. She also renewed her friendship with Max Lerner, now approaching 70, and he acted as some sort of technical adviser on her latest relationship.

According to Kitty Kelley, who interviewed Lerner, Elizabeth is claimed to have remarked of Wynberg, 'I know that no one else likes him, but I don't care . . . He fucks me beautifully, and I know he's not a big mind like you are, but he takes care of me, and that's what I need.' Peter Lawford was another regular visitor to the house, probably hoping that this affair would work out, if for no other reason than to keep Elizabeth away from his teenage son. What she did not know was that Wynberg was reported to be sneaking girls into the house when Elizabeth was not home.

Richard Burton might have been 'deteriorating fast', according to his friends in Switzerland, but his libido showed no signs of abating. In October 1974, he announced his engagement to 38-year-old Princess Elizabeth of Yugoslavia – tidings that resulted in his first

Elizabeth taking to bed with back pains, for which traction was prescribed, though she vehemently denied that she had invented the ailment to gain sympathy. The first to arrive to comfort her was Sara Taylor, living in Palm Springs since Francis's death, then Liza Todd and Christopher Wilding. Elizabeth also arranged for someone to infringe upon Burton and his new romance over the festive season. Her adopted daughter Maria, who had played a minor role in the Burtons' lives so far, was dispatched to Belgium. Maria stayed with Burton and Princess Elizabeth in Verviers, near Liège – whilst Howard Taylor and his family stayed at Elizabeth's chalet in Gstaad.

With Burton out of the picture and the media circus put on hold for the time being, Elizabeth's career progressed: for the first time in years, the critics took her acting seriously. She did a sterling job co-compèring *That's Entertainment!*, and, although the venture was a commercial flop, she was superb in George Cukor's *The Blue Bird* (1976).

Adhering closer to Maurice Maeterlinck's allegorical fairy tale than its predecessors, this $15-million remake was shot on location in and around Leningrad during the spring of 1975, finally realising Elizabeth's long-standing dream of working in Russia. She waived her fee, such was her eagerness, settling for a percentage of the box-office receipts, covered her own expenses and spent over $10,000 of her own money on her costumes. At points in the film, in which she plays four parts – Light, Mother, Witch and Maternal Love – she is almost unrecognisable. The British and American cast was headed by Ava Gardner (who on account of the studio's spartan conditions had to share her dressing-room), Robert Morley and Cicely Tyson. Playing one of the children Mytyl was seven-year-old Patsy Kensit, already a movie stalwart. Thirty years later, she told *Attitude* magazine's Andrew Fraser:

> She was my first encounter with gayness. She was surrounded by this gay mafia. Raymondo, her stylist, her make-up artists, all the other helpers – they would all dress in the same colour

as Elizabeth. If Elizabeth was in red, they'd all be wearing it. She was my first experience of divadom. The big diamond that Richard Burton bought her, she used to take it off her finger and say, 'Patsy, catch!'

Elizabeth was accompanied on the trip by Henry Wynberg – but only just. Her beau had recently been arraigned on several counts of grand theft, accused of turning back the milometer on cars he had sold. Following an appeal, these charges were commuted to misdemeanours, with a $1,000 fine and three years probation, which normally would have prohibited him from leaving the country. A second appeal appears to have overturned this to enable him to travel with Elizabeth, who might have vouched for him by declaring him to be professionally involved with *The Blue Bird* as its stills photographer.

Wynberg must have felt awkward when Elizabeth insisted upon stopping off en route to Russia at Gstaad to check up on Richard Burton. Princess Elizabeth had just discovered that he had been cheating on her whilst filming in Nice with a black *Playboy* model named Jeanne Bell. Not wishing to evoke a scandal – which prompts the question, why get involved with a known lecher like Burton in the first place? – the princess had broken off their engagement. In Leningrad, a possible reunion with her ex-husband occupied Elizabeth's every waking minute when she was not working, and Wynberg must have seen the writing on the wall as she feigned interest in him.

The Blue Bird wound up early in August – several weeks behind schedule due to Elizabeth being laid low with viral flu and then amoebic dysentery. Though illness had prevented her from eating properly whilst filming, and though her beauty would never fade, even in old age, she had piled on the pounds. Unflattering photographs – usually of her stuffing her face – began appearing in the press. Then, later in the month, everything fell apart for the Burton-Bell, Taylor-Wynberg liaisons when Burton and Elizabeth met up in Lausanne to discuss 'business affairs'. For her, living with a man was out of the question: despite her many affairs, she had been brought up to respect the sanctity of marriage and was still old-fashioned in this respect. What she now wanted, she told the press, was the *stability* of marriage. This, of course, had never worked before, and she was arguably too set in her ways for it to do so now. Cynics suggested that the rendezvous and its aftermath was a deliberate ploy to resurrect their respective flagging careers – particularly when they announced their plans to remarry almost at once.

According to Richard Burton, speaking later to *People* magazine, within days of their getting back together they were 'at it hammer and tongs' – proof enough that they had never stopped loving one another. Syndicated columns the world over published lurid details of their revived spats, along with extracts from their syrupy love letters. They travelled to Johannesburg for a charity poetry-reading event and from there to Botswana's Chobe National Park, on the banks of the Zambezi. It was there, in a 20-minute ceremony conducted by the district commissioner, that they were married for the second time, on 10 October 1975.

This time there was no exclusive Helen Rose outfit, and the 'limo' was a Land Rover. The bride wore a floor-length green gown decorated with guinea-fowl feathers, a gift from Burton's late brother, Ifor Jenkins. The groom wore white trousers and a scarlet sweater – he claimed to have been on the wagon for the past year but was sozzled at ten in the morning. His wedding gift this time around was a 25-carat *pink* diamond, reported to have cost $1.1 million – which Elizabeth announced she did *not* want! Hoping to curry favour with her critics, sharpening their quills in readiness for a renewed attack on the Burton-Taylor spending mania, she decided to sell the bauble and use the money for charitable purposes. Because Botswana had given her the happiest day of her life since marrying Burton the first time, she pledged $1 million towards building a clinic in Kasane, the town adjacent to the park. 'They need one more than I need another ring,' she told reporters. It was an impressive gesture, but nothing more. When the project was inexplicably cancelled – by which time Elizabeth and Burton were virtually history and the location no longer regarded in the same romantic light – the health ministry controlling the region was promised $45,000 but only received $25,000. It was a generous donation all the same but would have been more appreciated had this amount been promised in the first place, instead of the community's hopes being built up and then dashed as they had.

The honeymoon comprised a wildlife safari, too much for the ailing Richard Burton, who came down with malaria. His life was ostensibly saved by an Italian-Egyptian pharmacist who had to be flown in by helicopter. Around Elizabeth's age, her name was Chenima Samin; Elizabeth shortened this to Chen Sam and quickly formed a close bond with her, so much so that when the couple returned to London to celebrate Burton's 50th birthday, Chen Sam accompanied them. She remained an integral part of Elizabeth's entourage as her publicist (replacing Dick Hanley, Mike Todd's publicist, whom she had retained and who had died the previous year). Chen Sam would serve Elizabeth faithfully until her own death in 1996.

The new marriage lasted all of three months, and, as before, Burton was the one doing the straying. On the Swiss ski slopes, he met racing driver James Hunt's pretty 29-year-old wife Suzy, a leggy former model. In January 1976, when he opened in the Broadway production of Peter Shaffer's *Equus*, she was at his side. Not long afterwards, Suzy obtained a quickie Haitian divorce.

So ended arguably the most extravagant pairing in show business. Over the last decade, the Burtons had raked in an estimated $100 million from mostly mediocre movies and shrewd investments with heavy tax concessions. Seemingly without a care in the world or much thought for anyone but themselves, they had ploughed approximately three-quarters of this back into the economy with their greed for razzmatazz and the media spotlight.

Pretending not to be affected by Burton and his new love interest, Elizabeth played him at his own game by having a fling with a tall, dark and handsome 37-year-old Maltese advertising executive named Peter Darmanin. The pair met in The Cave, a disco in the basement of Gstaad's Hotel Olden. According to press reports, they danced all evening, despite Elizabeth's bad back. And according to Darmanin, Elizabeth summoned him to her chalet the next morning, and they made love at once. Their affair lasted all of seven weeks, with Darmanin telling *People* magazine in 1976 that with Elizabeth's constant demands and acute possessiveness it had seemed like seven years. 'She was passionate in bed,' he said, 'and I must confess we didn't sleep much during those seven weeks.' It all ended when Elizabeth slapped him during a barney and one of her diamonds slashed his forehead. Darmanin also claimed that, like her character in *Suddenly, Last Summer*, Elizabeth had once stubbed out a cigarette in the palm of his hand.

The break-up coincided with Richard Burton's escalating problems while in *Equus* in New York. His first stage performances in 12 years were well received by the critics, a far cry from most of the work he had done with Elizabeth. Even the feisty, frequently non-complimentary *New York Times*'s Bosley Crowther observed that *Equus* was the best thing that Burton had *ever* done. However, such plaudits coupled with his failed attempts to stay on the wagon placed Burton at an all-time low, and in February 1976 he called Elizabeth and begged her to fly out to New York. Incapable of resisting the command, she was on the next plane – only to discover that the real reason he wanted her there was to ask her to her face for a divorce so that he could marry Suzy Hunt. Elizabeth returned to California at once and 'reconnected' with Henry Wynberg as if nothing had happened since she had last seen him.

Wynberg, who had been shunted aside for Peter Darmanin and then Richard Burton, must have been a sucker for punishment, for no sooner had he and Elizabeth set up home – again – at a rented house in Los Angeles's exclusive Trousdale suburb than there was another contender for her favours. In March 1976, the two dined with Secretary of State Henry Kissinger and his wife (she and Burton had met them the previous year during a lightning charity trip to Israel), and it was Kissinger who added Elizabeth's name, but not

Wynberg's, to the guest list for another fund-raiser, this time in aid of the American Ballet Theater. The high-profile bash took place in April at Washington's Kennedy Center. Elizabeth wore over $1 million of jewels and, according to the *Washington Post*, 'swept into Washington like Cleopatra into Rome'. This was followed by another lavish party at the Iranian embassy, hosted by Ardeshir Zahedi, the country's ambassador to the United States.

Zahedi, a 48-year-old bachelor formerly married to the shah's daughter, always maintained that his relationship with Elizabeth was platonic. If this was the case, he did little at the time to convince the world. Over the next two weeks, the pair were virtually inseparable: they were snapped dancing in nightclubs, holding hands and kissing. Zahedi was Elizabeth's date for the New York premiere of *The Blue Bird*, and she was his 'special guest' when the US–Iran Air Service proposed a 140-strong celebrities-only inaugural flight to Tehran. Their relationship hit a serious snag, however, when rumours that Elizabeth might have been looking for husband number six reached the shah's ears. Having already suffered the extreme humiliation of Zahedi divorcing his favourite daughter, the shah was in no mood to tolerate his cultural representative being involved with a neo-Jewish woman of Elizabeth's reputation. Zahedi was instructed not just to sever ties with her, but to refrain from accompanying the guests on the flight to Tehran. Elizabeth travelled there anyhow, stayed at the Hilton and snarled at a reporter who erroneously addressed her as 'Mrs Burton' – this just about summed up her one and only trip to Iran. And, as before, she returned to Henry Wynberg.

The reunion was brief, Elizabeth learning that Wynberg had been recently arrested on 'undisclosed moral charges'. On 16 February, the *Los Angeles Herald-Examiner* (and numerous syndicated columnists who almost certainly would not have picked up on the story had it not been for his association with Elizabeth) reported that Wynberg had been questioned by police in regards to his conduct. As would later happen with Michael Jackson, Elizabeth dropped him like the proverbial hot brick. In February 1977, Wynberg was arraigned in Los Angeles for having a party with four girls, at which there was drugs and alcohol. He would later be found guilty of a criminal charge, serve ninety days in the Los Angeles County Jail and be put on probation for five years. Wynberg subsequently sued the *National Enquirer* over a story that he had 'exploited for commercial gain' his relationship with Elizabeth but lost when the federal judge noted that he had a criminal record and 'a reputation for taking advantage of women generally'.

During the early summer of 1976, Elizabeth began taking an active interest in American politics, having discovered that the Washington social register had just as much to offer as its Hollywood and New York counterparts. In New York, she attended a Democratic fund-raiser in support of Jimmy Carter during his run-up to the presidential candidate selections, declaring that she did not *dislike* his rival Gerald Ford, only that Carter was the more intelligent of the two! The following day she lunched with Vice-President Nelson Rockerfeller in Washington, then returned to New York to lend support to Congresswoman Bella Abzug.

It was by way of her political leanings that Elizabeth met the next important man in her life – and a member of the enemy camp. She and 49-year-old Republican John Warner had bumped into each other a couple of times on the society circuit. This was the year of the American bicentenary, and on 8 July 1976, to honour the occasion, President Ford and Queen Elizabeth hosted a dinner party at the British embassy in Washington. Anyone who was anyone was invited. Because she did not have a partner, Elizabeth was 'fixed up' with the six-foot, prematurely greying would-be politician, currently director of the Bicentenary Committee. This apparently did not sit well with the British ambassador Sir Peter Ramsbotham, who is thought to have instructed Elizabeth to dress down for the occasion and not to 'overdo' the jewels. Likewise, Warner was discreetly asked to keep her in check – the last thing Ramsbotham wanted was the queen of England being upstaged by the queen of the movies!

Born in 1927, the son of an Episcopalian minister, Warner shared Elizabeth's star sign; she believed that this was a lucky omen after her recent troubles. Warner had dropped out of high school to serve with the US Navy towards the end of the Second World War and had later served with the marines in Korea. Demobbed, he had studied law in his native Virginia, and in 1957 had been appointed an assistant US attorney for Washington. That year he had also married Catherine, daughter of the Pittsburgh multimillionaire philanthropist Paul Mellon. It was reputedly through Mellon's influence with the Nixon administration that Warner had been appointed secretary of the US Navy in 1972. The following year he and his wife had divorced, the major source of dissension between them being Warner's support of the Vietnam War, which Catherine opposed. Theirs had been the most amiable split imaginable. In return for Warner not contesting the action, Paul Mellon had awarded him custody of the three children for most of the year, the couple's $750,000 house in Georgetown, their 2,700-acre farm at Middleburg and a lifelong income from investment valued at around $7 million.

After the Washington bash, Elizabeth was invited to John Warner's farm, an hour's drive from the city. Pride of place went to the swimming pool he had built in one of the barns, his 600-strong herd of Hereford cattle and a 500-acre wildlife park. Very soon the place would be 'Taylorised', with the addition of a screening room and disco, and some of Warner's conservative prints would be replaced by her collection of grand masters.

Theirs certainly was a classic case of opposites attracting. Warner was as reserved in his tastes, beliefs and conduct as Elizabeth was boisterous, racy and forthright. She was also a converted Jew and a Democrat, which did not exactly fit in with some of his policies. They had a whirlwind romance – was there any other kind for Elizabeth? – and when Warner privately proposed marriage, she was not slow in accepting, even though her divorce from Richard Burton would not be finalised until the August of that year.

Meanwhile, Elizabeth flew to Vienna to shoot the film version of Stephen Sondheim's cult stage musical *A Little Night Music*. She played Desiree Armfeldt, an ageing actress who wants to retire from the stage and get married. Playing her mother was British acting institution Hermione Gingold, who had never hidden her disdain for Elizabeth during her adventure with Richard Burton, and fireworks were anticipated when these 'connoisseurs of gentlemen' met on the set. But Gingold surprised everyone by declaring Elizabeth to be 'absolutely adorable' and 'divine to work with'. Elizabeth sang 'Send in the Clowns' beautifully – better, in fact, than anyone other than Frank Sinatra, who took the song into the charts – and she also formed a close friendship with British actress Lesley-Anne Down.

The press, unable to report any catfights, made up for their disappointment by drawing attention to Elizabeth's appearance, especially her 'fuller' figure, highlighted in the film when her lover (Len Cariou) laments the fact that she is too attractive by crooning, 'If only she'd been faded . . . If only she'd been fat!' The *Daily Mirror*'s film critic observed after the March 1978 premiere:

> What brought us all dangerously close to rolling in the aisles was the forlorn attempt to squeeze Elizabeth Taylor's quart-sized goodies into a pint-sized ensemble. Tortuously nipped in here, flowing out there, heaving out you know where – it only required heavy dark-blue eye-shadow to complete the impression of a superannuated Madame.

In Vienna, Elizabeth was joined by Maria Todd, now 19, and, unusually for once, although still claiming to despise his mother's opulent lifestyle, Michael Wilding Jr turned up with new girlfriend Joanna and their baby Naomi. It was whilst she was enjoying this little family reunion that she received tidings of Richard Burton's marriage to Suzy Hunt on 22 August 1976. The newlyweds added insult to injury by having the ceremony in Arlington in Virginia, the state where *she* had found the recent love of her life. Suzy might also have had one of Elizabeth's wedding speeches at the back of her mind when she told reporters, 'I've promised that I'll be with him all the time and do all the things a good wife should.' Her efforts would be in vain: Burton, like Elizabeth, had never listened to reason and was too far gone in his habits to change.

Elizabeth called Burton at once, ostensibly to congratulate him, though her sincerity must be doubted. Robert Stephens, her co-star in *A Little Night Music* (1977), had just walked off the picture, and Elizabeth wanted Burton to replace him – arguably her first step in wooing him away from his new wife and mindless of her own feelings for John Warner. Unable to cope with what she regarded as Burton's ultimate rejection (though they would stay in close contact until the end), Elizabeth summoned Warner to Vienna, and on 10 October their engagement was made official. From this point in their relationship, there is little doubt that while Elizabeth was using Warner (as she had Wynberg and Darmanin) as a stopgap in the hope that Burton would be hers once more, her celebrity status was arguably beneficial to his aspiring political career, though his affection appears to have been genuine.

Elizabeth and John Warner were married on 4 December 1976 at the top of a steep incline on his land, where he had proposed to her, and which they had named 'Engagement Hill'. Later, she told the story of how they had driven there in his jeep to watch the sunset and been caught in a storm, and the moment had been too magical for him to ignore. Elizabeth dressed for the occasion in what passed for the typical garb of the farmer's wife: cashmere dress and turban, suede boots, and a fur-trimmed coat, all in her favourite shades of lavender and grey. The simple ceremony was conducted by Reverend Neale Morgan – the couple's second choice after one of his colleagues refused to officiate for a woman who had been married six times already. Reverend Morgan read Psalm 23 for Warner and a passage from the Book of Ruth for Elizabeth. The guests included Warner's son, a few friends and farmhands – and most of the Hereford cows, who followed the party up the hill. For the seventh time, Elizabeth told reporters that she had never felt this much love before – and, yes, this one would last the course. There was also a prenuptial agreement – one which, the couple said, would protect their children's futures, because neither would have to pay the other a penny in the event of a divorce. They also made arrangements to be buried together – Elizabeth had clearly forgotten that she had already reserved a place for her mortal remains next to Richard Burton.

Burton had wooed Elizabeth with paintings and jewels. John Warner gave her a corn silo emblazoned with 'John Loves Elizabeth', whilst she offered him a prize-winning bull and two cows. The honeymoon, extending over the Christmas period, was spent at Elizabeth's chalet in Gstaad – again, it was as if being in close proximity to Burton was obligatory. John Warner later claimed that he had never met any of Elizabeth's ex-husbands and that the only one worthy of her had been Mike Todd – no doubt because he was the only one who had never got around to divorcing her and was no longer around to broadcast what she had really been like to live with. He did meet Burton, however, during that festive season, and is on record as having said that he found him 'a fascinating individual'. Aware of Elizabeth's obsession with Burton, he was probably afraid of saying anything else.

In January 1977, John Warner embarked on his first political campaign, attempting to raise funds for the Republican Party and further his aims to become a senatorial nominee. When Elizabeth boarded his Greyhound bus – apparently the first time she had been on one – cynics suggested that having submitted herself to such a drop in standards, using what amounted to public transport, her marriage would have no chance of succeeding, because Warner would now expect her to slum it. She liked to believe this husband as dominant as some of her predecessors, telling *People* magazine, 'He can make me do anything he wants, except make me pregnant.' When it emerged that Warner had begun dictating to her how to conduct herself in public, it became pretty clear that their marriage *was* doomed. Asking Elizabeth to lay off the booze and not curse like a docker whilst on the campaign trail was one thing. Warner, however, not only forbade her to wear the famed Taylor-Burton jewels, he also ordered her not to dress in her favourite lavender, grey and purple – the latter, he declared, because this denoted royalty, which contravened the edicts of the Republican Party. For the time being, she complied, even selling the Taylor-Burton

Diamond for $3 million, three times the original purchase price.

There was a brief return to the Hollywood spotlight that spring when Elizabeth appeared in CBS's *An All-Star Tribute to Elizabeth Taylor*. For one evening, she stopped being a farmer's wife, donned her baubles and permitted herself to be feted by peers and colleagues. The evening, attended by the likes of June Allyson, Margaret O'Brien, Janet Leigh and the Paul Newmans – genuine friends who cared about her – raised over $100,000, which she donated towards a hospital wing that would bear her name. During the summer, she was paid $300,000 for a cameo appearance in television movie *Victory at Entebbe* (1976), her second outing with Helmut Berger. She handed over her salary to one of her Jewish charities as a tribute to those involved with the Israeli commando raid on the Ugandan town, which had ended the airport siege of 1976. It subsequently emerged (courtesy of a statement leaked by Simcha Dinitz, the Israeli ambassador to the USA) that Elizabeth had offered to fly to Kampala and personally negotiate with dictator Idi Amin for the release of the 104 hostages – if necessary, offering herself in exchange for their release. And she would have done so had it not been for the intervention of the Israeli troops. An admirable stance indeed.

The first cracks in the Warners' marriage appeared in February 1978 at a pre-46th birthday party thrown by Elizabeth's couturier Halston at New York's infamous Studio 54, an establishment renowned for its 'anything goes' attitude towards exhibitionist sex and drugs. Elizabeth must have had a very good idea how the evening would turn out and might have deliberately wished to wind up her strait-laced husband by trying to bring him into contact with the 'real' world. A dozen well-endowed hunks, naked but for sequined posing-pouches, and some with joints dangling from the corners of their mouths, scattered gardenia petals in the couple's path as they entered the auditorium with its glitter ball. Several more wheeled in a 500-pound chocolate cake, shaped like Elizabeth's busty upper half. She hugged Andy Warhol – now forgiven for trying to tape her in Rome – then picked up a knife and began portioning out the cake. Warhol later observed in his *Interview* magazine, 'She blew out the candles, sliced off her right tit and gave it to Halston. The television cameras zoomed in as he ate it – then John Warner ran away.' The dancing and fun continued until the early hours, the atmosphere heavy with the stench of poppers and Elizabeth bebopping with a bevvy of gay porn stars, until Warner put his foot down and said that they were leaving. For him, the writing was by then clearly on the wall.

On 6 January 1978, John Warner announced that he would be running for the Virginia senatorial Republican candidacy. Needless to say, he had to be seen to be living an unblemished life. His main rivals were Linwood Holton, a former governor, Nathan Miller, the state senator, and, the favourite, Richard D. Obenshain, former state GOP chairman. At that stage, most Virginians regarded Warner as the least likely candidate to win the election. To pay for his campaign, he is alleged to have sold off 40 acres of farmland.

During the balloting of 3 June 1978, most of Warner's rivals withdrew from the competition, including Linwood Holton, leaving Richard D. Obenshain in the clear lead, with Nathan Miller and Warner lagging behind. Two ballots later, Warner and Obenshain were the only two in the running. Then, after two more ballots, Warner's hopes were dashed when he lost to Obenshain at the Republican convention. Seemingly unperturbed, Elizabeth told a press gathering, 'I'm not worried. Something's bound to come up!'

Though disappointed by her husband's defeat, Elizabeth took some consolation in returning to work, flying to Hollywood to appear in another television drama, this time as its star. In *Return Engagement* (1978), she played a college professor of ancient history who falls in love with a student (Joseph Bottoms). Interviewed by the *Los Angeles Times*, she spoke of her own curiosity value – for example, during the Warner campaign trail, one overweight, unidentified matron (doubtless of media invention) is supposed to have quipped, 'All my life I've wanted to look like Liz Taylor, and now I do!'

'People are looking for wrinkles and pimples, and I don't disappoint them,' Elizabeth said. 'They want to see if my eyes are really violet, or bloodshot, or both. Then they can go home and say, "I saw Liz Taylor. And you know what? She ain't so hot!" And do you know what? They're right!' She was, of course, selling herself short: fat or thin, young or old, she never lost her looks.

No sooner had Elizabeth completed the film than Obenshain died in a plane crash, on 2 August 1978, remarkably similar to the one that had claimed Mike Todd. Within days of the tragedy, with the press repeating Elizabeth's chilling prediction 'Something's bound to come up!', Warner inherited the Republican candidacy, and the campaigning started all over again. The results, announced on 7 November, were close: Warner won by a majority of just 4,721 votes out of an estimated 1.25 million. But his victory was to be deferred for a recount, the results of which would not be announced until the end of the month. However, this never took place. A board of elections ruling stated that recounts had to be financed by the losing party, in this instance to the tune of $120,000. As the Democrat candidate could not afford this, his only option was to concede.

Warner's election to the Capitol sounded the death-knell on his already shaky marriage. His senatorial work would keep him away from home for long periods, and when they were together, Elizabeth – largely responsible for his redoubtable success – was compelled to take a back seat and watch someone else enjoy the limelight for the first time in her life.

In March 1979, the 'farmer and his wife' were interviewed in their kitchen by Barbara Walters for her television chat show – a potentially uneasy occasion, because Warner and Walters had once been an item. The scenario was staged to make the most of the rural setting: Warner's hacking jacket was slung over the back of the chair, and Elizabeth wore an old-fashioned smock to make her look a little more homely. When Walters intimated that marrying a serial divorcee might prove detrimental to his career, Warner's reaction was, 'I suppose that if she'd had six or seven consecutive marriages of just two or three years apiece, that might have frightened me away.' He then stated that Elizabeth had been married to Richard Burton for sixteen years and not ten. Obviously, Warner had not done his homework – otherwise he would have realised that the marriage to Nicky Hilton had lasted all of eight months and that *all* the others had very quickly hit much-publicised snags.

Neither did John Warner do Elizabeth any favours by publicly referring to her as 'My Little Heifer' and 'Chicken Fat' – following in the tradition of Montgomery Clift (Bessie Mae) and Mike Todd (My Jewish Broad), this simply was not funny, particularly as her passion for junk food had pushed her weight up to 180 pounds. The press were merciless: if Elizabeth's own husband could poke fun at her, then so could they. Before and after photographs appeared in newspapers and magazines. She was snapped looking obese but elegant during a soiree with Studio 54 owner Steve Rubell – this was the shot, reversed and with Rubell brushed out, that featured on the cover of Kenneth Anger's acclaimed *Hollywood Babylon II* (E.P. Dutton, 1984). Inside the book was a much less flattering 'study' of Elizabeth, caught unawares and literally stuffing her face, with the caption, 'Eat it, eat it, open your mouth and feed it.' Comedienne Joan Rivers famously quipped, 'Elizabeth Taylor has more chins than there are in the Chinese phone book!' On stage in Las Vegas, Debbie Reynolds offered dietary advice: 'Know what works for me, girls? I've stuck a photograph of Elizabeth Taylor on my refrigerator door!' Other comics joked that there was going to be a sequel to *Around the World in Eighty Days* – with Elizabeth playing the hot-air balloon.

Such remarks *must* have rankled, yet in her memoirs Elizabeth writes, 'Since I wasn't working as an actress, I felt there was no reason for me to look any particular way or weigh any particular amount.'

The Warners' political rallies were hugely successful, with record turnouts. Just as Eddie Fisher fans had latterly flocked to his shows to see *her*, so the voting public were more interested in the spectacle of Elizabeth Taylor than they were in her dour by comparison silver-haired consort. Over the coming months, she attended wives' groups, judged pie-making and baby contests, opened stores, fetes and charity drives, and was hospitalised several times for her efforts – following a fall from a horse, with recurrences of her old back problems, and with repetitive strain injury from shaking thousands of hands. More seriously, she very nearly choked to death on a chicken bone. Yet she claimed to have loved every minute, and there is no doubting the enormous impact she had in putting John Warner's name on the map. Even the somewhat stuffy *Wall Street Journal* observed, 'Mr Warner's rapid political rise is credited to the enormous publicity attracted by his famous wife – not only in Virginia, but also in the high society of neighbouring Washington.' She also asserted early in these campaigns that she was not going to be one of those politician's wives who sits back at rallies and lets her husband rant on, seemingly without opinions of her own. In February 1980, the *Sunday Express* covered the GOP's Tidewater Conference in Maryland. The topic was Warner's sexist opinion that only men should be allowed into the services if draft registration be reintroduced. The George and Martha-style bickering went as follows:

ELIZABETH: I'm a lady who likes to fight, and I think women should go into the trenches if they could.

WARNER: Elizabeth, you don't have a vote on this issue . . .

ELIZABETH: *You* invited me here!

WARNER: I'm sure that Abe Lincoln, the great emancipator, would see my view . . .

ELIZABETH: *Abe Lincoln*? How many years do you want to go back?

WARNER: I'm proud to say that when *I* was secretary of the navy, I opened up more jobs for women than they'd ever had before . . .

ELIZABETH: 'Rosie the Riveter', you mean? Women have been in active control since year one. Look at Margaret Thatcher. Look at Cleopatra!

She might have added, 'Look at Elizabeth Taylor!' had not Warner signalled for her to shut up. When he did this, she turned on him and said, 'Don't you *dare* steady *me* with that all-dominating hand of yours!' to a massive roar of appreciation from the crowd. If the writing had not been on the wall for John Warner after the Studio 54 party, it certainly was now.

THIRTEEN

IN THE FOOTSTEPS
OF TALLULAH

E LIZABETH'S ALWAYS DELICATE CONSTITUTION SUFFERED
a severe setback on 8 July 1979 when Michael Wilding died,
aged 67, of a brain haemorrhage following a fall at his Chichester
home. She flew with Liza Todd to England to join her sons, and the
eulogy she delivered at Wilding's funeral was heartfelt and genuine.
Unlike with Nicky Hilton and Eddie Fisher, there had been no
animosity between them since their divorce, and they had always
spoken of one another with great respect. Elizabeth was also upset
to learn, after the post mortem, that Wilding had had an aneurism
for many years – even whilst they had been married – which could
have killed him at any time.

She coped with this loss as she did most of the catastrophes in her
life – with an excess of pills and booze. Wilding's death, however,
triggered off another addiction that by the spring of 1980 looked
like spiralling out of control: comfort eating. She checked in at the
Palm Air Spa, at Florida's Pampano Beach, and within a month had
shed 28 pounds. Then she set about sifting through the scripts that
had accumulated during her absence.

Of all the films Elizabeth had made over the last three years, only *A Little Night Music* had attracted half-decent reviews, and as such she was naturally suspicious of taking the plunge again. It was Agatha Christie's *The Mirror Crack'd* (1980) that took her fancy the most, and she immediately signed the contract because she would be working once again with her great friend Rock Hudson, who had enjoyed tremendous success on the small screen since his career as a matinee idol had ended, most notably in *McMillan*. Now, he and Elizabeth (replacing Natalie Wood, at four times the salary Wood had been offered) headed a star-studded cast in this high-camp romp, filmed in England in May to June 1980, the action taking place close to the fictional village of St Mary Mead, home to the celebrated Miss Marple. Adding to the glittering roster were Tony Curtis, Edward Fox, Geraldine Chaplin and the scintillating Kim Novak.

It is a gem of a production, probably the best Elizabeth appeared in during her later career. It also provides another interesting actress-character juxtaposition, in this instance Elizabeth playing fading movie icon Marina Gregg, making her comeback after many years in the wilderness. The action takes place during June 1953, coronation month, when a group of Hollywood eccentrics take over an old mansion to shoot a movie about Mary, Queen of Scots – or 'Mary Queen of Sluts' as she is referred to – played by Novak, who Elizabeth could not stand. This only makes the banter between them more realistic and hilarious. Elizabeth is not just acting when she spits at her rival, 'In that wig, you could play Lassie. What are you supposed to be? A birthday cake? Too bad everybody's had a piece!' To which Mary responds, 'Chin up, darling– both of them!' Elizabeth also added one plum line herself, to 'punish' Rock Hudson for saying in an interview that Doris Day would always remain his favourite leading lady. Gazing at her reflection in the dressing-table mirror while he looks on, po-faced, she sighs, 'Bags, bags, go away. Come right back on Doris Day!'

Because of its glittering pantheon of stars, the Kent location of *The Mirror Crack'd* was a fiercely guarded secret – neither Rock nor Elizabeth were interested in speaking to reporters: he on account of the persistent gay slurs, she because of the rumour that her marriage was on the rocks. It was, and now that the big-screen acting bug had bitten again, Elizabeth realised what she had been missing since meeting Warner. In the July, she was at his side, feigning the role of dutiful wife at the Republican National Convention that nominated Ronald Reagan as the presidential candidate. Reagan had given up a successful acting career to enter the political arena, since which time his wife, former MGM contract player Nancy Davis, had done likewise to support him. Nancy, however, was not the world's biggest still-working movie star, and Elizabeth knew exactly where she belonged – and it was not in an environment far removed from the one she had spent 30 years monopolising.

Since their second divorce, Elizabeth had been on good terms with Richard Burton. His marriage to Suzy Hunt had floundered, and he returned to what he had done before Elizabeth burst into his life – a Broadway revival of *Camelot*. Taking Burton's advice that she would make a fine stage actress, Elizabeth began searching for a suitable role. Eventually, she plumped for Regina Giddens in Lillian Hellman's *The Little Foxes*, on an unprecedented salary of $50,000 a week. The director (her second choice upon learning that *Who's Afraid of Virginia Woolf?* director Mike Nichols was committed to another project) was Austin Pendleton. Her co-stars included Maureen Stapleton, Anthony Zerbe and Joe Panazecki.

The last major production of *The Little Foxes* had been in 1939 when Tallulah Bankhead had, in her own words, 'taken Broadway by the balls' and made a lifelong enemy of Bette Davis, Bette having been contracted for the film version. Tallulah (who died six months after watching Elizabeth 'murder' Flora Goforth in *Boom!*) had described Regina as 'a rapacious, soulless, sadistic bitch who would have cut her own mother's throat'. Back in 1939, months before the outbreak of the Second World War, the play, a Communist masterpiece, had had very powerful political implications. Hellman's Deep South characters, spearheaded by the obnoxious Regina, were capitalists who achieved their ruthless aims by deceiving, cheating, exploiting black labour, lying and even resorting to murder in order to make huge profits in their cotton mill. Times had changed, and parts of the script had to be amended to suit Elizabeth's less forceful on-stage persona.

Lillian Hellman had been so impressed by Tallulah Bankhead's performances – 408 in all – that she had forbidden anyone else to portray Regina on Broadway until that point, and given Elizabeth's generally bad reviews over the last few years it would appear that Hellman only favoured the Hollywood star because of the enormous revenue the hiked-up ticket prices would bring. To ensure that she raked in as much as possible from the production, Elizabeth formed her own theatre company with impresario Zev Bufman, who had recently triumphed in Washington with a revival of *Brigadoon*. The try-outs opened at the Florida Playhouse, Fort Lauderdale, on account of its proximity to the Spa, just in case Elizabeth needed to pop back there for treatment.

The premiere took place on 27 February 1981, Elizabeth's 49th birthday, and constituted her toughest challenge in years. Richard Burton had complained about her inability to project her voice during the early scenes of *Cleopatra*, so she was generally expected to die on her feet. Many people believed that she had accepted the play to court the necessary publicity in order to get another half-decent film role, and once she did, she would abandon Regina. Indeed, it was also thought that Bufman already had another 'Hollywood stalwart' waiting in the wings to take over. Others who had worked with her and experienced her 'indispositions' believed that her fickle health would not survive the course – even Bufman himself must have been worried that she would succumb to illness, because he took out a $125,000 insurance policy with Lloyds of London.

Those who had not seen Elizabeth in a while and who were expecting a fat frump to come stomping onto the stage were in for a surprise. By cautious dieting, she had lost 40 pounds and looked as svelte as she had throughout most of *Cleopatra*. In fact, she was so good as the bitchy, conniving Regina – with scarcely a jewel in sight – that by the time *The Little Foxes* opened at Washington's

Kennedy Center, all 47 performances had been sold out. The first-night audience was, courtesy of John Warner, a political showcase attended by President and Nancy Reagan, George Bush senior, the future president, and most of the senate.

The play transferred to New York's Martin Beck Theater on 7 May, where it would run until 6 September – 123 performances, barring a break when Elizabeth was laid low with respiratory problems. It then moved to Los Angeles for two weeks, a sojourn that enabled her to spend a few afternoons taping five episodes of *General Hospital*, her favourite daytime soap. She played the wealthy wife of an eccentric scientist who eventually bequeaths her fortune to the hospital – and promptly donated her $20,000 fee to two Virginia clinics.

In Los Angeles, there should have been an opening-night party hosted by Rock Hudson, but this was not to be. Rock had secretly complained of feeling unwell whilst shooting *The Mirror Crack'd* and during the flight back to Los Angeles, but his doctor – the ubiquitous Rex Kennamer – had diagnosed nothing more serious than the flu. We now know that this was the onset of heart disease, though he continued to work, still enjoying tremendous success as one of television's leading lights. *McMillan* had run its course, but he had starred in *The Martian Chronicles* with Roddy McDowall and, more recently, in the father-son detective series *The Devlin Connection* with Jack Scalia. He was halfway through taping the second series of this when he was hospitalised on 30 October 1981 with severe chest pains. Two days later, he underwent triple-bypass surgery – the prognosis was not good. His first visitor at Cedars-Sinai Hospital was Elizabeth, who was sufficiently concerned to consider pulling out of *The Little Foxes* to spend more time with him. Rock persuaded her not to and, against all odds, pulled through. The incident was a turning point in Elizabeth's life – from then on she who had thrived on unrelenting selfishness would begin to put others first.

Rock's first public outing following his illness was early in the December, when he accompanied Elizabeth to their friend Natalie

Wood's funeral. The star, aged 43, had mysteriously drowned off Catalina Island, though at the time – taking into account her lifelong morbid fear of water – there was much speculation over whether her death had been an accident or suicide, perhaps even murder. As such, the press were far less interested in Elizabeth, bloated and overweight once more, than they might ordinarily have been. With dignity and compassion, it would appear, Elizabeth allowed Natalie Wood her final moment of notoriety before announcing that she and John Warner had split. The statement was delivered to the press on 21 December 1981. 'There is sadness, but no bitterness,' it concluded. 'Neither party intends to seek a divorce.'

The move had been triggered largely by John Warner's hostile attitude towards Elizabeth's pets. Now that *he* had moved up in the world, Warner wanted to relocate to an apartment within his head office, Washington's Watergate building. This would mean selling the house in the city and possibly the farm Elizabeth had loved from day one. Worse still, the Watergate building did not allow dogs and cats. Faced with an ultimatum – her husband or her 'babies' – Elizabeth did not find the choice a hard one to make. She 'celebrated' her new-found freedom by treating herself to a new $2-million home – 700 Nimes Road, Bel Air, the former residence of Frank Sinatra's wife, the Nancy of the 'laughing face' – and she shelled out $150,000 for a customised Aston Martin Lagonda to drive back and forth to engagements.

On 23 February 1982, leaving several teams of workmen in charge of the renovations, Elizabeth flew to London to prepare for the British production of *The Little Foxes*. Richard Burton was already in town for a charity performance of *Under Milk Wood*, and four days later he accompanied his ex-wife to her 50th birthday bash at Legends disco. The press were unkind. Burton, now said to be in the latter stages of liver disease, could scarcely stand; one publication compared him to a 'large blob of pastry'. Elizabeth had left the theatre in a hurry, still wearing her stage make-up, and looked ghastly. There were loud guffaws when Burton introduced her to reporters as 'the fruit of my loins' – and the next day's tabloids compared her with Hattie Jacques, the loveable but overweight *Carry On* star.

Elizabeth was brutally honest when discussing her drink and drugs problem with the press in the UK. The British tabloids, more famed for their lurid exclusives than their American counterparts (the long-defunct *Confidential* and its near successor the *National Enquirer* being exceptions), were robbed of speculation by her insistence on spilling the beans at every opportunity. Elizabeth readily confessed her inability to face the world – in other words, theatre audiences – without her two Percodan washed down with liquor. Then, she claimed, she would take two more four hours later to stay on top of things. One biographer, Donald Spoto, went to the trouble of calculating that between 1980 and 1985 she had been prescribed 'more than 1,000 prescriptions for 28 different hypnotics (sleeping pills), anxiolytics (tranquillisers) and narcotics (painkillers) by three Californian doctors who were later reprimanded by a medical board'.

When the press questioned Elizabeth and Burton, individually, over rumours that they might be about to tie the knot for the third time, Burton claimed that he had taken her home after the party, 'cast out the homos and hangers-on' and had had his way with her – whilst Elizabeth's version of events was that he had been 'too drunk to make it to the bedroom'. Burton aside, she was romantically linked with Anthony Geary, the 30-something soap star she had met whilst guesting on *General Hospital*. It was he who escorted her on a nostalgic trip to Heathwood, the Hampstead house where she had been born. The kindly current owners allowed her to wander around the place – but refused to sell it to her, even when they were offered way over what would have been the asking price.

The Little Foxes opened on 11 March and was savaged by the critics. Elizabeth had gone to great pains to look good for the American production but had let herself go again since Rock's illness and the collapse of her marriage. The reviewer for the *Daily Express* thought she had made an entrance worthy of *The Muppet*

Show's Miss Piggy, whilst Robert Cushman of *The Observer* called the production 'as grisly as an undertaker's picnic'. Much of what was said, of course, had less to do with what one had witnessed on the stage than whether one loved or loathed Elizabeth Taylor. Indeed, cynics suggested that it was possible to determine the sexuality of these journalists simply by the positive or negative tone of their comments. *The Times*'s Irving Wardell offered a half-hearted compliment by observing, 'Miss Taylor looks in tip-top shape and has a strong line in reptilian Southern charm.' Nicholas de Jongh, writing for *The Guardian*, must have had at the back of his mind Tallulah Bankhead's infamously panned Broadway production of *Antony and Cleopatra*, which had been closed by John Mason Brown's cutting, 'Tallulah Bankhead barged down the Nile last night – and sank!' De Jongh's rewording of this was, 'Elizabeth Taylor sailed into London last night like some stately old galleon – almost submerging the play.' For once, adverse reviews were inconsequential: the largely gay audiences were not paying to be repelled by Regina Giddens's evil machinations; they were at the play expressly to see Elizabeth Taylor!

Even so, Elizabeth believed she was good and confidently announced that her next theatrical project would be better than this one because she had persuaded Richard Burton to co-star with her. Returning to Los Angeles, she met up with Zev Bufman, and two possibilities were discussed: Tennessee Williams' *Sweet Bird of Youth* and a stage revival of *Who's Afraid of Virginia Woolf?*. Whilst mulling things over, she divorced John Warner in November 1982 – cynics have suggested that it took him another twenty-one years to remarry because of the ordeal of living with Elizabeth Taylor. Then, acting on a whim, Elizabeth announced that she and Burton would be appearing in Noel Coward's already outdated *Private Lives*.

There was also a new man in Elizabeth's life, arguably her most mismatched coupling since Max Lerner. Victor Gonzalez Luna was an unattractive, balding, paunchy 55-year-old Mexican lawyer who had handled Elizabeth and Burton's property transactions in

Puerto Vallarta. Divorced, Luna had four daughters, whom, he said, were very excited at the prospect of having Elizabeth Taylor for a stepmother. Unfortunately, he apparently made the boast before discussing this with Elizabeth. Luna also had political aspirations and might rather have been hoping that being with her would offer him the same prestige as it had John Warner. Even so, she did not turn him down: with the proposal came a fabulous $250,000 diamond-and-ruby engagement ring.

Elizabeth next made an announcement of her own. Just as she and Richard Burton had attempted to end the Cold War by visiting Russia, so she and her latest fiancé would be 'doing their bit' to end the bloody conflict in the Middle East. She had, she claimed, arranged a meeting with the heads of the opposing factions – Israeli Prime Minister Menachem Begin and Lebanon's President Amine Gemayel. Some people might have thought this an admirable idea – anything to end the suffering and fighting was worth a try – but the powers that be in Washington were horrified. The State Department issued a statement declaring their opposition to the project, condemning Elizabeth for interfering in a delicate political issue – whilst the world's press mocked her with such headlines as 'Cleopatra's Latest Peace Initiative' and for having more money than sense to be able to finance such a foolhardy mission. Even so, she refused to compromise, and she flew to Tel Aviv on 27 December 1982, accompanied by Victor Luna.

The trip turned out to be a farce: just another disappointing, self-centred headline-grabbing stunt. Elizabeth had agreed to meet hundreds of sick and injured children at the Tel Aviv Hilton; secretly, she was planning to adopt one. Typically, she arrived two hours late, dripping in diamonds and laden with gifts, tossing these into the crowd, according to one syndicated report, 'like she was feeding scraps to a pack of starving dogs'. The afternoon she had set aside for this event was reduced to just 15 minutes, whilst local journalists eagerly pointed out that she was more in her element on New Year's Eve, hobnobbing with the elite and wearing more jewels than most of them had ever seen at a political ball. What was actually said to her by the sponsors – or if she got around to meeting Prime Minister Begin and President Gemayel – is not known. Her adoption plans also failed when the father of her 'earmarked' baby, whose wife had died during the conflict, changed his mind and decided to raise the child himself. The visit ended prematurely, and on 6 January 1983 Elizabeth and Luna flew home.

At the end of the month, Elizabeth flew to Canada, where she filmed *Between Friends* (1983) for pay-for-view television. Her co-star was Carol Burnett. Elizabeth played a wealthy divorcee who spends much of her on-screen time drinking and engaging in 'dirty girl-talk' with man-hungry Burnett. It was a paltry effort, best summed up when the two actresses held a pre-shoot press conference. Elizabeth told the *Los Angeles Times*, 'She's the nympho – I'm the drunk!'

Then it was straight into rehearsals for *Private Lives*. The plot of the play revolves around the absurdly snobbish lovers Amanda Prynne and Elyot, who like Elizabeth and Burton (and Elizabeth and all the other men in her life) have separated after an impossible-to-live-with-or-without affair and who meet up again years later after they have each found someone else. The original production with Noel Coward and Gertrude Lawrence had played in New York in 1931 and had been old hat then – it had eventually closed not because of falling ticket sales but because the actors had become bored with it. Tallulah Bankhead had revived it, touring extensively between 1948 and 1950, including 250 performances on Broadway. She had incurred Coward's waspish wrath by deliberately camping up every line, effectively *improving* the piece. One line, 'I believe in being as gay as possible, darling,' had sent her largely homosexual audience into paroxysms of laughter.

If Tallulah had purposely sent up *Private Lives*, Elizabeth and Burton only did so unintentionally when the play opened in Boston on 7 April 1983. The critics (some of whom still referred to the pair as the Burtons) loathed and lambasted it to the last man, not that this prevented every performance from selling out. The play transferred to New York's Lunt–Fontanne Theater on 8 May, almost two years to the day since Elizabeth had opened on Broadway with *The Little Foxes*, by which time she was exhausted. The curtain rose half an hour late, and the interval lasted about an hour whilst she rested. Twelve performances would be aborted on account of Elizabeth's fatigue, aggravated by bronchitis. She was, of course, insanely jealous and watchful of her co-star, who by now had a new love in his life: Sally Hay, a 34-year-old production assistant he had met in London whilst filming a mini-series about Richard Wagner for the BBC. Burton took advantage of one of Elizabeth's indispositions on 3 July to whisk Sally off to Las Vegas, and when they returned to New York, it was as man and wife. Elizabeth expressed her 'delight' to the press, though from then on sharing the stage with Burton became increasingly traumatic. They still hit the town each night after the show, but now it was with separate entourages. *Private Lives* ground to a halt in Los Angeles on 6 November, by which time Elizabeth was on the verge of physical and mental breakdown.

In the December of that year, Elizabeth publicly announced that she was addicted to drink and drugs, and checked into the Betty Ford Clinic at Rancho Mirage. A fellow patient was her friend and former MGM co-star Peter Lawford, now terminally ill with liver and kidney disease – he died a few months later. Many people, even the ones who disliked her, applauded Elizabeth's courage for using words such as 'drunk' and 'junkie'. The harsh regime that accompanied her treatment – including 'menial' tasks such as cleaning her room, doing the laundry and taking out the garbage – did her much good, and she emerged from the clinic in the middle of January looking more like the Elizabeth Taylor of old, returning to her by now completely refurbished Bel Air home.

Most people would have wished to put the whole unpleasant experience of rehabilitation behind them, but hoping that others might learn from her mistakes – and everything in her life had to be chronicled for posterity with the maximum drama – she insisted upon appearing on ABC's *Good Morning America*. Fighting back the tears, trembling a little and slightly slurring her speech on account of her nerves, she took a very deep breath and delivered her 'confession':

> I was a stumbling, stuttering, incoherent. I needed sleeping pills for 25 years. I'd learned to rely on them. I'm an addictive kind of person. It's a disease. I was terrified when I first went there – I'd never felt so alone in my entire life. There's been a lot of genuine pain in my life, and I learned to rely on drugs. I thought I could control it . . . but it's much more fun being lucid. You don't have to worry about forgetting what you've said!

Kenneth Anger viewed the situation differently in *Hollywood Babylon II*, published later that year with the aforementioned 'obesity shot' on its cover:

> Liz Taylor's latest health spa check was not so much to knock off some pounds – though after they laughed at her in *Private Lives*, the joke went 'like trying to squeeze ten pounds of shit in a five-pound bag' – but to try to get a handle on the rainbow coalition of pills she was dropping every night and day. *Pillhead Liz*, would you believe? And the health spa clinic made her sign up for S&M Psychodrama I, a wacko Hollyweird therapy involving floor scrubbing à la Joan Crawford . . .

Richard Burton had also spent some time in rehab. At just 58, his were the ravaged features of an old man, and he had been crippled with back pains for months. For once, he said, he had a wife who could take care of him, though the marriage to Sally proved short-lived. On 4 August 1984, Burton suffered a massive cerebral haemorrhage, brought about by his excesses, and he died in a Geneva hospital the next day.

To say that Elizabeth was heartbroken was an understatement. As had happened with Mike Todd – though Burton's death had by no means been unexpected – she went completely hysterical. Matters were made infinitely worse when she learned that his widow Sally would be burying him in the tiny churchyard at Céligny. Until then,

Elizabeth had never really regarded him as anyone else's husband but hers, and not being in charge of the funeral arrangements – and actually being requested to stay away for fear of turning a solemn occasion into a media event – only added to her grief, which some of her friends genuinely believed might send her over the edge.

No one had the right, of course, to exclude Elizabeth from her ex-husband's funeral, but she complied with Sally's wishes until 14 August, when she flew out to visit the grave. How the press found out about this, if they were *not* alerted to the fact by the sensation-seeking Elizabeth herself, remains a mystery. She and Liza Todd turned up at six in the morning, wearing heavy disguises, yet within minutes they were besieged by scores of photographers. The following week, she went to offer her condolences to Burton's family in Pontrhydyfen and stayed at his sister's terraced house. In all the years these ordinary folk had known her, they had never passed judgement, and they welcomed her with open arms. On 30 August, black-clad and genuinely grieving, she joined the Jenkins, Sally and hundreds of Burton's friends, colleagues and acquaintances in London for his memorial service at St Martin-in-the-Fields. Sally unfairly dismissed this as an intrusion into her private mourning. She was also miffed by the amount of press attention Elizabeth received – but this was only to be expected. It was her divine right! Elizabeth Taylor and Richard Burton had been the world's number-one show-business couple for more than a decade, and for another decade after that they had grabbed the headlines whenever they had met up simply because people had refused to believe they would ever really go their separate ways. It is an undisputed fact, and by no means disrespectful to the other love interests in his life, that whenever the subject of Richard Burton crops up, the first and frequently *only* woman mentioned is Elizabeth.

Burton left the bulk of his $3.5-million estate to Sally (with one-tenth going to adopted daughter Maria), enabling her to enjoy a near royal lifestyle that continues to this day. Many observers believed she had earned this by nursing him through his final months, but others believed that had Burton lived a few more years Sally would not have ended up quite so wealthy, because he would have gone looking for someone else, as had always happened in the past. Indeed, one of Elizabeth's friends believes there *would* have been a third-time lucky marriage.

Neither did Burton bequeath anything to Elizabeth or her other children, heeding Elizabeth's wishes. *She* had enough already, most importantly her memories, and *they* were already wealthy in their own right, mainly thanks the trust funds their mother had set up. The Wilding boys had settled down somewhat, now that they were in their 30s. Michael Jr, now an actor, had married Jack Palance's daughter Brooke, whilst Christopher was enjoying a successful career as a photographer. Liza Todd had married and was working as a sculptress, and Maria Burton was a clothes designer.

In 1988, Sally Burton would sell the property in Céligny, which had meant so much to her husband, and move back to London. To date, she remains single. Unlike Elizabeth, however, she has contributed more to Richard Burton's memory than just standing on a podium, feeling sorry for herself and telling the world how wonderful he was. In recent years, having no use for them herself, she has dispensed with his vast library of books and donated the money to some of his favourite theatrical charities. And in August 2004, on the 20th anniversary of his death, as head of the Burton Trust, she announced that a theatre would be built in his name at the Royal Welsh College of Music and Drama in Cardiff. Even so, in just about every newspaper or magazine article commemorating the event, the accompanying photographs were of Elizabeth and Burton. 'Elizabeth, being so publicly in love with him for so long, will always be the keeper of his dreams,' Sally told the *Mail on Sunday*'s Denai Brook, adding, unable to resist the dig, 'Perhaps I am the keeper of his reality, having restored him to reality.'

Exactly who broke off their relationship – Elizabeth or Victor Luna – is not clear. The press came to the conclusion that because she would never have Richard Burton again, in her grief she had convinced herself that she would never have anyone else, and Luna was, therefore, sent packing as a form of revenge for Burton having deserted her. In October 1984, Luna told the British *Sunday People* that *he* had ended their relationship, adding, 'She was completely out of control. I realised how deeply tied she was to this man, how vital a role he had played in her life, that I could never have that special place in her heart she keeps for Burton.'

As usual, a replacement was waiting in the wings – several, if the press were to be believed. Elizabeth only had to be seen with a friend – even a gay one like Roddy McDowall – and they were predicting wedding bells. Fifty-two-year-old Dennis Stein ran a faded-denims empire and had financial interests in numerous other companies, including Technicolor. Again, it was a high-speed romance: by November, Stein had presented her with a 20-carat sapphire engagement ring; by January 1985, it was all over. He had entered history as just another notch on the Elizabeth Taylor bedpost, and she was back on the shelf, about to face one of the most harrowing, tide-turning episodes of her life.

FOURTEEN

GOODBYE ROCK...
HELLO LARRY

T HE WORK TRICKLED IN SLOWLY BUT SURELY. THERE WAS
a cameo appearance in the glitzy soap-style drama *Hotel*
(1984) alongside Roddy McDowall, and she played Louella Parsons
opposite Jane Alexander's Hedda Hopper in Gus Trikonis's TV
movie *Malice in Wonderland* (1985). The casting might have been
near perfect, but the scriptwriter made the unforgivable mistake
of transforming Hollywood's resident harridan hacks into genteel,
witty, respectable matrons when they had been anything but. Then,
in March 1985, Elizabeth was paid $100,000 for a day's work,
playing a brothel madam in an episode of the television mini-series
North and South. It was at this time that she came to the rescue
of Lesley-Anne Down.

Down and Elizabeth had much in common. Born in Wandsworth,
London, in 1954, Down had become a household name at the age
of 18, playing the flighty Lady Georgina Worsley in television's
Upstairs, Downstairs. Soon afterwards, she had been paid a
staggering $5 million to become the face of Estée Lauder, and
Hollywood had beckoned. Though no great shakes as an actress,
with her limited expressions and stilted delivery, there had been

no shortage of work. Down's career had peaked in 1976, the year before she first met Elizabeth, when she had starred opposite Peter Sellers in *The Pink Panther Strikes Again*. In 1980, she had wed Argentinian director Enrique Gabriel. This had not worked out, and two years later she had married *The Exorcist* director William Friedkin, almost 20 years her senior.

In September 2004, speaking to *Night & Day*, Down revealed that she had begun taking cocaine and drinking heavily to cope with the (she alleged) mental cruelty inflicted upon her by her husband. She added that she had been saved on the set of *North and South* by Elizabeth and the show's cameraman Don FauntLeRoy, whom she subsequently married. First she had to cope with Friedkin's public attacks denouncing her. Elizabeth, who had championed other 'lost causes', such as James Dean, Montgomery Clift, Rock Hudson and Roddy McDowall, had never taken a young woman under her wing before. Perhaps she recognised a little of her younger rebel self in the 30-year-old British actress. 'She was the lone voice of friendship and reason,' Down told *Night & Day*, adding that Elizabeth had taken her, her mother, her young son and Don FauntLeRoy into her Bel Air home. Of her saviour, she further observed, 'Liz is this blousy, ballsy, wonderful woman who encouraged me to stand up to my bullying husband. She swears like a trooper and is just hysterical. She was a dear friend and remains so to this day.'

As a special treat to cheer her up, Elizabeth loaned Lesley-Anne Down her Krupp Diamond ring for the evening – which she very nearly lost when it slipped off her finger and fell into the toilet in a ladies' rest room. 'To this day,' Down said, 'I've never dared tell how I nearly flushed her most prized possession away!' It was Elizabeth who introduced the younger star to celebrity divorce lawyer Mervin Nicholson, and for another two years Elizabeth would stand by Down while Nicholson fought to clear her name – even though she herself was going through one of the toughest periods of her life.

For some time, Elizabeth had realised that all was far from well with another of her friends: Rock Hudson was seriously ill. Since

Natalie Wood's death, he had made just one film, *The Ambassador* (1984), shot on location in Israel with Robert Mitchum. He had, however, made a big impression on the small screen, playing rancher Daniel Reece in *Dynasty*. Then, in June 1984, he had been diagnosed as suffering from AIDS, a secret he had kept from most of his intimate friends, even Elizabeth.

She had always known that Rock was gay but, like just about everyone else during the early days, knew little about the disease other than that it seemed to almost exclusively affect homosexual men. The scenes in *Dynasty* in which he had appeared had been filmed haphazardly. As a result, Rock's physical appearance varies to such an extent that he gives the impression that he is fading before our very eyes. Prior to shooting, he had received treatment at a Paris hospital experimenting in a drug that doctors there hoped might slow down the progression of the disease – though his official reason for being in France had been to visit Deauville for the film festival. So far as the press and Rock's peers were concerned, his gaunt appearance and drastic weight loss – from 223 to 180 pounds – was down to something he might have picked up in Israel, some kind of recurrent influenza, though many people speculated that he might have cancer or even anorexia.

So far as is known, Elizabeth learned of Rock's AIDS status in January 1985 when he escorted her and Liza Minnelli to the Golden Globe Awards. How she reacted to the news, so soon after losing Richard Burton, is not hard to ascertain. Being told that she must keep the fact under wraps and therefore be unable to seek help, solace and advice must also have been difficult. From then on, Rock was never out of her thoughts.

On 16 July 1984, Rock guested on *Doris Day's Best Friends*, his *Pillow Talk* co-star's first television show in years. The media made much of this, though once the programme had aired and pictures of Rock circulated around the world it was Rock's appearance and not the important reunion between one of Hollywood's top comedy duos of the 1960s that hit the headlines. Rock looked so frail in what would be his final celluloid appearance that many fans found it hard to watch what was supposed to be a comedy sketch without shedding tears.

A few days after the show, Rock flew to Paris for more treatment – by now the press favoured the anorexia story. The diagnosis was revised when he collapsed in the VIP lounge at Orly Airport and was admitted to the American Hospital in Neuilly. A spokesman there announced that he was suffering from acute liver disease, with little chance of recovery. Then, on 25 July, it was officially announced that he had AIDS.

Rock was flown home to Los Angeles to die, and amongst his first visitors at the UCLA Medical Center were Elizabeth and Roddy McDowall. They, like his other friends, were counselled before being ushered into his room – it was essential that Rock should not see how shocked they were by his ghastly appearance or repeat what was being written about him in the press, arguably the worst vilification of a celebrity in show-business history. Elizabeth and McDowall helped Rock wade through 30,000 letters and cards from well wishers – the ordinary fans who far from judging and condemning him for his lifestyle just wished for the impossible: for him to be well again. There were dozens of telegrams from show-business pals and acquaintances – some of the gay ones preferring to remain anonymous in the wake of a renewed wave of homophobia.

Elizabeth put Rock in touch with the Shanti Foundation, a Los Angeles-based organisation that had set up a telephone helpline for AIDS sufferers who did not wish to be seen visiting their centre. Even this was lampooned by the tabloids, who dubbed it 'Hudson's Hotline of Death'. Elizabeth went to see him almost every day, despite the fact that he could keep nothing down much of the time and mindless of the overpowering stench of the sickroom.

Rock's indefatigable champion always managed to stay calm whilst she was with him, but press reports and photographs suggest that she went to pieces the moment she left. In a climate of extreme homophobia and ignorance, Elizabeth was literally putting her career on the line by having anything to do with a homosexual actor suffering from the so-called 'gay plague'. Many of Rock's actor friends wanted to see him but were terrified of being ostracised if they did. Nancy Reagan, America's First Lady, risked the wrath of her husband's administration by speaking to him on the phone, whereas President Reagan is acknowledged as never once publicly uttering the word 'AIDS' until after Hudson's death. Elizabeth, never less than a law unto herself, had no intention of changing now. She did not care what the press thought. She had stuck by one friend, Monty, through thick and thin, and would do so again with Rock.

On 19 September, Elizabeth and Shirley MacLaine, who had already raised a vast amount of money for AIDS charities, organised a benefits dinner for Rock in Los Angeles. Prior to sending out the invitations, they overconfidently (they thought) announced that they would achieve their $250,000 target, though some of Elizabeth's and Rock's gay friends – including Roddy McDowall – who gave generously insisted upon anonymity and did not show up on the evening, fearful of being outed by the press.

Rock Hudson died on the morning of 2 October 1985, just short of his 60th birthday. Within 30 minutes of the newsflash, the gates of the Castle – his sumptuous home on Beverly Crest Drive – were besieged by a media circus rivalling that witnessed at Mike Todd's funeral. Elizabeth was having none of it and sent a crack team of security men to deal with the situation. For months, she continued to refer to her friend in the present tense. She told reporters on the day of his death, 'I love him, and he is tragically gone. Please God that he has not died in vain.'

What made Rock's death harder to bear, for Elizabeth and for most of us, was his horrendous treatment at the hands of the press. In England, more so than in the USA, the tabloids could not have been more inhuman and undignified. 'He was one of the gentlest, kindest men in Hollywood,' Marlene Dietrich told me. 'All those journalists should burn in hell for the bile they printed about him when he died. I've never liked Elizabeth Taylor, but I *admired* her tremendously for the way she stuck up for him, the way she risked her career by supporting him.'

Elizabeth and Tom Clarke – Rock's ex-lover and latterly his right-hand man – were unable to arrange the funeral. The Public Health Department insisted that Rock's remains be cremated within hours of his death, and he was taken through the gates of the Castle in a tiny van, with his feet sticking out of the rear doors, a purposely undignified exit stage-managed by the undertakers and the press, who were hoping to get a shot of the corpse. Elizabeth's security men prevented this, and she and Tom Clarke gave their friend the send-off he so richly deserved – a celebration of his life that took place at the Castle on 19 October. It was Elizabeth who determined that the most fitting service for a lapsed Catholic should be a Quaker one; having missed Montgomery Clift's funeral, this was her way of paying tribute to them both. Elizabeth, Carol Burnett and Tab Hunter read the eulogies. The next day, she helped scatter Rock's ashes at sea, off Catalina Island.

The shock of Rock Hudson's rapid deterioration and his press-maligned death had brought Elizabeth to her senses so far as her own health was concerned. For the time being at least, alcohol and pills looked like being a thing of the past. At 53, she had regained the figure that had wowed audiences and sent men wild with desire 30 years earlier. She also began dictating her memoirs, *Elizabeth Takes Off* (Guild Publishing, 1987) – though this barely skimmed the surface of her complex, busy life. Backed by a promotional campaign said to have been in excess of $10 million, she launched her own range of perfumes (Passion and White Diamonds, retailing at up to $100 per one-ounce bottle) and cosmetics.

In *There Must Be a Pony* (1986), which began shooting in May 1987, Elizabeth played a has-been movie star on the comeback trail. Marguerite Sidney, who is the antithesis of Marina Gregg, ends up in the loony bin rather than killing herself. Before this happens, there are several episodes that suggest a link between the actor and the character: the brutal husband, the broken engagements, the neurosis that frequently courts the major star. A touching scene occurs when former child-star Marguerite is reunited with her former co-star: Mickey Rooney, playing himself! Elizabeth's leading man in the television movie was Robert Wagner, who co-produced it for his own company. This being a James Kirkwood story, there was also a gay subplot involving Marguerite's son (Chad Lowe) and a decent mad scene for her to get her teeth into.

There was also a new man in Elizabeth's life: Memphis-born Lothario actor George Hamilton. Seven years her junior, and one of Hollywood's most eligible bachelors, Hamilton had scored a big hit playing an effete young man in his first film *Home From the Hill* (1959), but major success had evaded him until 20 years later with his Dracula send-up *Love at First Bite* (1979). Handsome but peculiar looking *en profile* on account of his thick lips, Hamilton was signed to appear with Elizabeth in a television movie called *Poker Alice* (1987).

Elizabeth's salary for the production was undisclosed, but the press made much of her contractual demands. These included $100,000 to be set aside for 'gifts for the leading lady' – one to be presented to her on each day of the four weeks of shooting. She squealed with juvenile delight each time the director Arthur Allan Seidelman 'surprised' her with some little trinket she had commissioned: diamond earrings, necklaces, a $10,000 travelling clock. However, as television movies go, this was one of her best. The fine supporting cast included *M*A*S*H* (1970) actor Tom Skerritt, as well as David Wayne, Susan Tyrrell and character-actor Richard Mulligan, better known as Bert from the television comedy series *Soap*. The movie also contains a first, an Elizabeth Taylor catfight with a love-rival whore, the likes of which had not been seen in a comedy Western since the one between Marlene Dietrich and Una Merkel in *Destry Rides Again* (1939).

In February 1987, Elizabeth celebrated her 55th birthday, which coincided with her strangest friendship of all – with 28-year-old introverted pop star Michael Jackson. Wacko and Liz would rarely, if ever, meet without the press having been previously alerted, the occasion invariably having been orchestrated because of some ulterior motive: for financial gain or to draw attention to some self-inflicted drama. Linked with Elizabeth, Jackson attempted to pass himself off as some mega-rich but normal star-struck 'Stage Door Johnny'. Elizabeth, similarly, considered herself 'hip' to be seen in the company of one of the world's wealthiest and most flamboyant entertainers, even going so far as to attend some of his concerts and – the mind boggles at the thought of the spectacle – accompanying him to the races. Secretly, of course, thousands of fans, and even some of her closest friends, believed that there must have been something radically wrong with her to want to be involved with such an eccentric oddity in the first place. 'That's the kind of person she was,' Marlene Dietrich told me afterwards. 'Anything for a free ride. Michael Jackson tried to get in with me around the same time – wanted to come here [to my Paris apartment] and coax me out of retirement. I told whoever it was who called that I don't do interviews with monkeys!'

Elizabeth and Michael Jackson were in many ways still children, never having really grown up, accustomed always to having their own way in adulthood because no one ever got round to telling them that they were wrong. Perhaps this was because of overt sycophancy and fear of being ousted from the court, the hangers-on always aware that another lackey was waiting in the wings to take their place. She was Velvet Brown, eternally searching for that elusive crock of gold at the rainbow's end, never satisfied until she had brought about the storm guaranteed to drive it a little further out of reach. He was Peter Pan, the little boy so wrapped up in his own fantasies that he was unable to distinguish between the real world and what we more rational people call cloud-cuckoo-land.

Elizabeth became a regular visitor to his usually off-limits Neverland Ranch in the Santa Ynez Valley, a hundred miles north-west of Los Angeles. Contained within its 2,750 acres was a full-sized amusement park with Ferris wheel and roller coaster, and a zoo containing an assortment of animals, including an elephant named Gypsy, a surprise gift from Elizabeth. Neverland provided the perfect lure for children of all ages and in the not-too-distant future the setting for alleged events that would furnish the world's tabloids with some of their most lurid headlines since the AIDS-related deaths of Rock Hudson and Freddie Mercury.

In 1993, Jackson said of Elizabeth (*Elizabeth Taylor*, Biography Channel), 'We had a similar childhood . . . we shared a quest in search of acceptance from an adoring public.' Elizabeth responded, much to her later embarrassment, 'Michael is like a son to me. He has a quality of innocence we would all like to attain.' Nothing could have been further from the truth. Elizabeth might have had a restricted childhood – indeed, like all Hollywood child stars, she had been subject to studio-related restrictions that were not just obligatory but the law – but she had always been loved, and she and never been physically abused, as Jackson claimed he had. Neither did Jackson fit into the 'disenchanted' category into which Elizabeth had slotted Jimmy, Monty, Rock and Richard – genuinely troubled souls who, it might be argued, had not been the sole causes of their woes and tribulations. Indeed, in the eyes of many people, Elizabeth had taken a tumble from her authority-of-the-human-condition pedestal by adding Jackson's name to this gilded quartet.

Elizabeth's first party masterminded by Michael Jackson did not take place at Neverland but at the home of the composer Burt Bacharach. Ageing screen legend Bette Davis was amongst the guests, and it was she who strode up to one of ubiquitous reporters to 'show off' her latest trinket: a glass copy of the Taylor-Burton Diamond that had been presented to every female invited. This was etched with the initials 'E.T.'. 'In honour of Mr Jackson,' Bette drawled. 'Extra-Terrestrial!'

By now, Elizabeth had ended her relationship with George Hamilton and was 'seeing' 67-year-old Malcolm Forbes, the billionaire publisher of the magazine that bore his name, founded by his father in 1917 as the only business magazine in the USA. Forbes was a divorced grandfather whose interests outside his work included sailing, hot-air ballooning, owning the world's largest collection of Fabergé eggs – and the pursuit of 'chickens', or teenage boys who were paid for sexual favours.

For Elizabeth, besides being a valuable odd-bod friend, Malcolm Forbes was an invaluable society tool in the stamp of a Mike Todd or an Aristotle Onassis. She headed the 1,000-strong guest list for *Forbes* magazine's 70th anniversary party and managed to steal the show – and, she hoped, the host's heart. Had it emerged at the time that Forbes, a senior citizen, liked having sex with underage boys, he would have been ruined – and what better way, for him, of proving to the world that he was a 'red-blooded male' than to be seen on the arm of acknowledged man-eater Elizabeth Taylor?

In May 1987, accompanied by Forbes, Elizabeth flew to Paris to receive one of France's top accolades, the *Légion d'Honneur*. When she learned that the late Duchess of Windsor's jewels were being auctioned and the proceeds being donated to the Pasteur Institute for research into a cure for AIDS, she bought the famous Prince of Wales's feathers piece for $450,000. She then flew to Rome, where she had been contracted to make *Young Toscanini* (1988) with Franco Zeffirelli.

In arguably her most ridiculous role to date, Elizabeth played the soprano Nadia Bulichoff. As high camp as anything she did in *Suddenly, Last Summer* and *Boom!* is the scene in which Bulichoff (whose singing voice was provided by Aprile Millo) is performing *Aida* in Rio de Janeiro in 1886 – a true event – when halfway through 'Ritorna Vincitor' she stops the orchestra and, surrounded by her Nubian servants, makes an impassioned plea for the abolition of slavery. The project was doomed when the backers withdrew their funding and there was no one else to step into the breach. The film was completed but received such a critical panning after its only screening at the Venice Film Festival that it was never put on general release.

The movie's failure coincided with Elizabeth's autobiography-of-sorts, *Elizabeth Takes Off*, a bestseller throughout the western world. She travelled just about everywhere to promote it, almost always with Malcolm Forbes, who grasped every opportunity to 'buy in' from the rent-boy population of whichever city they visited. Reporters everywhere raved about how well Elizabeth looked, but when she arrived back in Los Angeles in July 1988, she was on the verge of collapse – downing pills and back on the bottle. By the end of October, she was back at the Betty Ford Clinic, this time booked in for six weeks' treatment. Her condition was aggravated by her mother's failing health. Now 92, the woman responsible for sowing the seeds of neurasthenia within Elizabeth in the first place was a patient at the nearby Eisenhower Medical Center. Amongst other things, Sara was suffering from bleeding ulcers and was reported to be dangerously ill. Elizabeth was allowed out of rehab for three hours each afternoon – one hour to be spent with her mother, the other two for visits to her hairdresser, beautician and couturier so that the press, alerted by her aides, could snap her looking her best. Sara recovered, and on 10 December Elizabeth was also given a clean bill of health and discharged.

Being in love, Elizabeth declared, had helped her through her tough rehabilitation routine. Though discouraged from getting involved with other patients at the Betty Ford Clinic, she had been unable to keep her eyes off hard-case Larry Fortensky, a 36-year-old former truck driver, currently on three years probation after being convicted of drink-driving and possession of drugs. As usual with Elizabeth, it was love at first sight – the difference being that the copper-haired hunk was from the opposite side of the fence from her, culturally, politically and professionally. As the film critic Alexander Walker later observed, 'To some, the sight of Elizabeth and Larry Fortensky offering each other mutual sympathy and support recalled the set-up for her film *Boom!*, where Flora Goforth, the world's richest woman, welcomes a passing beach bum with the gifts of life and death into her world of affluence and illness.'

Fortensky's personal history was sufficiently complex to make him the perfect consort for the former queen of Hollywood. Born in California, he had dropped out of school and at the age of 18 had married and enlisted for Vietnam in the same week. Discharged from military service a matter of months later, he had returned home in time for the birth of his daughter, but the marriage had not survived. Fortensky had quickly remarried, and upon her divorce the second Mrs Fortensky had told the court that her husband had tried to strangle her during a drunken rage. Clearly, he was a good match for the bust-up-loving Elizabeth, who was advised by Malcolm Forbes to steer clear of him. In Forbes's opinion, Fortensky was vulgar, inarticulate and decidedly bad news, just about everything Elizabeth admired in a man. By the end of the year, he had moved in with her, swearing that being with her would not change him and that he would never give up his new job as a construction worker. As such, his attitude was likened to that of a lottery winner who insists that life will go on as before. Elizabeth dutifully packed his lunch box each morning and waved him off at the door – initially not appearing to mind if he stopped off after his shift for a few beers with his buddies. Larry was entitled to his freedom and a life of his own, she said, and in any case she was too busy with her career to worry about what he might be getting up to whilst they were apart.

In the spring of 1989, Elizabeth appeared opposite Mark Harmon in the television movie of Tennessee Williams' *Sweet Bird of Youth* – the play she had wanted to do with Richard Burton. Her role, playing Princess Alexandra de Lago, the fading screen icon who seeks comfort in drugs, alcohol and much younger men, seemed appropriate in her current position. 'I'm a great success at playing has-beens,' she later told the *Daily Mail*.

In the August, Elizabeth and Fortensky flew to Gstaad – his first overseas trip – and she travelled on to Tangiers to host Malcolm Forbes's 70th birthday party. Forbes had recently donated $1 million to the American Foundation for AIDS Research (AmFAR), one of her projects, and convinced Elizabeth that Fortensky would be surplus to requirements for the $2-million birthday extravaganza, on the pretext that another substantial donation would be forthcoming so long as his wishes were adhered to. Fortensky was, therefore, instructed to house-sit in Gstaad. Once again, it would appear, Elizabeth had found herself a caddy who did not mind being ordered around so long as the pickings were good. Then, on 24 February 1990, Malcolm Forbes suddenly died at his New Jersey estate, and Fortensky must have gleaned some satisfaction from reading some of the lurid exposés in the tabloids concerning the extra-curricular activities of a man who had considered *him* something of an embarrassment and not good enough for Elizabeth.

That year there were also numerous hospitalisations – the most serious being an attack of viral pneumonia that laid Elizabeth low in the April and saw her back on the critical list. When she checked into the Daniel Freeman Hospital in Marina del Rey under the name Ruth Warner, some of the tabloids speculated that she might have done so to undergo tests for HIV, perhaps passed on by one of her bisexual friends. Indeed, when her condition deteriorated, forcing her to be transferred to the better-equipped St John's Hospital in Santa Monica, it was speculated that she might even have developed AIDS. Her costume designer Halston and her personal secretary Rother Hall had the disease. Lending credence to their suspicions was the fact that one of the doctors treating Elizabeth was Patricia Murray, a specialist in infectious diseases known to have treated several high-profile AIDS patients. Rather than ignore these hacks, Elizabeth played straight into their hands by telling a press conference, 'I feel that it is important that people are not afraid to be tested for AIDS. I have an annual physical and have been tested for the disease, and the results are negative.' Even so, at least one banner headline proclaimed 'Liz Taylor in AIDS Scare'.

On 26 July, Elizabeth and Larry Fortensky announced their engagement, she making cracks to the press that in remaining single for the past nine years she had been aiming for some sort of record. The wedding preparations were not all plain sailing, as the tabloids delved into the prospective groom's 'shady' background, claiming to be acting in Elizabeth's interests after hearing that Fortensky had signed a prenuptial agreement wherein he would be paid $1.25 million should the marriage fail. Few observers had any doubt that it would, considering the fate of his predecessors. Taking this into consideration, Fortensky was clearly onto a good thing. First, the press printed various exclusives from his two ex-wives, who had little to say about him that was positive. Then it was revealed that he had ignored his previous court order by walking out of the aforementioned rehabilitation programme soon after meeting

Elizabeth. The obvious joke doing the rounds at that time was that the self-taught jewellery expert had found herself a rough diamond.

Next, the press drew attention to Fortensky's family and the fact that several dubious characters would be rubbing shoulders with the Reagans and the cream of Hollywood society. Fortensky's (unnamed) best man was found to have had several convictions for robbery and drink-driving. Another relative had recently served a prison term for reckless conduct on the road. Other family members were deemed similarly suspect, and this resulted in a hasty trimming of the guest list.

How Larry Fortensky reacted to this media assassination is not on record. He was so besotted with Elizabeth, no doubt bedazzled by the opulence she had represented since before he had been born, that he might have perceived little if anything beyond the dollar signs, although there seems little doubt that he genuinely loved her. He also brought out her maternal instincts, dormant since the deaths of Montgomery Clift and Richard Burton, as was to be expected with the 20-year age gap. As Fortensky's Svengali, Elizabeth subjected the rough-and-ready hard-hat labourer to the ultimate Hollywood makeover, which, under differing circumstances, he might have found difficult to take: manicures, highlights, a designer-label wardrobe, teeth capping and the like. Fortensky was roped into the White Diamonds launch, a ten-city tour intended to test him out in the public arena. Naturally, he passed with flying colours as the crowds turned out in their thousands and roared their approval.

The couple were given a 'fairy tale' wedding on 6 October 1991 at Michael Jackson's Neverland Ranch. No expense was spared, with Jackson – who picked up the reported $1.5-million tab – ensuring that attention was focused on himself at all times, and not the bride and groom. The fiasco had begun several weeks earlier when the Cartier invitation cards had been sent out: 'Mr Michael Jackson requests the pleasure of your company at the marriage of his beloved friend', etc. The press at once latched onto the fact that this was an elaborate publicity stunt, with the singer alleged to have invested heavily in Elizabeth's White Diamonds perfume enterprise. By being seen to be publicly supporting her on this the happiest day of her life (for the eighth time), the press further inferred that Jackson was hoping that he would no longer be lampooned as a freak. Unfortunately, as the day progressed, the chances of that happening were greatly diminished.

The 160 guests included Franco Zeffirelli, Gregory Peck, Brooke Shields, Liza Minnelli, David Hockney, Bob Hope, Roddy McDowall, Eva Gabor, Rod McKuen, Frank Sinatra and Elizabeth's brother Howard, who is said to have been against the event. On Michael Jackson's orders, all were frisked by members of a 300-strong security force that included a detachment of Israeli commandos hired by Elizabeth. A number of cameras were confiscated – even from Sinatra and his mafioso bodyguard. Having read of the hoo-ha in the press, former Presidents Ford and Reagan, along with their wives, sent their apologies. Ninety-five-year-old Sara Taylor, now confined to a wheelchair, was guest of honour. The media were represented by all-powerful columnist Liz Smith, photographer Herb Ritts – and 15 not unexpected helicopters chartered by various television networks.

Elizabeth's final walk down the aisle might not have seemed out of place in a Carry On or Monty Python movie. The ceremony itself took place at 6.15 p.m. (45 minutes late) under a white gazebo festooned with gardenias and daisies, conducted by Marianne Williamson, a self-proclaimed high priestess whose voice, along with the piano and violin accompaniment, was completely drowned out by the din from the hovering helicopters. Whatever the press reported had been said, few had actually heard.

Elizabeth and Michael Jackson had previously issued separate statements proclaiming that the wedding was to be 'a quiet affair'. Obviously, it had been meticulously worked out to be anything but – hence the helicopters and a biplane from which a photographer parachuted, landing on the lawn just as Elizabeth was about to make her entrance. Had none of this been anticipated, there would have been no need for the helium balloons, which were sent up to dispel these 'unwelcome invaders', adding to the excitement and guaranteeing more column inches. Screaming profanities, Elizabeth entered the arena wearing an ankle-length yellow lace Valentino gown (an alleged freebie). She was escorted by Michael Wilding Jr but was given away by Jackson, clad in black, wearing silver space boots and garish make-up. Bubbles, his pet chimpanzee, toddled behind eating a bag of peanuts. Larry Fortensky, in a white tuxedo, is reported to have been bemused by it all. His last-minute best man was Elizabeth's hairdresser, José Eber, wearing his trademark straw hat, dyed black to match his suit.

Without trying too hard, Elizabeth had succeeded in making a fool of herself. Then all hell broke loose as she rushed towards the photographer, threatening him with a fate worse than death. The poor man was manhandled by several Israeli commandos, who would not have been required in the first place had the wedding really been planned as a clandestine affair.

The honeymoon was comprised of a series of trips at home and abroad to raise money for Elizabeth's AIDS charities and to promote her perfume. When asked to describe White Diamonds, she told the press, 'It's as white hot as the depths of a diamond with an endless brilliance. A profusion of living Amazon lily and Italian *neroli*, heightened by modern notes – Egyptian tuberose, living narcissus and a haunting blend of amber and precious woods.' Wow!

One of the AIDS events was presided over by Princess Margaret, who was virtually ignored as the press clamoured to interview and photograph the newlyweds. This time no promises had been made that the marriage would last forever – indeed, with Larry Fortensky having been offered a huge financial incentive in the event of Elizabeth divorcing him, cynics were saying that he might not have *wanted* it to work out.

FIFTEEN

SAINT ELIZABETH

ON 27 FEBRUARY 1992, ELIZABETH CELEBRATED HER 60th birthday at Disneyland. The guest of honour should have been Michael Jackson, but he was said to be suffering from depression in the wake of a recent disastrous tour of South Africa, cut short because he had been lambasted by the press for holding his nose each time he had been introduced to someone important, suggesting they smelled. The *National Enquirer* further upset him by putting forward another reason for his strange behaviour: 'He was picking his nose because he was bothered by the effects of repeated plastic surgery.'

Amongst the 650 guests instructed to wear identity badges were Tom Selleck, Shirley MacLaine and Dionne Warwick. All were presented with goodie bags containing an Elizabeth Taylor sweatshirt and a flacon of White Diamonds. Everyone made a fuss of her, but she persistently reminded them how much she was missing Michael Jackson. She told Liz Smith, 'Michael said to me, "I can't bear to see anyone. They're all going to laugh at me and everyone is going to start asking questions. I just want to crawl into a hole and die!" But I'm thinking about him all the time, and this birthday is for the child in me.' Of her new-found happiness with Larry Fortensky, *People* magazine reported her as saying, 'His main concern is that I'm a star, and he thinks he's a nonentity. But I'm *not* a star any more. For the first time in my life, I'm a housewife, and I'm enjoying it immensely.'

The 'housewife' later described her typical day: undergoing two hours of massage and beauty treatment each morning, arranging her daily mini-truckload delivery of flowers, conducting business meetings and fielding telephone calls, enjoying home-prepared meals (though not cooked by her), and spending whatever time was left in front of the television with Larry, watching her favourite sitcoms soaps. She subsequently found the time to appear in a quartet of these (*High Society, The Nanny, Murphy Brown, Can't Hurry Love*), her on-screen characters promoting her latest fragrance, Black Pearls.

Whilst she had been in London the previous November, Elizabeth had heard rumours that the rock group Queen's front man Freddie Mercury was dying of AIDS. After a little investigating on her part, she discovered that the rumours were true. And so began a repetition of the poisonous tabloid journalism that had preceded Rock Hudson's death, except that in Freddie's case he survived for just one day following his press statement that he had the disease. So far as is known, Elizabeth never met the flamboyant singer, but she had heard much about him from Rock Hudson.

In 1980, Rock and Freddie had met in The Glory Holes (aka South of Market Club), the notorious Los Angeles gay establishment brought to the 'uneducated' world's attention in Armistead Maupin's *Tales of the City* novels. The Glory Holes (subsequently shut down by the Public Health Department) consisted of several bars and a number of plywood booths, each with several holes through which customers could insert their penises in anticipation of gratification from the other side. But if the recipient had no idea who was pleasuring him, the hundreds of men assembled on the balcony that overlooked the booths were able to observe and applaud every movement. Rock and Freddie had both been offered membership of The Glory Holes: both had declined.

For some reason speculating that she would be the only one capable of getting the safe-sex message across to a 72,000-strong audience of mostly under-30s, the promoters asked Elizabeth to participate in the Freddie Mercury Tribute Concert for AIDS Awareness, which took place at Wembley Stadium on 20 April 1992. The line-up included the three surviving members of Queen, but most of the supporting acts were second-rate. 'Don't worry, I'm not going to sing,' Elizabeth joked, but truthfully she could have done better than most of those who appeared! Even Annie Lennox, David Bowie and Liza Minnelli put in execrable performances – only George Michael and Elton John were any good, the latter so moving Elizabeth that she later presented him with a silver-and-red-rhinestones AIDS brooch.

A shock item on the bill had to be Guns N' Roses, a group that Freddie Mercury and anyone sensibly and genuinely connected with the gay community and AIDS awareness positively loathed. In 1988, one of their songs had contained the deeply unpleasant line 'immigrants and faggots spread disease', said to have been aimed at Freddie himself. The group were booed throughout their set, and some of their fans heckled Elizabeth whilst she was on stage. 'I'll *get off* in a minute,' she shouted back, earning a huge cheer from the crowd. 'I have something to *say!*'

In her five-minute speech, delivered entirely off the cuff, Elizabeth urged the world to practise safe sex and not share syringes. She concluded:

> We are here to celebrate the life of Freddie Mercury, an extraordinary rock star who rushed across our cultural landscape like a comet shooting across the sky. We are also here to tell the whole world that he, like others we have lost to AIDS, died before his time. The bright light of his talent still exhilarates us, even now that his life has been cruelly extinguished. It needn't have happened – it shouldn't have happened. Please, let's not let it happen again . . . There's 70,000 people in this stadium. Look at yourselves. Look at how many you are. In two short weeks,

there will be as many new infections as there are people here tonight. Please don't let it happen to you. You are the future of our world. You are the best and brightest. You are the shining light that will illuminate a better world tomorrow . . . Protect yourselves, love yourselves, respect yourselves, because until you do I won't give in, and I won't give up, because the world needs you to live! You see, we really love you. We really *care!*

Rock Hudson's death had only been the beginning. The Freddie Mercury tribute concert was another turning point in Elizabeth's life. Henceforth, she would be much less interested in loving one particular man than she would these thousands of unseen, maligned men – and women – around the world. She had become *Saint* Elizabeth.

There was drama on 6 May – the day Marlene Dietrich died – when a number of extremely cutting anti-Elizabeth notes were found pinned to Marlene's bedroom wall, including one which read, 'You have done enough harm to great men like Burton, Todd and Wilding. Why don't you swallow your fucking diamonds and shut up!' This was the *politest* thing Marlene had written about her – during a visit to her avenue Montaigne apartment, my wife Jeanne and I had roared with laughter over some of the others, particularly one which had read, 'Elizabeth Taylor has two cunts – one of them is called Richard Burton.'

On the same day, Elizabeth's adopted daughter, Maria Burton Carson, delivered a stillborn baby boy in New York. Only days before, Elizabeth – 3,000 miles away in Los Angeles – had organised a $20,000 pre-natal shower for Maria at a New York hotel. Later, she would auction the baby's designer wardrobe for orphaned children. Maria, she claimed, had intended to name her son Richard, in honour of his late grandfather.

Early in 1993, Elizabeth was presented with the Jean Hersholt Humanitarian Award for her outstanding charity work. Then, on 11 March, in a ceremony hosted by Carol Burnett at the Beverly Hills Hilton, she became only the fourth woman to receive the

American Film Institute's Lifetime Achievement Award – the others had been Lillian Gish, Barbara Stanwyck, Ingrid Bergman and Bette Davis. As Peggy Lee sang 'Fever', the 'who's who' in Hollywood were treated to a potpourri of newsreel clips: Elizabeth's various marriages, the scenes of hysteria that had greeted her appearances around the world, the fan proudly sporting the 'Liz's Weddings' T-shirt. Then Elizabeth, wearing black and less jewels than usual, made her way through the auditorium towards her table, smiling radiantly, shaking hands, but kissing only the by-now-ever-present Michael Jackson. Extracts were shown from her films, including a rare clip of her singing with Alfalfa in *There's One Born Every Minute*. James Dean and Montgomery Clift were greeted with warm applause. There were congratulatory speeches from Angela Lansbury, Dennis Hopper and her friend Roddy McDowall, who told her, 'It has been wonderful over the years watching you matriculate as a human being, as an actress and as a major contributor to the welfare of mankind.' And unlike some of its predecessors, Elizabeth's acceptance speech was unscripted and delivered from the heart:

> When I first heard about the award, I went into a state of shock. I guess it's a long time since I've thought of myself as an actress. I, along with the critics, have never taken myself very seriously – my craft, yes, but as an actress, no. But I wasn't all that bad, was I? You've made me realise how much I really do miss it. But my life is full and good. It has taken so many diverse twists and turns, and I have grown into what I do . . .

At this point, Elizabeth paused and gazed at the sea of celebrity faces – a good many of those present genuinely cared about what was coming next, but there were more than a few there who could not have cared less, in particular a minority of closeted stars (including one performer whom she had turned her back on in the wings) who often attempted to camouflage their homosexuality with homophobic comments:

I am filled with pride – proud that I am part of this community, proud of you as a community, helping as many others, especially in the world of AIDS. We have come a long way in the last decade, and I know you are willing to go the whole mile and do whatever it takes.

Thanking everyone in the film industry who had helped her to get where she was today – though, truthfully, the only ones who deserved such recognition were her mother and her fans – she concluded:

My mind goes especially to four magnificent men, who, had they lived, might have stood here and received this award: Monty, Rock, Jimmy and, of course, Richard. Oh, I was so lucky to have known them, to have learned so much from them, to have loved them. Thank you all for making me feel so special tonight. It's a memory that I will have next to my heart for the rest of my life.

In July 1994, Elizabeth appeared on the big screen for the last time – as Fred Flintstone's unfortunately named mother-in-law, Pearl Slaghoople, in *The Flintstones*. She was only on screen for seven minutes but managed to make a big impression in a new Hollywood era when special effects all too frequently overshadowed acting requirements – in this instance, the prehistoric 'gadgets' that had monopolised the Hanna–Barbera animated television series upon which the film was based.

Elizabeth plays the archetypal mother-in-law from hell. John Goodman later confessed that he had found it extremely difficult to walk up to Elizabeth Taylor and growl, 'What's that old fossil doing here?' And in a party scene, the harridan *becomes* Elizabeth Taylor, turning up in furs and Burton jewels, and leading everyone into the conga.

The Flintstones was all good, clean fun, and many people expected more such roles to come Elizabeth's way. Sadly, they did not, and once more she began focusing her energies on her personal problems, most of them self-inflicted. Her marriage was all but falling apart at the seams. This time around she had married a malleable, star-struck man who allowed himself to be pushed into the background, or so it seemed, for the privilege of being Elizabeth Taylor's husband. Because of their age difference, she became even more possessive than usual, terrified that he might leave her, particularly as she grew older and more infirm.

At the end of August, allegedly under tremendous pressure to do so, Larry Fortensky accompanied Elizabeth on a 'mercy dash' to Singapore to rescue Michael Jackson, reported to have been on the verge of mental breakdown in the wake of allegations of drug abuse and, more seriously, child molestation. The news of the lawsuit filed at the Los Angeles Superior Court had caught up with the singer whilst he had been performing in Russia. The *New York Times* ran the exclusive that a 13-year-old boy had accused him of sexual abuse and had taken out a civil action. The boy's family were now in the process of seeking a trial by jury and 'unspecified monetary damages' from Jackson, who, of course, was denying the charge. The newspaper further reported, on 15 September, that Jackson had also been previously investigated by the Los Angeles Police Department but that he had not yet been charged with any misdemeanour.

Jackson was virulently defended by his security consultant, Anthony Pelliciano, who contended that the alleged victim's father had tried to extort $20 million from the singer. 'The first demands were for money, and the latter demand is for money,' the *New York Times* reported Pelliciano as having said. 'The police are still conducting their investigation appropriately.' Elizabeth lashed out like an angry lioness protecting her injured cub, although she had absolutely no idea what might or might not have actually transpired behind the walls of Jackson's ultra-high-security Peter Pan's palace. 'This is the *worst* thing that could happen to a man like Michael, who *loves* children,' she told a reporter from *Newsweek*, adding that she would do everything within her power to help him and saying that she fully understood why Jackson had allegedly turned to narcotics, because she too had once been hooked on prescription drugs.

Jackson avoided criminal charges in this instance by settling the civil suit filed by the boy's father out of court for a reputed $15–20 million – enough in itself for many observers to assume that the accused must have had something to hide, otherwise he would have had no fear in seeing the matter through to its legal conclusion. And Elizabeth would go on supporting what, with equal cynicism, was often referred to as her latest pet project. Once his tour of the Far East was over, she persuaded Jackson to seek treatment and counselling at a London clinic. Later, she installed a private line at her home, similar to the helpline she had opened for AIDS victims in the wake of Rock Hudson's final illness, except that this one was connected to one person only – the increasingly fragile man–child whose gratitude was expressed by the creation of an Elizabeth Taylor shrine: Jackson decorated the walls of his toy-filled bedroom with dozens of Andy Warhol prints of her and had the woodwork painted the exact shade of violet as her eyes. What Larry Fortensky had to say about this excessive fanaticism – if indeed he was permitted to express his opinions aloud without being cried down, particularly when Jackson claimed himself to be so happy now the charges had been dropped that *he* would ask Elizabeth to marry him *should* she divorce Fortensky one day – is not on record. One can only speculate wildly about what the press would have made of a Jackson-Taylor wedding should it ever have taken place! Jackson had already taken steps to *look* like Elizabeth, including plastic surgery, and the media would have afforded them absolutely no mercy.

Elizabeth and Fortensky spent Christmas 1993 in Gstaad, and there were several visits to Richard Burton's grave, which must have been unsettling for Fortensky, who appears to have been hanging on to his wife by the skin of his teeth. Whilst there, Elizabeth took a tumble on the ice, aggravating her old back and hip injuries. For three months, she suffered in silence, but in March 1994 she went into hospital for hip-replacement surgery. (This left her with one leg slightly shorter than the other, until a follow-up operation to replace the other hip.) Fortensky stood by her through a painful recuperation process, and she had barely recovered from this when Sara Taylor died at the Rancho Mirage complex, Palm Springs, on 11 September 1994, aged 98. Elizabeth had her interred next to Francis at the Westwood Memorial Park.

By then, Elizabeth and Larry Fortensky were said to be sleeping in separate rooms, and he was spending more and more time with his drinking pals. Sometimes, if Elizabeth was out of town, they would party all night long at her Bel Air home and leave the place looking a mess. The marriage, which many of her intimates declared should never have happened in the first place, took its first step towards ending in May 1995. Any number of reasons emerged about why Fortensky packed his bags and moved into the Beverly Hills Hotel: topping the list were his smoking (Elizabeth had stopped, taking her doctors' advice, the previous year), his mood-swings and his excluding her from the drinking parties with his friends.

There were also rumours, albeit unsubstantiated, of a new man in Elizabeth's life. Bernard Lafferty was the former butler of Lucky Strike tobacco heiress Doris Duke, who had died at Falcon's Lair (Rudolph Valentino's former mansion) in October 1993. Duke had named the cross-dressing, pony-tailed Irishman executor of her $1-billion estate, and this had caused concern amongst her relatives. Besides having a serious drink problem, Lafferty was semi-literate with learning difficulties and was therefore declared by them incapable of taking on such a huge responsibility. (*Bernard and Doris*, a biopic starring Ralph Fiennes and Susan Sarandon, was released in 2007. The producers had deliberated over whether to include Elizabeth's character whilst she was still alive, bearing in mind that she had taken legal action in the past to prevent herself being interpreted on the screen during her lifetime, and decided not to take the risk.)

The tabloids speculated about how Bernard Lafferty had managed to penetrate Elizabeth's near impenetrable inner circle. Was he, they wanted to know, hoping to fleece her the way Doris Duke's family believed he had wormed his way into their relative's affections? Was Lafferty amorously interested in her, despite his homosexuality, and sufficiently so to wish to oust Larry Fortensky? Did he wish to run Elizabeth's financial affairs the way he had his late employer's? Elizabeth had almost certainly extended the hand of friendship because Lafferty had used his privileged position to persuade Doris Duke to donate $1 million to Elizabeth's AIDS foundation, with the promise of more to come – and it is likely that Elizabeth had genuinely grown to like him and wanted him around. We shall probably never know for sure.

One suspects that the real reason for the failure of Elizabeth's eighth marriage was boredom on Fortensky's part – here was a young man in the prime of life compelled to stay home most of the time, and Elizabeth's near manic demands never to be left alone, along with her failing health, had worn the both of them down. Fortensky emerged form the situation laughing all the way to the bank. His lawyers advised him to reject the $1.25-million settlement detailed in his prenuptial agreement, saying that a kiss-and-tell account of his relationship with Elizabeth Taylor would bring in many more times this amount – that is, if he planned to do the dirty on her. Though there is no evidence of this, Elizabeth must not have discounted the possibility and was taking no chances. If the press reports are to be believed, the final pay-off to ensure Fortensky's silence was impressive, consisting of the original payment of $1.25 million plus an additional $2 million in stocks and shares, a $2-million beach house, $250,000 for 'immediate expenses', and an alimony-type payment of $600,000 a year for ten years – *and* two Harley-Davidsons that had taken his fancy!

With Larry Fortensky out of the picture, and with no more serious relationships, Elizabeth gradually sank deeper and deeper into reclusion, although each time she emerged from her self-inflicted cocoon it was with great panache, and she always provided a feast for the pre-informed media. In May 1996, she attended an AIDS benefit at the Cannes Film Festival, sponsored by Cher – another massive gay icon – who was forced to take a back seat as Elizabeth stole the show. Later in the week, Elizabeth caused controversy by walking out halfway through a gala premiere of an adaptation of Jane Austen's *Emma* (1996), declaring it to be boring! The following year, she was diagnosed with a brain tumour 'the size of a golf ball', submitted to her most serous operation so far and insisted upon being photographed with a bald head to minimise the stigma of cancer. Her doctors advised her of the dangers of dying her hair when this grew back; for several years, she was a silver-blonde but no less beautiful than before, even in old age. Her slow recovery was aided by her friendship with Rod Steiger; the pair were seen in public but denied any romance.

In 1996, Elizabeth patched up her quarrel with Sybil Burton, whom she had not seen since they had crossed swords whilst shooting *Cleopatra*. The two met again at the bedside of Roddy McDowall, their mutual friend, now dying of cancer. It is said that Richard Burton's name was never mentioned, though he was foremost in her thoughts on 16 May 2000 when Elizabeth flew to London to be made a Dame Commander of the Order of the British Empire. Elizabeth was photographed outside Buckingham Palace with Julie Andrews, there to receive the same honour. The two sat next to each other in the ballroom whilst the band of the Grenadier Guards played a selection from *Mary Poppins* (1964) – which Elizabeth confessed she had never seen! Then, looking slightly dumpy but every inch the star in pale-blue slacks, a matching patterned lavender surcoat and just a few jewels, she told the queen, whilst receiving her medal, 'I wish Richard could have been here with me today, ma'am!'

The honour was commemorated by the BBC's celebration of her life *England's Other Elizabeth*, for which she agreed to tell her own story and bare her soul in front of the cameras. There were, however, certain conditions. During the 60-minute documentary, narrated by Nigel Hawthorne, she would speak *only* of the men in her life whom she could recall with genuine fondness: Mike Todd, Richard Burton, Monty, Jimmy and Rock. Similarly, only those who truly respected her were asked to participate: Shirley MacLaine, Angela Lansbury,

Rod Steiger and her AmFAR co-founder, Dr Mathilde Krim. These friends applauded her emotional intelligence, keen survival instincts, bravery in the face of adversity – and unswerving loyalty to those close to her, particularly those amongst the gay community. Slightly tremulous and still a little on the plump side, Elizabeth nevertheless looked *fabulous*!

Of her first roles as a child star, Elizabeth said, 'I had a great imagination, and I just slid into it. It was like a piece of cake!' Of Monty, she said, 'There was such energy to the man – what was coming out of his eyes, his body. It was, I suppose, like sitting next to an electric chair.' Recalling Monty's accident, even five decades on, still traumatised her. She recalled intimate moments with Jimmy Dean when he confided in her things that she said would stay locked in her heart for ever: 'Wouldn't you *love* to know?' She wept whilst reliving Mike Todd's death, cursed the studio for making her return to *Butterfield 8* and dismissed the film as 'a piece of shit'. Of Richard Burton, she claimed that he taught her how to be a better actress – but the other husbands did not get a mention.

Elizabeth closed her interview by sounding her own trumpet (and rightly so) about her work for AIDS victims, how she visited hospices anonymously and how, up to that point, she had helped raise over $180 million for her cause. 'You *can* put your arms around them,' she insisted, begging for tolerance, understanding and help. 'You *can* kiss their face, you can ruffle their hair. You're not gonna get it – you're not gonna die. It doesn't cost you one nickel to be of use!' The documentary then ends with a 1981 out-take from *General Hospital*, in which Elizabeth fluffs her lines. 'I'm sorry, folks,' she quips, 'I'm not used to acting!'

The biggest feud of Elizabeth's career – a feud of over 40 years standing, brought about by her stealing Eddie Fisher from Debbie Reynolds – was 'put to rights' in 2001 when Debbie's and Fisher's actress daughter Carrie came up with the script for *These Old Broads* and co-produced the television movie. Portraying the cast members of *Boy Crazy*, a 1960s feel-good film that is enjoying a tremendous box-office revival, were Debbie, Shirley MacLaine and (replacing Julie Andrews) Joan Collins. And Fisher pulled a scoop by casting Elizabeth as their hard-as-nails Jewish manager!

In fact, it is not entirely clear that Elizabeth and Debbie actually met during filming: in their scenes together, when one is facing the camera, we see only the other's back – rather like Marlene Dietrich's scenes in her final film *Just a Gigolo* (1978) when she met none of her co-stars. On the other hand, Elizabeth's obvious condoning of the Taylor-Fisher scandal being used as the butt of the film's funniest jokes, considering the gravity of the situation at the time, suggests that she can only have agreed to bury the hatchet. Similarly, episodes in Joan Collins and Shirley MacLaine's lives that they might have wanted obliterating from history are mercilessly resurrected by Carrie Fisher and her scriptwriting partner Elaine Pope, with hilarious effect. Virtually every scene contains an actress–character juxtaposition that is far from flattering.

The man responsible for getting the *Boy Crazy* gang back together again 40 years later is Wesley (Jonathan Silverman), the adopted son of Kate (MacLaine), who has not spoken to him in years. And to make Wesley's job that much more difficult, the three women hate each other for running off with each others' partners. Art mostly reflects real life as Kate tours flea-pit theatres, whilst Piper (Reynolds) sits on a golden throne in her Vegas casino, surrounded by cardboard cut-outs of herself in *Singin' in the Rain*. Reynolds parodies herself even further by confessing that she had to fight her way back to the top after being swindled by her manager. Her second husband, Harry Karl, gambled away $8 million of her fortune prior to their 1973 divorce.

The final member of the trio is Addie (Collins), the ex-sitcom star who has been living as a recluse for ten years since the incarceration of her mobster lover. 'I would rather get a barium enema on live TV than work with that tramp again,' Kate says of Addie, and when Wesley fails to reunite the trio, he turns to their former mentor, Beryl (Taylor), whose CV reads, 'Stays in bed all day, eating and talking on the phone, smoking pot and watching documentaries about dead people.' Surrounded by Andy Warhol portraits of herself, Elizabeth also wears the Krupp Diamond.

The first composite scene between Beryl and Piper dredges up the Taylor-Fisher-Reynolds scandal. It is revealed that Beryl, feeling low after having her tonsils out, stole Piper's husband during a week-long bender:

BERYL: It all happened so long ago, when we were so young.

PIPER: Just drop it, OK? I forgave you years ago, so let's move on. Besides, everyone knows you're a very sick woman, a card-carrying nymphomaniac . . .

BERYL: *Nympho*! Hah, you think any woman who had a normal, healthy sex life was a *nym-pho-maniac*?

PIPER: I enjoy sex. But you, if a man was on fire, you'd stamp him out and screw him!

BERYL: Piper, I did you a favour by taking away Freddie . . .

PIPER: A favour is doing something for someone that they're unable to do for themselves. I was perfectly capable of losing Freddie all on my own!

Beryl manages to get the three co-stars back together for a one-off TV special, and the bitching resumes: 'One more facelift and she'll blow her nose through her forehead'; 'Excuse me, Mrs Munster'; and 'Look, it's Queen Elizabeth and her mother, Ethel.' The scriptwriters even get away with referring to Joan Collins as the 'British Open'. Mike Todd and Eddie Fisher are combined in the character Tony the Meatpacker (so named for obvious reasons): he escapes from prison and gives Addie 'multiples' before expiring during Tantric sex – suffering from post-mortem priapism as the girls smuggle his body from her room, with Piper crooning 'Arrivederci, Tony', a direct reference to Fisher's closing number during the time of the scandal! When rebuking Piper, Addie also borrows a line from

Fisher's autobiography, telling Piper, 'You're so frigid, you've never had an orgasm,' before adding a line of her own: 'Pretending to be that little goody two-shoes when you were just as big a whore as we were!' The ensuing fight see the girls walking off the production, prompting Beryl to turn into Elizabeth Taylor as a means of getting her own way – faking an illness (a coronary) to get them back together again.

This was Elizabeth's final celluloid appearance, and how lovely she looks, smiling radiantly, swathed in lavender furs, her violet eyes and diamonds sparkling as she coerces the audience into giving her girls a standing ovation by drawling, 'Get off your asses for these old broads!' There could have been no finer swansong for the queen of Hollywood!

SIXTEEN

THE FADING STAR

AFTER *THESE OLD BROADS*, ELIZABETH RARELY EMERGED from her self-enforced solitude other than for the odd lawsuit or the all-too-frequent hospitalisations. Towards the end, there were the occasional sorties with friends and appearances at AIDS benefits, almost always to hammer home the same point: that she was still a force to be reckoned with when it came to personal or political issues, and to refute media claims that she was dying when, sadly, she slowly was.

Elizabeth's team always tried to ensure that her entrances were fanfared and spectacular. This did not happen, however, when, decked out in $5 million worth of diamonds, she 'dropped in' on one of Britain's most famous dysfunctional families, the Osbournes, when they held an AIDS fundraiser at their Los Angeles mansion. Because she was confined to a wheelchair, she had to enter the house via the cluttered garage, but she still managed to shine.

Despite her traumas, Elizabeth retained her glamour, courage and ever-present smile until the very end. The term 'mutton dressed as lamb', commonly applied to some of her Botox-enhanced colleagues from the same generation, was never once applied to her. In February 2005, despite ill-health, she attended the Oscars ceremony. By then, walking unaided was extremely difficult, yet she insisted on getting out of her wheelchair and shuffling unassisted – and still managed to look stunning in a silver, rhinestone-studded outfit, whilst many of the modern-day actresses clustered around her looked like they had been kitted out courtesy of the local nickel-and-dime store. 'I want to make sure that people know I'm still alive,' she told reporters.

Elizabeth's final round in the fight to prove herself a force to be reckoned with and a prima donna par excellence began on 19 March 2003 when, speaking at an AIDS benefit in Los Angeles, she laid into President Bush for demanding that Saddam Hussein flee his country on the eve of the Iraqi war. 'I can't imagine the thought of us going into World War III,' she said. 'I think it's so *stupid*! How can we expect this man who is a dictator and probably the most vain man in the world to leave his palace and his country in 24 hours? If that proposal was given to President Bush, can you see *him* packing his bags?'

There were more fireworks on 21 May, when Elizabeth was guest of honour at a special screening of *Giant* at the Cannes Film Festival. She arrived at the venue in a foul mood, turned her back on the sea of photographers and screamed, 'You want pictures, then you show me the money!' The instant Rock Hudson's face appeared on screen, she burst into tears and insisted on leaving, though this time she did not yell at the press, explaining that recalling Rock, and the terrible manner of his death, always got her overwrought – and that the demand for cash had been to augment her AIDS charity.

Towards the end of the following year, this indomitable war-ravaged old battleship once more sailed to the rescue of Michael Jackson, who was facing charges of child molestation for a second time. On 20 November 2004, the press reported that Jackson had handed himself in to the Santa Barbara police following the serving of an arrest warrant alleging that he had 'committed lewd and lascivious acts' with a child under the age of 16. Released on a $3-million bail bond, Jackson had gone into seclusion 'somewhere in the Las Vegas area' and immediately began defending himself on the mjnews.us Internet site. 'The charges recently directed at me are terribly serious,' he opined at the start of a five-page statement prepared by his public relations officer. 'They are, however, predicated on a big lie. This will be shown in court, and we will put this horrible thing behind us.'

The 'we' referred to Michael Jackson, his family and those fans who were so in awe of him that in their blinkered eyes it was inconceivable that he could be anything but innocent. And Elizabeth herself was still sufficiently star-struck to count herself amongst them. Since his earlier accusation of child abuse, Jackson had endured two lampooned marriages, including one to Elvis Presley's daughter, Lisa Marie – which Elvis's fans did not doubt would have had the King spinning in his grave. There had also been a much-publicised and criticised episode that had seen Jackson attacked by parent groups when the singer had been filmed dangling his baby precariously over a balcony. So far as Jackson's detractors were concerned – and these by far outweighed the fans – nothing was inconceivable until the courts proved otherwise.

This time the matter was taken to the US Supreme Court, with the very real possibility that Jackson would face a long jail sentence if found guilty – with his fragile constitution, that was an ordeal many people believed he would not survive. 'He is absolutely *innocent*,' Elizabeth's 2 November press statement read, adding of the media, 'Their whole attitude is that he is guilty. I thought the law was "innocent until proven guilty"? I *know* he's innocent, and I hope they all eat crow!' What everyone wanted to know, as they had the last time Jackson had been accused, was how Elizabeth could be so sure when she had not been there when the alleged offences had taken place? Once again, she was setting herself up for public ridicule.

There was also considerable speculation as to whether Elizabeth would be summoned to court as a character witness– it was only when Jackson's office declared that she would be subpoenaed if she failed to put in a good word for her friend that the media began doubting the authenticity of their friendship. Equally, there were conflicting reports over how she might react should the jury reach a guilty verdict. Had this happened, she would never have got away with remaining Jackson's ally – that is if they were still friends and Elizabeth's defensive outburst was not just another of her publicity stunts to attract attention to her fading star.

In any event, Elizabeth's presence was not required to augment the media circus. Following an unusually lengthy and fraught deliberation process, to which some believed the adage 'no smoke without fire' applied, the man universally referred to as 'Wacko Jacko' was acquitted of all charges.

'Holocaust Heirs Sue Star Liz for £10 Million Van Gogh Looted by Nazis' screamed the headline in the *Daily Express* on 15 October 2004, suggesting that at some time Elizabeth had been engaged in nefarious activities. Five months after Elizabeth had submitted a claim to a Los Angeles court stating ownership of the 1889 masterpiece, the descendants of one of its previous owners, the late Margarete Mauthner, were claiming that it had been stolen by the Nazis in 1939 and that under the rules of the 1998 Holocaust Victims Redress Act it should be returned to her heirs or auctioned off and the proceeds handed over.

Mauthner's great-grandson, Canadian lawyer Andrew Orkin, declared in his press statement, 'We are asserting that Ms Taylor was negligent and careless when she bought the painting. Our complaint charges that she ignored numerous conspicuous "red flags" in 1963 that it had likely been confiscated from a victim of Nazi persecution.' In fact, Elizabeth's father had purchased *View of the Asylum and Chapel at Saint-Remy* on her behalf, for an estimated $255,000, from Sotheby's of London.

The case dragged on for months, with Elizabeth's representatives counterclaiming that Mrs Mauthner, a German Jew, had sold the masterpiece in 1933, six years before fleeing to South Africa when the Nazis had seized her property. As there seemed to be no proof of this, or that Francis Taylor (who had amassed a fortune out of buying such works at rip-off prices from their owners, but never from the Nazis) had been aware of the painting's history, the judge dismissed the lawsuit on 2 February 2005, and Elizabeth got to keep her Van Gogh.

Elizabeth is said to have been 'utterly devastated'– she never did emotions by halves – by two interviews given by Sally Burton (one to the *Mail on Sunday*'s Danae Brook, the other to the *National Enquirer*) in August 2004 to mark the 20th anniversary of Richard Burton's death. The widow claimed in both interviews that Elizabeth's overwhelming presence had driven her to the brink of suicide, resulting in her being made an inpatient for six weeks on an intensive drugs programme. Her downward spiral had begun, she claimed, when Elizabeth had turned up at Burton's graveside only days after his funeral, thereby intruding upon her mourning. Elizabeth must have been delighted by the British paper's decision to complement the feature with over half a page of Taylor-Burton photographs and just a tiny picture of Sally.

'Elizabeth has her fantasies, and that's fine,' Sally told the *National Enquirer*, 'but I thought, "My God! All I'm ever going to be is one line on the end of the great Burton–Taylor romance!"' This of course echoed the sentiments of the whole world that, despite their two divorces, Elizabeth Taylor – and only Elizabeth Taylor – had been the love of Richard Burton's life.

In the spring of 2005, Elizabeth co-founded the House of Taylor Jewellery with Jack and Monty Abramov of Mirabelle Luxury Concepts, Los Angeles. The company, it was announced, would supply traditional jewellery at affordable prices, along with 'commissioned couture' pieces costing in excess of $1 million. The press announcement read:

> Elizabeth Taylor is synonymous with beauty, humanity, talent and exquisite jewellery. It is an unbelievable honour to partner the most iconic woman of our time and to build our entire company around her exquisite taste. To collaborate with her and design for her is one of the greatest dreams of any designer.

Elizabeth's passion for jewellery and her mania for one-upmanship even extended as far as her wheelchair. Having broken her back for the fifth time the previous August, she was reported as having placed an order with a Beverly Hills wheelchair company for a gold-plated model, studded with diamonds and with emerald-inlaid armrests. Her aim, she said, was to 'get one over' on the porn-baron Larry Flynt, the victim of an assassination attempt, whom she had seen riding around town in a solid-gold wheelchair. 'I want the Ferrari of wheelchairs,' Elizabeth told a reporter. 'Money's not a problem. Flynt travels in style, and so must I!' Such extravagance was defended by Elizabeth's spokesman, who explained in an 'official' statement, 'The point of acquiring a wheelchair is to enhance her mobility. Ms Taylor is still a very active campaigner and fund-raiser, and wants to do more. She remains a woman of tremendous style.' This might have been true, but there were many critics who questioned the morality of forking out $504,000 for an item that, although essential, need not have cost so much and pointed out that the money could have been better spent augmenting one of her charities.

In March, Elizabeth granted her first interview, via fax, to a French reporter in a decade. The lucky man was Christophe Martet of *Têtu*, the country's leading quality gay publication. She might have been slowing down her activities owing to increasingly poor health, but she was as vociferous as ever regarding the fight against AIDS:

> Our government *must* invest more money in research. At the moment, all the passion and hard work is down to individuals and private foundations. I've always detested being famous. Fame was something I tried to evade, but that was totally impossible. Then when I began my fight against AIDS, for the first time ever I was able to put my star status to good use. Because of it, people listened to me. My fame opened all doors. And you know that I have such affection for the gay community. These men are my *brothers* . . .

By the autumn of 2005, these brothers and Elizabeth's other fans around the world were distressed to learn that she was reported to be 'despairing, depressed, sleeping 14 hours a day and close to death'. Though it was often near impossible to differentiate between genuine truth, hearsay and plain attention seeking, what was certain was that her doctors had diagnosed osteoporosis – which certainly explained her falls and broken vertebrae – and, much more seriously, congestive heart disease.

Elizabeth's Bel Air home was reported to have been turned into a one-patient nursing home. With railed walls throughout, it was staffed around the clock. A special bed with cot-sides to prevent her from falling out had been installed in her room. 'It is as if she's thrown in the towel and admitted she has nothing to live for,' an unnamed close friend told the *Daily Express*. Another was quoted as having said, more prosaically, 'Elizabeth asked me what heaven was like. She couldn't wait to go there. She told me with tears in her eyes, "I won't hurt any more. I'll be with Richard." That's all she really cares about.'

Richard Burton's niece, Sian Owen, to whose home in Pontrhydyfen Elizabeth had sent a Fortnum & Mason hamper every Christmas since Burton's death, told *The Observer* on 30 October 2005, 'She's a believer. She does think that once she dies she will be together with him again. They were soulmates, but they just couldn't live together. It was like a Shakespearean tragedy.'

Fearing that the end might be near, Elizabeth began to finalise plans for her funeral, once more obsessing over Richard Burton. Her friend Mel Ferrer claimed early in November that she had confided in him, saying, 'Soon there will be no pain any more, and I'll be with Richard.'

Elizabeth had of course been close to death on more occasions than anyone cared to remember – sometimes genuinely so, often speculatively or inventively. Most recently, fearing that she might have been having a heart attack, her aides had rushed her to hospital, but this had turned out to be a false alarm – chest pains brought on by a severe cold. This time she was taken seriously.

Initially, Elizabeth wanted to be buried in the plot that she and Richard Burton had reserved in the Methodist cemetery at Pontrhydyfen – casually overlooking the fact that she had converted to Judaism. And if Sally Burton would not agree to having him re-interred, Elizabeth would lie next to Burton's parents, Edith and Richard Jenkins. Alternatively, she would be cremated and her ashes scattered across his grave in Switzerland. The plan to be buried in Pontrhydyfen was reaffirmed by Burton's brother, Graham. Speaking to the *Daily Mail*, he declared, 'She says that although Richard's body is buried in Switzerland, his heart belongs to Wales, and it is her wish to be buried here.'

This prompted the PerezHilton.com website to post a get-well message, which is said to have tickled her no end:

Dear Liz. You can sleep when you're dead! You need to snap out of it. Maybe a nice little cruise will cheer you up. Bring along Liza Minnelli and Debbie Reynolds (Oh, the drama!) and the fags will pay thousands to be at sea with you legends. All proceeds will go to AmFAR, of course. Feel better, Maggie. May you be purring again soon!

These ups and downs in Elizabeth's health continued throughout the winter of 2005–06, with some reports stating that she had Parkinson's disease – additionally, that she was in the preliminary stages of Alzheimer's. Then on 30 May 2006 came the so-called 'Deathbed Interview' for CNN, a forty-five-minute grilling (with no less than six commercial breaks) conducted by chat-show host Larry King, who certainly was intent on exacting his pound of flesh.

Like Elizabeth, seventy-two-year old King had been around the block a few times: he'd had seven marriages (two to the same woman) and several much-publicised affairs, including one with Angie Dickinson. The interview, pre-recorded and one suspects vetted by Elizabeth before being heavily edited, made the front pages of most of the world's major newspapers the next day, with the emphasis placed on Elizabeth's well-being. 'Oh come on,' she yelled at King, 'Do I *look* like I'm dying? Do I look or sound like I have Alzheimer's?'

On first impression, one would have said not. Elizabeth looked good, nowhere near 74, but if you study the interview in its entirety before the cuts have been made, the tell-tale signs are there – much of her personal appearance has to do with cast-iron self-control and, meticulous grooming. Elizabeth wears the most horrendous lime-green kaftan and enough jewellery to sag a Christmas tree. This deflects from her puffed, blotchy features and corpulent (by way of overmedication) figure. Prior to the interview, when we observe her being pushed into the studio in her wheelchair – her little dog, Daisy, sitting on her lap – she really does resemble a little old lady, still astonishingly beautiful and smiling radiantly, but very fragile and seemingly a little confused by it all. Later, when she faces the host across his desk, there is no audience. Next to her there are cue cards and a box of tissues, should all this get to be too much for her and she feel a tear coming on. Elizabeth has done this sort of thing before, constantly reminding her interrogators that she is first and foremost an *actress*, therefore allowing viewers to decide for themselves if she is telling the truth or merely playing her most famous role – that of Elizabeth Taylor. On this occasion, her speech is slightly slurred. Has she been drinking? *Does* she have Alzheimer's? Or is she merely nervous? These are the questions the viewer most frequently asks.

Once she has theatrically denied having one foot in the grave, Elizabeth attacks the tabloids for prompting the rumours in the first place. 'They have nothing else dirty to write about anybody else. They won't let me retire,' she laments. Then she contradicts herself by declaring that she does not *want* to retire – which brings up the *real* purpose of this interview: she is promoting the 15th-anniversary edition of her White Diamonds perfume and is also about to head for Las Vegas to launch the latest batch of jewellery that she has designed.

In the meantime, King asks her if she would take on another movie role. Without hesitation, she replies that she would, providing it was 'juicy, spicy and challenging'. Then it is back to the subject of her health. She has been confined to a wheelchair, she says, on account of the severe back pain that has plagued her her whole life. She was born with scoliosis (double curvature of the spine) and admits to having osteoporosis, a condition her publicist has recently denied, which prompts the question: if he denied this, what is to say that Elizabeth is not suffering from the other ailments that have also been denied? King asks her if she is afraid of death and she says that she is not, because she has died four times already (her illness whilst shooting *Cleopatra*) and that she firmly believes that the spirit lives on after death. She speaks briefly about her conversion to Judaism, confessing that she did this to be closer to Mike Todd after his death, from which she has never recovered.

Elizabeth is less forthcoming about certain aspects of her love life. In previous interviews, the subject of husbands has always been rigorously taboo, particularly Nicky Hilton and Eddie Fisher, though she grimaces through a clip from *Butterfield 8* in this instance. The only husbands she has ever wanted to talk about have been Todd and Burton: losing them was traumatic, and if anything has sustained Elizabeth over the years, cynics might observe, it has been a good old-fashioned trauma, with the promise of a breakdown thrown in for good measure.

Elizabeth reacts with angry reticence when King demands to know which husband was her biggest soulmate: 'Oh, aren't *you* scratchy? I'm not going to tell *you* the truth!' With this, she was shooting herself in the foot. If she had no intention of divulging the truth about the men in her life, how sure were we – again – that she was not trying to pull the wool over our eyes regarding her health? Once more, the audience had to remind themselves that Elizabeth Taylor is first and foremost a thespian who has been doing this sort of thing her whole life.

As with her recent interview with *Têtu*, Elizabeth pretends not to care for terms such as 'icon' and 'legend', which she rightfully concedes are too liberally applied. 'An icon is someone who's dead, with a wooden plaque on the wall,' she opines. 'A legend is something you read about in the past tense.' Here she was definitely selling herself short: even her worst enemies would have agreed that Elizabeth was a *living* legend, and some.

Elizabeth says that she has much respect for some of her co-stars. She loved Paul Newman, and Jimmy Dean and Rock Hudson were wonderful, but it upsets her so much reflecting on these two that King avoids mentioning Monty Clift. Brando, she says, was 'full of rubbish', intimidating everyone by fluffing his lines, but she adored him just the same. Then she spoils it all by having too much enthusiasm for Michael Jackson, whom she believes was deliberately set up by the press.

'I've never been so *angry* in my life,' she growls when questioned about the allegations of child abuse, concluding that Jackson (then self-exiled in Bahrain) had sworn never to perform in the United States again because the media there had treated him like dirt. Recalling an occasion when she, Jackson and his nephews had laid on the bed in his room watching Disney movies, she went on, 'There was nothing abnormal about it. There was no touchy-feely going on. There was nothing *odd* about it!' Cynics would again suggest, of course, that *had* any untoward activity taken place *chez* Jackson, it certainly would not have been in Elizabeth's presence. This is a cue for Elizabeth to dip into the aforementioned box of tissues and for King to announce the next commercial break.

Next, Larry King takes calls from listeners, all female, all telling Elizabeth how wonderful they think she is. The stars she had looked up to in her formative years, she says, were Katharine Hepburn and Spencer Tracy. Her favourite amongst her films was *Who's Afraid Of Virginia Woolf?* And regarding her constant back pain, she advises a fellow sufferer, 'If you want to go on functioning, you grin and bear it!'

Next comes the precise reason for the interview: the House of Taylor's latest collection, about to go on show in Las Vegas. She refuses to put a price on each piece: what it is worth, how much customers will have to pay to have some little trinket personally designed by her. King sucks up to her by pretending not to know what a tiara is. The pieces, she says, have been made in Bangkok and other parts of the Far East, which might confirm the real reason behind Elizabeth's and Larry Fortensky's visit to Singapore 'to comfort Michael Jackson' at around the time she put together her first collection – combining business with a mercy dash to acquire maximum publicity for the former.

For the benefit of CNN's viewers, Elizabeth has also brought along several items from her personal collection: the Krupp Diamond, nine diamond bracelets, and a diamond-necklace-and-earrings set given to her by Mike Todd. Collectively, these are valued at over $10 million, and it is almost obscene when Elizabeth pretends not to know what they are worth. As for the items she has designed, it will subsequently emerge that the huge House of Taylor ruby-and-diamond brooch she is modelling will retail for $82,500 and the diamond necklace for a cool $179,000. And just to remind viewers that she is not lacking in humility, on King's desk next to these items are Elizabeth's reading glasses – which she claims she bought from a 99-cents store!

The final phone call comes from Elizabeth's business partner, Kathy Ireland, who might be excused her acute sycophancy, because what she says could not be more apt: the ultimate tribute to a remarkable woman for all the right reasons. Elizabeth in her heyday might have represented all that was spoilt, reckless, grasping and selfish about a product of Hollywood's studio system, but as an ambassadress for the gay community in the wake of AIDS – at the time of the Larry King interview, she had raised over $300 million for the cause – she absolutely and unquestionably *was* the new Messiah.

Revealing how bigoted 'friends' had hung up on her and how Elizabeth's gay-friendliness had put her own career at risk, Ireland concludes:

Today we have people who are living with HIV. When Dame Elizabeth began her battle, everyone infected died of AIDS, and she's responsible for saving millions of lives. And so for

being courageous, for being someone we all love and adore,
Dame Elizabeth, you will always be my hero and the Joan
of Arc of AIDS.

The interview ends on a jovial, yet still theatrical note: Elizabeth
having a fit of giggles. King wants to know if there is any possibility
of her marrying again. *She* wants to know if *he* is proposing before
delivering a resounding, 'No!' 'Well,' he responds, 'For someone
on her death-bed with Alzheimer's, you did amazingly well. For
someone so tragically ill, I've never seen more courage!'

In August 2006, Elizabeth's attention – though not it would seem
her anger – was drawn to the fact that I was writing this book.
She did not appear to mind my describing her as being, in her
heyday, 'the most self-centred star in the firmament, whose excesses
were obscene'. The publicity sheet that ended up on her desk also
referred to her as 'the last truly great Hollywood superstar, in the
wake of whom every single one of today's so-called "headliners"
fades into oblivion'.

Her spokesperson told me over the phone: 'Though I wouldn't
doubt she would bawl you out if you've written any shit about
her, she'd be the first to want to give you a hug for all the praise
you've heaped upon her. Elizabeth's seen some of your books,
and she approves of the honest approach you have. She says that
David Bret is a shit, but a loveable shit!'

Faced with more speculation over her health, and in a last-ditch
attempt to prove that she was still fit as the proverbial fiddle –
for which she must only be commended – in the September, while
holidaying in Hawaii, Elizabeth excelled even herself by making a
spur-of-the-moment decision to go swimming with sharks!

Days earlier, the Australian naturalist Steve Irwin had died after
being attacked by a stingray, prompting one website to now run the
headline 'Krikee! Elizabeth Taylor Is The New Crocodile Hunter!'
Sitting in her wheelchair and wearing a T-shirt reading 'Shark
Bait', she was photographed being manoeuvred into the boat for
the two-hour crossing to Oahu, where she was loaded into a

10 x 8 foot Plexiglas cage and lowered below the surface. After paddling around with the sharks for 30 minutes, she resurfaced looking an absolute mess and panting for breath but exhilarated by the experience. Later, she dashed off a postcard to the *New York Post*'s Liz Smith, the doyenne of gossip columnists. 'For someone who has been in bed with a bad back, I have done all the things I've dreamed of,' she wrote, adding that it had been the most exciting day of her life.

And Liz Smith's own reaction to this book, attacking me and my publisher for what she had yet to read, appeared in her *New York Post* column of 19 October 2006. 'Oh pul-leeze,' she crowed, 'I challenge them to find one scandalous revelation we haven't heard. Miz Liz survives all. The recent Randy Taraborrelli book galvanised her to get up and swim with sharks. What will this one do? Send her to arm-wrestle a giant squid?'

However, no sooner had Elizabeth settled this latest rumour about her health than, with contrary aplomb, she started them all up again by announcing that she was selling some of her jewels, memorabilia, art work, clothing and personal possessions. 'She wants the things she's cared about over the years to go to good homes,' a Christie's spokeswoman told me. 'She feels the end is nearer than ever before and doesn't want people squabbling over her possessions when she's dead.'

The media had by now lost count of the number of times Elizabeth's publicist had 'leaked' the news that she was at death's door, only to just as quickly state that she was hale and hearty – anything to keep the publicity machine rolling. Arguably the biggest stunt so far occurred when the press reported that she was about to wed for the ninth time!

The story broke in the *Sunday Express* on 15 October 2006, when a 'close friend' was reported as saying:

> She has known some terribly dark days, but it's amazing how she's bounced back. She has rebounded straight into the arms of a man, and it's wonderful to see them together. For some

stars it's work, family, even shopping. But for Liz, romance has always been a driving force.

The lucky 'groom-to-be' was Iranian portrait artist Firooz Zahedi, at 57, 17 years Elizabeth's junior. A graduate of Georgetown University, he had studied photography at the Corcoran School and worked for Andy Warhol's *Interview* magazine in the mid-1970s. At around this time he had met Elizabeth and on the strength of their friendship had relocated to Los Angeles, where he had become her personal movie-stills photographer and, over the next three decades, worked for *Vanity Fair*, *Esquire* and *Time*. He had also developed a coterie of celebrity friends, including Meryl Streep and Barbra Streisand.

Zahedi remained tight-lipped about the affair, though there were others willing to speak on his behalf – mainly to stress that he was not a gold-digger. One story (which no one believed, even after the reportedly genial atmosphere of *These Old Broads*) circulated that Elizabeth had confided in her 'old movie-star friend' Debbie Reynolds that she was thinking of marrying again, adding, 'He isn't scared of being number eight.' And inevitably there was also the 'close pal who cannot be named' who predicted that Zahedi would be 'popping the question' at the end of the month when he accompanied Elizabeth to her next business meeting in Hawaii.

Of course, after the confession came the denial. Elizabeth's spokesman confirmed the relationship with Zahedi – and before the ink dried on the newspapers, Elizabeth hit the roof, declaring, 'We are not, never have been and never *will* be romantically involved! My private life and my plans at this time *remain* private!' The refutation was delivered with such aggression that, in the end, no one knew what to believe, and few really cared. For ten years, since she'd divorced Larry Fortensky, there had been no regular man in her life – a bonus, one of her friends told me, adding, 'Without the added complications of love, Elizabeth's that much easier to be around. Let's hope that it stays that way until the end!'

In the summer of 2007, with her usual defiant attitude that

the show must go on no matter what, Elizabeth announced two ambitious projects – one which attained fruition, the other which never had any hope of doing so. Later in the year, she appeared with James Earl Jones in a single performance of A.R. Gurney's stage play *Love Letters*, a project that raised $500,000 for her AIDS foundation. Her character, an extension of herself, appeared in a wheelchair, and the show did not place too much strain on her health.

The monstrously difficult role of Norma Desmond, in the movie remake of *Sunset Boulevard*, was quite another matter. For one thing, the sponsors would have had a tough task getting anyone to insure her when she was persistently fighting off rumours that she virtually had one foot in the grave. The original film, made in 1950, had starred Gloria Swanson and – after Montgomery Clift had turned it down – William Holden. Again, it was difficult to separate truth from hearsay. Paramount released a statement claiming that they had reached 'an advanced stage of negotiation' with Elizabeth's manager, Barbara Berkowitz, and had offered her a fee of $5 million. To add credence to the idea that Elizabeth was 'demonstrating to Tinseltown her improbable recovery', Paul Scott's report in the *Daily Mail* contained a recent photograph of her descending the steps of a plane, in his words, 'looking like a geriatric Ali G, adorned ridiculously in rapper-style bling crucifixes, gold chains and sporting a trucker's cap made by hip-hop designer Ed Hardy'. A Paramount spokesman told me, however, that Elizabeth had made up the story and had never even been considered for the part, and that the last thing any studio wanted was a multmillion-dollar lawsuit brought about by one of the greatest stars on the planet dying on them mid-production. So, what did Elizabeth do to convince the studio that this would not happen? The same friend who had talked to me about Firooz Zahedi said, 'She pretended that she was fighting fit by putting out the story that she was thinking of getting married again!'

This latest instalment in the 'Is Liz dying or not?' saga got under way in Hawaii when she planned a 'low-key private dinner' with her friend Jason Winters, a black entrepreneur who at 47 was

28 years her junior. Of course, where Elizabeth was concerned there was no such thing as low key. The staff at the restaurant were instructed not to breathe a word of who their special guest was going to be on 28 September – while Elizabeth called Liz Smith and announced that there was a new man in her life: 'Jason Winters is one of the most wonderful men I've ever known, and that's why I love him. He bought us a beautiful house in Hawaii, and we visit it as often as possible!' Then she hired a huge black limousine, along with a police escort complete with screaming sirens, to drive her to the venue, and added further excitement to the proceedings by having it park outside the restaurant while she fixed her make-up. Throughout the meal, according to a Reuters report, 'Elizabeth repeatedly caressed the face of her millionaire friend.' Wearing an ankle-length satin gown, a white mink stole, the Krupp Diamond and '$4 million's worth of trinkets', she posed for the crowd in her wheelchair, then rushed home to complain to the press about their having intruded on her evening!

The next day, a 'close friend' of Elizabeth, who naturally asked not to be named, told Reuters, 'Liz is madly in love with Jason, and he feels the same way. It's taken us all by surprise, but we are happy for her. She didn't think she'd fall in love again, but since Jason came into her life, all that has changed.' It was, of course, the start of another of those attention-seeking campaigns for which Elizabeth had always been known. No sooner had the ink dried on the 'Liz Plans To Marry Husband Number Nine' headlines than the denials came rolling in. Martin Delaney, the founder of a San Francisco AIDS charity of which Winters was patron, told the *Daily Mail*:

> I don't know how a marriage between them could take place. That's not the kind of relationship they've got. Elizabeth is friends with Jason and his long-term friend, Erik Sterling. Jason and Erik are both on the board of the charity, and *they* have a house in Hawaii. The idea of them marrying is silly stuff.

The 'romance' quickly played itself out.

Throughout 2008, there were numerous hospitalisations. At one stage, Elizabeth became so ill that her family were summoned to her bedside and told to expect the worst. In October, there was a setback when her former co-star Paul Newman died. The papers reported her as being 'utterly heartbroken', but once again this was mostly attention seeking; she and Newman had neither seen nor spoken to each other for years.

Elizabeth's biggest 'drama-fest' since the death of Richard Burton centred on the demise, on 25 June 2009, of 50-year-old Michael Jackson. By now, her friendship with 'Wacko Jacko' had cooled somewhat – there had been too many child molestation stories since she had last leapt to his defence for her to be certain that he would ever be completely exonerated of all the charges, rumours and facts levelled against him. Even so, this now sadly deluded old lady went into extreme emotional overdrive upon hearing the news, reportedly collapsing and being rushed to hospital – though no one seemed to know which one – and issuing a statement which partly read:

> My heart, my mind, they are broken. I loved Michael with all my soul, and I can't imagine life without him. We had so much in common, and we had such loving fun together . . . I still can't believe it. I don't want to believe it. It can't be so . . . He will live in my heart, but it's not enough . . . I don't think anyone knew how much we loved each other. The purest, most giving love I've ever known . . .

Elizabeth claimed that she had been in the middle of packing her suitcases, ready to travel to London for the opening night of Jackson's imminent European tour. This was not true. Elizabeth had never packed a suitcase in her life, and her doctors had expressly forbidden her to fly for fear that she might have a heart attack on board the plane. The *Wall Street Journal* was the first to point out that Elizabeth had referred to *herself* 23 times in the 162-word statement, bringing the comment from the popular *I Hate The*

Media! website, 'There's one thing in Taylor's statement that cannot be disputed. Her mind is definitely broken.'

In the wake of the hysteria surrounding Jackson's death, and to ensure that as much emphasis as possible was placed upon *her* as a self-professed key figure in the singer's life, Elizabeth declared that she would not be attending his memorial service or his funeral. 'I just don't believe that Michael would want me to share my grief with millions of people. I cannot be part of the public whoopla,' she announced on Twitter. In fact, there were reports that the Jackson clan did not want her there, their excuse being that she had been a friend of Michael's, not theirs, but in reality because they were well aware that what was supposed be the combination of a solemn occasion and a celebration of their son's life did not need to be turned into an Elizabeth Taylor extravaganza, where she would be centre of attention.

There was no way, of course, that Elizabeth was going to miss out on such an important media fest. She attended the ceremony whether she was welcome or not and afterwards did attempt to steal the limelight – obviously forgetting her earlier promise to Richard Burton – by announcing that, when her time came, she now wanted to be buried next to Michael Jackson!

The next big drama occurred on 22 September 2010: Eddie Fisher died, aged 82, and once again Elizabeth was reported to be 'devastated'. This cut no ice with Fisher's family and friends. Speaking to the press, the singer's daughter Carrie declared that Elizabeth had never loved him, rather that he had been no more than a shoulder to cry on after the death of Mike Todd.

Then, on 11 February 2011, Elizabeth was admitted to Cedars-Sinai Hospital, where she is now known to have suffered a slight stroke. As with every drama in recent years, her spokesman was there to deny that she was as gravely ill as the hospital claimed. Sadly, this time it really was serious. For a few days, she seemed to rally – there was even talk of her being discharged.

The end came suddenly, at 1.28 a.m. on Wednesday, 23 March, just three weeks after she had celebrated her 79th birthday. 'I was tending to her when she opened those big, beautiful violet eyes,' a hospital spokeswoman said. 'She was surrounded by her family and offered a weak, almost timid smile. Then she was gone, perhaps the biggest star Hollywood has ever known.'

EPILOGUE

WE, THE FANS AND LOVED ONES, HAD ANTICIPATED THE end for a long, long time. Even so, the news came as a tremendous shock. Hers had been a traumatic life, made more so by self-inflicted dramas, persistent ill health – and arguably not just too many men but almost always the wrong kind of man. Maybe had Elizabeth married her first sweetheart, Glenn Davis, and given up her career as he had wanted her to, there would have been far less tragedy in her life. And then, of course, the world would never have witnessed one of the truly spellbinding talents not just of her generation but of any other.

Long before dawn on 23 March, hundreds of fans gathered on Hollywood's Walk of Fame. Many had swooped on the city's florists to snap up violets, the colour of Elizabeth's eyes, and a massive wreath of these was erected over her star. In London, simple bunches of daffodils were left next to the gates of the house where she had been born.

The tributes and eulogies were legion and could easily form a book of their own. Michael Caine, Angela Lansbury, director Michael Winner, singer George Michael, dozens of minor stars of whom Elizabeth had probably never heard, politicians and heads of state all rushed to their phones to pay their last respects within an hour of her death. Elton John wept at the news and said, 'We have just lost a Hollywood giant. More importantly, we have lost an incredible human being.' Liza Minnelli said, 'As a friend, she was always, always there. I'll miss her for the rest of my life.'

Now-retired chat-show host Larry King called her 'a great star and a gutsy woman, the likes of which we will never see again'. Whoopi Goldberg called her 'a great broad and a great friend'. Joan Collins announced, 'There will never be another star who will come close to her luminosity and generosity.'

Barbra Streisand, that other indefatigable champion of the gay man who has also raised millions for her charities, wrote, 'She was so funny. She was generous. She made her life count. It's the end of an era. It wasn't just her beauty or her stardom. It was her humanitarianism. She put a face on HIV/AIDS.' Debbie Reynolds, who had once been a part of the 'enemy camp', but who had long since made her peace with Elizabeth, called her death 'a blessing in disguise', adding, 'God bless her, she's on to a better place. I'm happy that she's out of her pain because she was in a lot of pain. This was a blessing in disguise . . . she's in heaven and she's in a heavenly place and she's happy.' Debbie's daughter, Carrie Fisher, who had brought about their reunion many years after the affair, said, 'If my father had to divorce my mother for anyone, I'm so grateful that it was Elizabeth.'

And Jarrett Barrios, president of GLAAD (the Gay and Lesbian Alliance Against Defamation), observed, 'Dame Taylor was an icon not only in Hollywood but in the LGBT community, where she worked to ensure that everyone was treated with the respect and dignity we all deserve.'

Elizabeth's son Michael Wilding Jr spoke eloquently and touchingly when announcing her death to the media:

> My mother was an extraordinary woman who lived life to the fullest, with great passion, humour and love. Though her loss is devastating to those of us who held her so close and so dear, we will always be inspired by her enduring contribution to our world. Her remarkable body of work in film, her ongoing success as a businesswoman and her brave and relentless advocacy in the fight against HIV/AIDS all make us all incredibly proud of what she accomplished. We know, quite simply, that the world

is a better place for Mom having lived in it. Her legacy will never fade, her spirit will always be with us and her love will live for ever in our hearts.

It is an indisputable fact that Elizabeth Taylor was the very last of the Hollywood greats. Most of her contemporaries – Garbo, Streisand and Dietrich excepted – were compelled to walk in the shadow of her sun. Of today's stars, *not one* may be deemed worthy of stepping even within a mile of that shadow.

APPENDIX

THE FILMS OF ELIZABETH TAYLOR

There's One Born Every Minute, Universal, 1942 (Harold Young), with Peggy Moran, Carl Switzer, Scott Jordan

Lassie Come Home, MGM, 1943 (Fred Wilcox), with Roddy McDowall, Donald Crisp, Dame May Whitty, Edmund Gwenn, Nigel Bruce

Jane Eyre, 20th Century Fox, 1944 (Robert Stevenson), with Orson Welles, Joan Fontaine, Margaret O'Brien

The White Cliffs of Dover, MGM, 1944 (Clarence Brown), with Irene Dunne, Alan Marshal, Dame May Whitty, Gladys Cooper, Peter Lawford, Roddy McDowall

National Velvet, MGM, 1944 (Clarence Brown), with Mickey Rooney, Donald Crisp, Angela Lansbury

Courage of Lassie, MGM, 1946 (Fred Wilcox), with Frank Morgan, Harry Davenport, George Cleveland

Cynthia, MGM, 1947 (Robert Z. Leonard), with George Murphy, S.Z. Sakall, Mary Astor, Spring Byington

Life with Father, Warner Bros, 1947 (Michael Curtiz), with William Powell, Irene Dunne, Edmund Gwenn

A Date with Judy, MGM, 1948 (Richard Thorpe), with Wallace Beery, Jane Powell, Robert Stack

Julia Misbehaves, MGM, 1948 (Jack Conway), with Greer Garson, Walter Pidgeon, Peter Lawford

Little Women, MGM, 1949 (Mervin LeRoy), with June Allyson, Peter Lawford, Margaret O'Brien, Janet Leigh, Rossano Brazzi

Conspirator, MGM, 1949 (Victor Saville), with Robert Taylor, Robert Flemyng, Thora Hird

The Big Hangover, MGM, 1950 (Norman Krasna), with Van Johnson, Edgar Buchanan, Gene Lockhart

Father of the Bride, MGM, 1950 (Vincente Minnelli), with Spencer Tracy, Joan Bennett, Don Taylor

Father's Little Dividend, MGM,
1951 (Vincente Minnelli), with
Spencer Tracy, Joan Bennett,
Don Taylor

Quo Vadis (cameo), MGM, 1951
(Mervyn LeRoy), with Robert
Taylor, Deborah Kerr, Leo Genn

A Place in the Sun, Paramount,
1951 (George Stevens), with
Montgomery Clift, Shelley
Winters, Anne Revere, Keefe
Brasselle, Raymond Burr,
Shepperd Strudwick

Callaway Went Thataway (cameo),
MGM, 1951 (Norman Panama,
Melvin Frank), with Fred
MacMurray, Dorothy McGuire,
Howard Keel

Love Is Better Than Ever,
MGM, 1952 (Stanley Donen),
with Larry Parks, Josephine
Hutchinson, Ann Doran

Ivanhoe, MGM, 1952 (Richard
Thorpe), with Robert Taylor,
Joan Fontaine, George Sanders,
Emlyn Williams

The Girl Who Had Everything,
MGM, 1953 (Richard Thorpe),
with Fernando Lamas, William
Powell, Gig Young

Rhapsody, MGM, 1954 (Charles
Vidor), with Vittorio Gassman,
John Ericson, Louis Calhern

Elephant Walk, Paramount, 1954
(William Dieterle), with Dana
Andrews, Peter Finch

Beau Brummel, MGM, 1954
(Curtis Bernhardt), with Stewart
Granger, Peter Ustinov, Robert
Morley

The Last Time I Saw Paris, MGM,
1954 (Richard Brooks), with
Van Johnson, Walter Pidgeon,
Donna Reed, Eva Gabor

Giant, Warner Bros, 1956
(George Stevens), with Rock
Hudson, James Dean, Mercedes
McCambridge, Jane Withers,
Carroll Baker, Sal Mineo,
Dennis Hopper, Chill Wills

Raintree County, MGM, 1957
(Edward Dmytryk), with
Montgomery Clift, Eva Marie
Saint, Lee Marvin, Rod
Taylor, Nigel Patrick, Agnes
Moorehead, Tom Drake

Cat on a Hot Tin Roof, MGM,
1958 (Richard Brooks), with
Paul Newman, Burl Ives, Judith
Anderson, Jack Carson

Suddenly, Last Summer,
Columbia, 1959 (Joseph
Mankiewicz), with Montgomery
Clift, Katharine Hepburn,
Albert Dekker, Mercedes
McCambridge, Gary Raymond,
Mavis Villiers

Holiday in Spain (aka **Scent of
Mystery**) (cameo), Michael
Todd Jr Productions, 1960
(Jack Cardiff), with Denholm
Elliott, Peter Lorre, Paul Lukas

Butterfield 8, MGM, 1960 (Daniel
Mann), with Laurence Harvey,
Eddie Fisher, Dina Merrill

Cleopatra, 20th Century Fox,
1963 (Joseph Mankiewicz),
with Richard Burton, Rex
Harrison, Roddy McDowall,
Pamela Brown, Martin Landau

The VIPs, MGM, 1963 (Anthony
Asquith), with Richard Burton,
Louis Jourdan, Elsa Martinelli,
Margaret Rutherford

The Sandpiper, MGM, 1965
(Vincente Minnelli), with
Richard Burton, Eva Marie
Saint, Charles Bronson

Who's Afraid of Virginia Woolf?, Warner Bros, 1966 (Mike Nichols), with Richard Burton, George Segal, Sandy Dennis

The Taming of the Shrew, Columbia, 1967 (Franco Zeffirelli), with Richard Burton, Cyril Cusack, Michael Hordern

Doctor Faustus, Columbia, 1967 (Nevill Coghill), with Richard Burton, Andreas Teuber, Elizabeth O'Donovan

Reflections in a Golden Eye, 1967, Warner Bros (John Huston), with Marlon Brando, Robert Forster, Julie Harris

The Comedians, MGM, 1967 (Peter Glenville), with Richard Burton, Alec Guiness, Peter Ustinov, Lillian Gish

Boom!, Universal, 1968 (Joseph Losey), with Richard Burton, Noel Coward, Michael Dunn

Secret Ceremony, Universal, 1968 (Joseph Losey), with Mia Farrow, Robert Mitchum, Peggy Ashcroft

Anne of the Thousand Days (cameo), Hal Wallis Productions, 1969 (Charles Jarrott), with Richard Burton, Geneviève Bujold, Irene Papas

The Only Game in Town, 20th Century Fox, 1970 (George Stevens), with Warren Beatty, Charles Braswell, Hank Henry

Under Milk Wood, Altura Films, 1971 (Andrew Sinclair), with Richard Burton, Peter O'Toole, Glynis Johns

Zee and Co., Columbia, 1972 (Brian Hutton), with Michael Caine, Susannah York

Hammersmith Is Out, Cornelius Crean Films, 1972 (Peter Ustinov), with Richard Burton, Peter Ustinov, Beau Bridges, George Raft

Divorce His, Divorce Hers, ABC-TV, 1973 (Waris Hussein), with Richard Burton, Carrie Nye, Barry Foster

Night Watch, Avco Embassy, 1973 (Brian Hutton), with Laurence Harvey, Billie Whitelaw, Tony Britton

Ash Wednesday, Paramount, 1973 (Larry Peerce), with Helmut Berger, Henry Fonda, Keith Baxter

That's Entertainment, MGM, 1974 (Jack Haley), with Fred Astaire, Bing Crosby, Gene Kelly, Peter Lawford

The Driver's Seat, Avco Embassy, 1974 (G. Patroni Griffi), with Guido Mannari, Ian Bannen

The Blue Bird, 20th Century Fox, 1976 (George Cukor), with Ava Gardner, Jane Fonda, Patsy Kensit, Robert Morley

Victory at Entebbe, ABC, 1976 (Marvin Chomsky), with Kirk Douglas, Burt Lancaster, Richard Dreyfuss

A Little Night Music, New World Pictures, 1977 (Harold Prince), Lesley-Anne Down

Return Engagement (aka **Repeat Performance**), NBC-TV, 1978 (Joseph Hardy), with Joseph Bottoms, Peter Donat, Allyn Ann McLerie

Winter Kills, Avco Embassy, 1979 (William Richert), with Jeff Bridges, John Huston, Anthony Perkins, Eli Wallach

The Mirror Crack'd, EMI Films,

1980 (Guy Hamilton), with
Rock Hudson, Tony Curtis,
Kim Novak, Edward Fox,
Geraldine Chaplin, Angela
Lansbury

Between Friends, HBO-TV, 1983
(Lou Antonio), with Carol
Burnett, Barbara Rush, Stephen
Young

Malice in Wonderland, ITC-TV,
1985 (Gus Trikonis), with Jane
Alexander, Richard Dysart,
Joyce Van Patten

North and South (TV mini-series),
ABC-TV, 1985 (Richard T.
Heffron), with Kirstie Allie,
Patrick Swayze, Lesley-Anne
Down

There Must Be a Pony, Columbia
TV, 1986 (Joseph Sargent), with
Robert Wagner, James Coco,
Ken Olin

Poker Alice, New World
Television, 1987 (A.A.
Seidelman), with Tom Skerritt,
George Hamilton

Il giovane Toscanini, Carthago
Films, 1988 (Franco Zeffirelli),
with C. Thomas Howell, Sophie
Ward

Sweet Bird of Youth, NBC-TV,
1989 (Nicolas Roeg), with
Mark Harmon, Valerie Perrine

The Flintstones, Universal, 1994
(Brian Levant), with John
Goodman, Rick Moranis, Rosie
O'Donnell

These Old Broads, ABC-TV,
2001 (Matthew Diamond),
with Debbie Reynolds, Shirley
MacLaine, Joan Collins, Peter
Graves, Jonathan Silverman

BIBLIOGRAPHY
& SOURCES

The American Film Institute. *Dialogue On Film: George Stevens,* 4, May/June 1975.

Anger, Kenneth. *Hollywood Babylon.* San Francisco: Straight Arrow Books, 1981.

Anger, Kenneth. *Hollywood Babylon* II. New York: Dell Publishing, 1984.

Antonio (Maria Callas' chauffeur). Interview with David Bret, September 1977.

Astor, Mary. *Life On Film.* New York: Delacorte Press, 1967.

Bacon, James. *Made In Hollywood.* New York: Warner Books, Inc., 1978.

Bast, William. *James Dean: A Biography.* New York: Ballantine Books, 1956

Belsten, Mick. "Rock Hudson, Health Report." *Gay Times,* September 1985.

Bosworth, Patricia. *Montgomery Clift: A Biography.* New York: Harcourt Brace Jovanovich, Inc., 1978.

Bret, David. *Freddie Mercury: Living on the Edge.* London: Robson Books, 1996.

Bret, David. *Joan Crawford: Hollywood Martyr.* London: Robson Books, 2006.

Bret, David. *Marlene, My Friend: An Intimate Biography.* London: Robson Books, 1993.

Brodsky, Jack, and Nathan Weiss. *The Cleopatra Papers.* New York: Simon & Schuster, 1963.

Burton, Richard. *Meeting Mrs. Jenkins.* New York: William Morrow, 1964.

Cohn, Art. *The Nine Lives of Mike Todd.* New York: Random House, 1958.

Collins, Joan. *Past Imperfect: An Autobiography.* London: Coronet Books, 1979.

Considine, Sean. *Bette & Joan: The Divine Feud.* New York: Warner Books, Inc., 1992.

Cottrell, John, and Fergus Cashin. *Richard Burton: Very Close Up.* Englewood Cliffs, NJ: Prentice Hall, 1971.

Dalton, David. *James Dean: The Mutant King.* New York: St. Martin's Press, 1987.

David, Lester, and Jhan Robbins. *Richard & Elizabeth.* New York: Funk & Wagnalls, 1977.

Davidson, Bill. *Spencer Tracy: Tragic Idol.* London: Sidgwick & Jackson, 1987.

Devilliers, Marceau. *James Dean on Location.* London: Sidgwick & Jackson, 1987.

Dietrich, Marlene. Interviews with David Bret, various.

Dmytryk, Edward. *It's A Hell of A Life, but Not a Bad Living.* New York: New York Times Books, 1978.

Downing, David. *Marlon Brando.* London: W.H. Allen, 1984.

Eames, John Douglas. *The MGM Story.* New York: Crown Publishers, 1975.

Edwards, Anne. *Katharine Hepburn: A Biography.* London: Coronet, 1987.

Ferber, Edna. *Giant.* New York: Doubleday, 1952.

Ferris, Paul. *Richard Burton.* London: Weidenfeld & Nicholson, 1981.

Fisher, Eddie. *My Life, My Loves*. London: W.H. Allen, 1982.

Gates, Phyllis (with Bob Thomas). *My Husband, Rock Hudson*. Sydney: Angus & Robertson, 1987.

Geist, Kenneth L. *Pictures Will Talk: The Life & Films of Joseph L Mankiewicz*. London: Frederick Muller, 1978.

Greene, Myrna. *The Eddie Fisher Story*. New York: Paul S. Eriksson, 1978.

Hersh, Burton. *The Mellon Family*. New York: William Morrow, 1978.

Hickey, Des, and Gus Smith. *The Prince: The Public & Private Life of Laurence Harvey*. London: Leslie Frewin Publishing, 1975.

Hirsch, Foster. *Elizabeth Taylor*. New York: Pyramid Publications, 1973.

Holley, Val. *James Dean*. London: Robson Books, 1995.

Hopper, Hedda. *From Under My Hat*. New York: Doubleday, 1952.

Hopper, Hedda. *The Whole Truth & Nothing But*. New York: Doubleday, 1962.

Hudson, Rock (with Sara Davidson). *Rock Hudson: His Story*. New York: Bantam Books, 1987.

Huston, John. *An Open Book*. New York: Ballantine Books, 1981.

Jenkins, Graham. *Richard Burton, My Brother*. London: Michael Joseph Ltd., 1988.

Joseph, Joan. *For Love Of Liz*. New York: Manor Books, 1976.

Kazan, Elia. *Elia Kazan: A Life*. London: André Deutsch, 1988.

Kelley, Kitty. *Elizabeth Taylor: The Last Star*. New York: Simon & Schuster, 1981.

Kensit, Patsy. Interview with *Attitude*, 2006.

LaGuardia, Robert. *Monty*. Westminster, MD: Arbor House, 1977.

Maddox, Brenda. *Who's Afraid Of Elizabeth Taylor?* New York: M. Evans & Co., 1977.

Mankiewicz, Joseph L. Near-Death Experience Speech. July 1961.

Medved, Harry, and Michael Medved. *The Golden Turkey Awards*. Sydney: Angus & Robertson, 1980.

Morley, Sheridan. *Elizabeth Taylor: A Celebration*. London: Pavilion Books, 1988.

Nickens, Christopher. *Elizabeth Taylor: A Biography in Photographs*. New York: Doubleday, 1984.

Quinlan, David. *Quinlan's Illustrated Directory of Film Character Actors*. London: Batsford Ltd., 1995.

Reynolds, Debbie, and David Patrick Columbia. *Debbie: My Life*. London: Sidgwick & Jackson, 1988.

Roen, Paul. *High Camp: A Gay Guide to Camp and Cult Films, Volumes I and II*. San Francisco: Leyland Productions, 1994.

Schary, Dore. *Heyday*. New York: Little, Brown & Co., 1979.

Sheppard, Dick. *Elizabeth: The Life & Career of Elizabeth Taylor*. New York: Warner Books Inc., 1975.

Stone, Paulene, and Peter Evans. *Laurence Harvey: One Tear Is Not Enough*. London: Michael Joseph, 1975.

Taylor, Elizabeth. *Elizabeth Takes Off*. London: Macmillan, 1988.

Taylor, Elizabeth. *Elizabeth Taylor*. New York: Harper & Row, 1964.

Taylor, Elizabeth. *Nibbles & Me*. New York: Duell, Sloan & Pearce, 1945.

Taylor, Elizabeth. Interview (alleged) with *Hollywood Reporter*, October 1943.

Taylor, Elizabeth. Interview with *Ladies Home Journal*, February 1976.

Taylor, Elizabeth. Freddie Mercury speech, April 1992.

Taylor, Sara. Interview with *Ladies Home Journal*, February 1954.

Todd, Michael Jr. *A Valuable Property: The Life Story of Mike Todd*. New York: Arbor House, 1983.

Vermilye, Jerry, and Mark Ricci. *The Films of Elizabeth Taylor*. New York: Citadel Press, 1976.

Vatican statement. *L'Osservatore Della Dominica*, March 1962.

Winters, Shelley. *Shelley, Also Known As Shirley*. New York: William Morrow, 1980.

Walker, Alexander. *Elizabeth*. London: Orion Books, 1997.

Walker, Alexander. Interviews with Elizabeth Taylor, various.

Walker, Alexander. *Sex In The Movies*. London: Pelican Books, 1966.

Warhol, Andy, and Bob Colacello. *Andy Warhol's Exposures*. New York: Grosset & Dunlap, 1979.

Waterbury, Ruth. *Elizabeth Taylor: Her Life, Her Loves, Her Future*. New York: Popular Library, 1964.

Waterbury, Ruth. *Richard Burton: His Intimate Story*. New York: Pyramid Publications, 1965.

Wigg, David: "Elizabeth Taylor Interview." *Good Housekeeping*, February 1977.

Wilding, Michael (with Pamela Wilcox). *Apple Sauce*. Crows Nest, NSW: Allen & Unwin, 1987.

Zec, Donald. *Liz, the Men, the Myths, and the Miracle: An Intimate Portrait of Elizabeth Taylor*. London: Mirror Books, 1982.

Zec, Donald. *Put The Knife In Gently: Memoirs of a Life with Legends*. London: Robson Books, 2003.

INDEX